W9-CAH-380

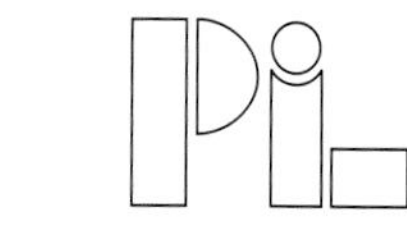

Publications International, Ltd.

Louis Weber, CEO
Publications International, Ltd.
7373 North Cicero Avenue
Lincolnwood, Illinois 60712

Some of the products listed in this publication may be in limited distribution.

Front cover photography by Peter Walters Photography/Chicago.

Pictured on the front cover: Choco-Caramel Delights *(page 154),* Festive Fruited White Chip Blondies *(page 249),* Moons and Stars *(page 348),* Flourless Peanut Butter Cookies *(page 352),* Brownie Caramel Pecan Bars *(page 219),* Raspberry Almond Sandwich Cookies *(page 132),* Loaded Oatmeal Cookies *(page 48),* Peanut Butter and Chocolate Spirals *(page 16),* Danish Raspberry Ribbons *(page 280)* and Chocolate Macadamia Chewies *(page 90).*

Pictured on the contents page: Peanut Butter Chocolate Chippers *(page 88).*

Pictured on the back cover *(clockwise from top):* Spritz Christmas Trees *(page 276),* Mini Kisses™ Coconut Macaroon Bars *(page 208)* and Crayon Cookies *(page 344).*

ISBN: 0-7853-4363-6

Library of Congress Catalog Card Number: 00-100574

Manufactured in China.

8 7 6 5 4 3 2 1

Microwave Cooking: Microwave ovens vary in wattage. Use the cooking times as guidelines and check for doneness before adding more time.

Preparation/Cooking Times: Preparation times are based on the approximate amount of time required to assemble the recipe before cooking, baking, chilling or serving. These times include preparation steps such as measuring, chopping and mixing. The fact that some preparations and cooking can be done simultaneously is taken into account. Preparation of optional ingredients and serving suggestions are not included.

Contents

Cookie Basics	4
Cookie Jar Classics	8
Chockful of Chips	62
Out of the Ordinary	104
Brownie Bonanza	168
A Bevy of Bars	204
Holiday Treats	258
Almost Homemade	310
Especially for Kids	344
Acknowledgments	374
Index	375

Cookie Basics

Baking cookies is a much-loved, time-honored American tradition. What other food could welcome children home from school, star at community bake sales, and help celebrate countless holidays and special occasions? Cookies are everywhere! Whether you're whipping up a quick snack for your family or putting together a beautiful gift basket, the more cookie recipes you have, the better. You'll find all the great cookie recipes you could ever want right here in this book, along with helpful information on preparing, baking and storing your cookies.

General Guidelines

Take the guesswork out of cookie baking by practicing the following techniques:

- Read the entire recipe before beginning to make sure you have all the necessary ingredients and baking utensils.
- Remove butter, margarine and cream cheese from the refrigerator to soften, if necessary.
- Toast and chop nuts, peel and slice fruit, and melt chocolate before preparing the cookie dough.
- Measure all the ingredients accurately and assemble them in the order they are called for in the recipe.
- When making bar cookies or brownies, use the pan specified in the recipe. Prepare the pans according to the recipe directions. Adjust oven racks and preheat the oven. Check oven temperature for accuracy with an oven thermometer.
- Follow recipe directions and baking times exactly. Check for doneness using the test given in the recipe.

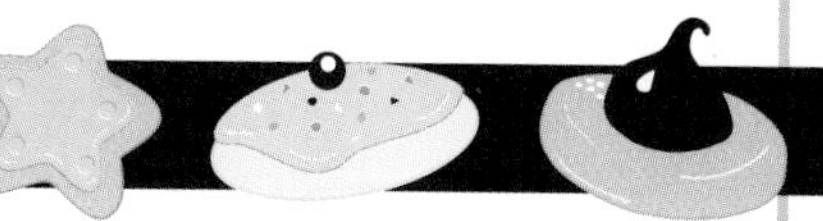

Melting Chocolate

Make sure the utensils you use for melting chocolate are completely dry. Moisture makes the chocolate become stiff and grainy. If this happens, add ½ teaspoon shortening (not butter) for each ounce of chocolate and stir until smooth. Chocolate scorches easily, and once scorched cannot be used. Follow one of these three methods for successful melting.

Double Boiler: This is the safest method because it prevents scorching. Place the chocolate in the top of a double boiler or in a bowl over hot, not boiling, water; stir until smooth. (Make sure the water remains just below a simmer and is one inch below the top pan.) Be careful that no steam or water gets into the chocolate.

Direct Heat: Place the chocolate in a heavy saucepan and melt over very low heat, stirring constantly. Remove the chocolate from the heat as soon as it is melted. Be sure to watch the chocolate carefully since it is easily scorched with this method.

Microwave Oven: Place an unwrapped 1-ounce square or 1 cup of chips in a small microwavable bowl. Microwave on High (100%) 1 to 1½ minutes, stirring after 1 minute. Stir the chocolate at 30-second intervals until smooth. Be sure to stir microwaved chocolate since it retains its original shape, even when melted.

Preparation

The seemingly endless variety of cookies can actually be divided into five basic types: bar, drop, refrigerator, rolled and shaped. These types are determined by the consistency of the dough and how it is formed into cookies.

Bar Cookies: Bar cookies and brownies are some of the easiest cookies to make—simply mix the batter, spread it in the pan and bake. These cookies are also quick to prepare since they bake all at once rather than in batches on a cookie sheet.

Always use the pan size called for in the recipe. Substituting a different pan will affect the cookies' texture: a smaller pan will make the bars more cakey, while a larger pan will produce flatter bars with a drier texture.

Most bar cookies should cool in the pan on a wire rack until barely warm before they are cut into squares. Try cutting bar cookies into triangles or diamonds for a festive new shape. To make serving easy, remove a corner piece first, then remove the rest.

Cookie Basics

Drop Cookies: These cookies are named for the way they are formed on the cookie sheet. The soft dough mounds when dropped from a spoon and then flattens slightly during baking. Space the mounds of dough about 2 inches apart on the cookie sheets to allow for spreading unless the recipe directs otherwise.

Cookies that are uniform in size and shape will finish baking at the same time. To easily shape drop cookies into a uniform size, use an ice cream scoop with a release bar.

Refrigerator Cookies: Refrigerator doughs are perfect for preparing in advance. Tightly wrapped rolls of dough can be stored in the refrigerator for up to one week or frozen for up to six weeks. These rich doughs are ready to be sliced and baked at a moment's notice.

Always shape the dough into rolls before chilling. Shaping is easier if you first place the dough on a piece of waxed paper or plastic wrap. If desired, you can gently press chopped nuts, flaked coconut or colored sugar into the roll. Before chilling, wrap the rolls securely in plastic wrap so that air cannot penetrate the dough and cause it to dry out. Use gentle pressure and a back-and-forth sawing motion when slicing the rolls so the cookies will keep their nice round shape. Rotating the roll while slicing also prevents one side from flattening.

Rolled Cookies: Rolled or cutout cookies are made from stiff doughs that are rolled out and cut into fancy shapes with floured cookie cutters, a knife or a pastry wheel.

Chill the cookie dough before rolling for easier handling. Remove only enough dough from the refrigerator to work with at one time. Save any trimmings and reroll them all at once to prevent the dough from becoming tough.

Shaped Cookies: These cookies can be simply hand-shaped into balls or crescents, forced through a cookie press into more complex shapes or baked in cookie molds.

By using different plates in a cookie press, spritz cookies can be formed into many shapes. If your first efforts are not successful, just transfer the dough back to the cookie press and try again.

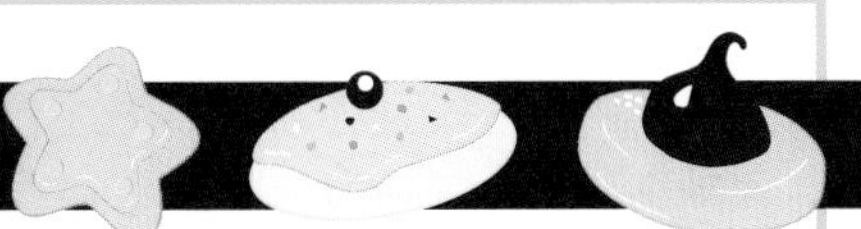

Baking

The best cookie sheets to use are those with little or no sides. They allow the heat to circulate evenly during baking and promote even browning. Another way to promote even baking and browning is to place only one cookie sheet at a time in the center of the oven. If you do use more than one sheet at a time, rotate the cookie sheets from top to bottom and front to back halfway through the baking time.

When a recipe calls for greasing the cookie sheets, use shortening or a nonstick cooking spray for the best results. Lining the cookie sheets with parchment paper is an alternative to greasing. It eliminates cleanup, bakes the cookies more evenly and allows them to cool right on the paper instead of on wire racks. Allow cookie sheets to cool between batches; the dough will spread if placed on a hot cookie sheet.

Most cookies should be removed from cookie sheets immediately after baking and placed in a single layer on wire racks to cool. Fragile cookies may need to cool slightly on the cookie sheet before being moved. Always cool cookies completely before stacking and storing. Bar cookies and brownies may be cooled and stored in the baking pan.

Storing

Unbaked cookie dough can be refrigerated for up to one week or frozen for up to six weeks. Rolls of dough should be sealed tightly in plastic wrap; other doughs should be stored in airtight containers. Label dough with baking information for convenience.

Store soft and crisp cookies separately at room temperature to prevent changes in texture and flavor. Keep soft cookies in airtight containers. If the cookies begin to dry out, add a piece of apple or bread to the container to help them retain moisture. Store crisp cookies in containers with loose-fitting lids to prevent moisture build-up. If they become soggy, heat undecorated cookies in a 300°F oven for 3 to 5 minutes to restore crispness. Store cookies with sticky glazes, fragile decorations and icings in single layers between sheets of waxed paper. Bar cookies and brownies may be stored in their own baking pans, covered with aluminum foil or plastic wrap when cool.

Cookie Jar Classics

Double Chocolate Walnut Drops

- ¾ cup (1½ sticks) butter or margarine, softened
- ¾ cup granulated sugar
- ¾ cup firmly packed light brown sugar
- 1 large egg
- 1 teaspoon vanilla extract
- 2¼ cups all-purpose flour
- ⅓ cup unsweetened cocoa powder
- 1 teaspoon baking soda
- ½ teaspoon salt
- 1¾ cups "M&M's"® Chocolate Mini Baking Bits
- 1 cup coarsely chopped English or black walnuts

Preheat oven to 350°F. Lightly grease cookie sheets; set aside. In large bowl cream butter and sugars until light and fluffy; beat in egg and vanilla. In medium bowl combine flour, cocoa powder, baking soda and salt; add to creamed mixture. Stir in "M&M's"® Chocolate Mini Baking Bits and nuts. Drop by heaping tablespoonfuls about 2 inches apart onto prepared cookie sheets. Bake 12 to 14 minutes for chewy cookies or 14 to 16 minutes for crispy cookies. Cool completely on wire racks. Store in tightly covered container.

Makes about 4 dozen cookies

Variation: Shape dough into 2-inch-thick roll. Cover with plastic wrap; refrigerate. When ready to bake, slice dough into ¼-inch-thick slices and bake as directed.

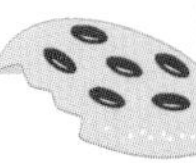

Double Chocolate Walnut Drops

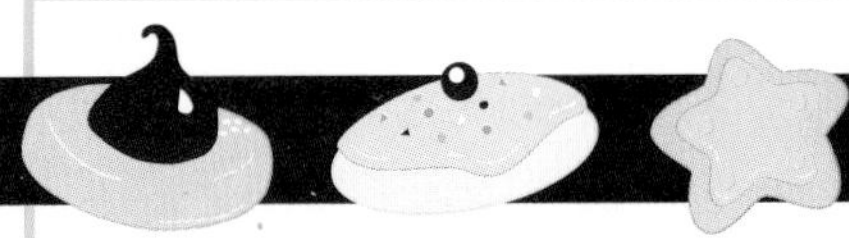

Peanut Gems

- **2½ cups all-purpose flour**
- **1 teaspoon baking powder**
- **⅛ teaspoon salt**
- **1 cup butter, softened**
- **1 cup packed light brown sugar**
- **2 eggs**
- **2 teaspoons vanilla**
- **1½ cups cocktail peanuts, finely chopped**
- **Powdered sugar (optional)**

Preheat oven to 350°F. Combine flour, baking powder and salt in small bowl.

Beat butter in large bowl with electric mixer at medium speed until smooth. Gradually beat in brown sugar; increase speed to medium-high and beat until light and fluffy. Beat in eggs, one at a time, until fluffy. Beat in vanilla. Gradually stir in flour mixture until blended. Stir in peanuts.

Drop heaping tablespoonfuls of dough about 1 inch apart onto ungreased cookie sheets; flatten slightly with hands.

Bake 12 minutes or until set. Let cookies stand on cookie sheets 5 minutes; transfer to wire racks to cool completely. Dust cookies with powdered sugar, if desired. Store in airtight container. *Makes 30 cookies*

Chocolate-Dipped Oat Cookies

- **2 cups uncooked rolled oats**
- **¾ cup firmly packed brown sugar**
- **½ cup vegetable oil**
- **½ cup finely chopped walnuts**
- **1 egg**
- **2 teaspoons grated orange peel**
- **¼ teaspoon salt**
- **1 package (12 ounces) milk chocolate chips**

Combine oats, sugar, oil, walnuts, egg, orange peel and salt in large bowl until blended. Cover; refrigerate overnight.

Preheat oven to 350°F. Lightly grease cookie sheets or line with parchment paper. Melt chocolate chips in top of double boiler over hot, not boiling, water; keep warm. Shape oat mixture into large marble-sized balls. Place 2 inches apart on prepared cookie sheets.

Bake 10 to 12 minutes or until golden and crisp. Cool 10 minutes on wire racks. Dip tops of cookies, one at a time, into melted chocolate. Place on waxed paper; cool until chocolate is set. *Makes about 6 dozen cookies*

Peanut Gems

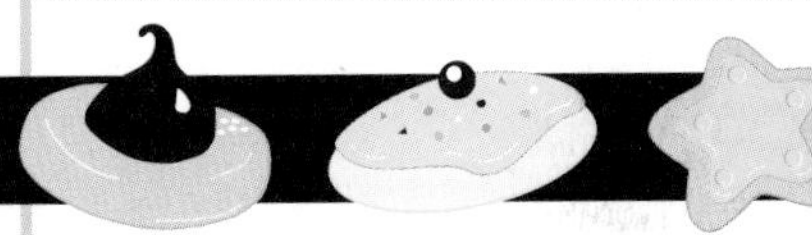

Baker's® Coconut Chocolate Jumbles

- **½ cup (1 stick) butter *or* margarine**
- **½ cup granulated sugar**
- **¼ cup firmly packed brown sugar**
- **1 egg**
- **½ teaspoon vanilla**
- **1 cup flour**
- **1 teaspoon baking soda**
- **¼ teaspoon salt**
- **6 squares BAKER'S® Semi-Sweet Baking Chocolate Squares *or* BAKER'S® Premium White Baking Chocolate Squares, chopped**
- **1 package (7 ounces) BAKER'S® ANGEL FLAKE® Coconut (2⅔ cups)**
- **1 cup *each* chopped, toasted walnuts and raisins**

HEAT oven to 350°F.

BEAT butter and sugars in large bowl with electric mixer on medium speed until light and fluffy. Beat in egg and vanilla. Mix in flour, baking soda and salt. Stir in chocolate, coconut, walnuts and raisins.

DROP by rounded tablespoonfuls, 1½ inches apart, onto ungreased cookie sheets.

BAKE 10 to 12 minutes or until golden brown. Cool 2 to 3 minutes; remove from cookie sheets. Cool completely on wire racks. Store in tightly covered container.

Makes about 3 dozen cookies

Prep Time: 15 minutes
Baking Time: 12 minutes

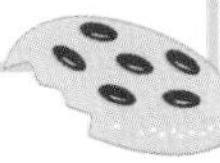

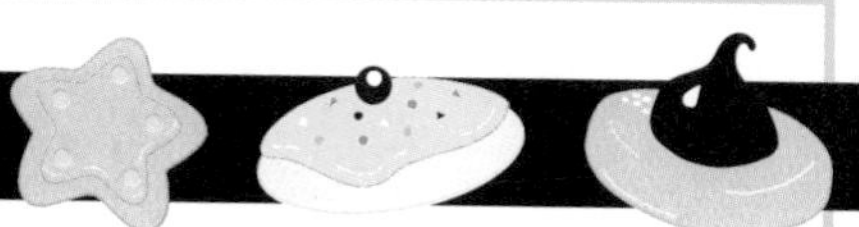

Hermits

MAZOLA NO STICK® Cooking Spray
3 cups flour
2 teaspoons pumpkin pie spice
¾ teaspoon baking powder
¾ teaspoon baking soda
¼ teaspoon salt
½ cup (1 stick) MAZOLA® Margarine, softened
1 cup packed brown sugar
2 eggs
½ cup KARO® Dark Corn Syrup
1 cup raisins
1 cup coarsely chopped walnuts
2 tablespoons finely chopped crystallized ginger (optional)

1. Preheat oven to 350°F. Spray cookie sheets with cooking spray. In medium bowl combine flour, pumpkin pie spice, baking powder, baking soda and salt.

2. In large bowl with mixer at medium speed, beat margarine and brown sugar until fluffy. Beat in eggs and corn syrup. Reduce speed; beat in flour mixture until blended. Stir in raisins, walnuts and ginger.

3. Drop by heaping teaspoonfuls 1½ inches apart on prepared cookie sheets.

4. Bake 12 minutes until golden and lightly browned at edges. Cool several minutes before removing from pan. Remove; cool completely on wire rack.

Makes about 4 dozen cookies

Note: *Soft or chewy cookies such as Hermits should always be stored in an airtight container to keep them fresh. If tightly wrapped in moisture-proof packaging, these cookies will keep well in the freezer up to 6 months.*

Prep Time: 25 minutes
Bake Time: 12 minutes, plus cooling

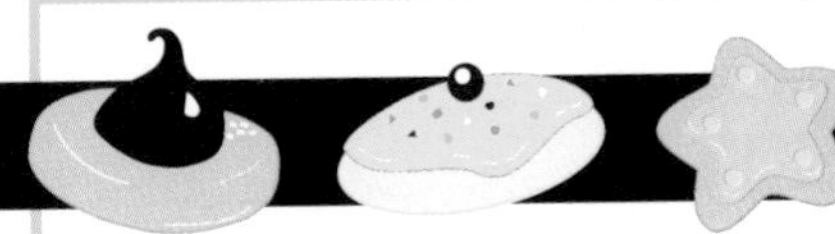

Classic Refrigerator Sugar Cookies

1 cup butter, softened
1 cup sugar
1 egg
1 teaspoon vanilla
2 cups all-purpose flour
2 teaspoons baking powder
Dash nutmeg
¼ cup milk
Colored sprinkles or melted semisweet chocolate* (optional)

**To dip 24 cookies, melt 1 cup chocolate chips in small saucepan over very low heat until smooth.*

Beat butter in large bowl with electric mixer at medium speed until smooth. Add sugar; beat until well blended. Add egg and vanilla; beat until well blended.

Combine flour, baking powder and nutmeg in medium bowl. Add flour mixture and milk alternately to butter mixture, beating at low speed after each addition until well blended.

Shape dough into 2 logs, each about 2 inches in diameter and 6 inches long. Roll logs in colored sprinkles, if desired, coating evenly (about ¼ cup sprinkles per roll). Or, leave rolls plain and decorate with melted chocolate after baking. Wrap each roll in plastic wrap. Refrigerate 2 to 3 hours or overnight.

Preheat oven to 350°F. Grease cookie sheets. Cut logs into ¼-inch-thick slices; place 1 inch apart on prepared cookie sheets. (Keep unbaked logs and sliced cookies chilled until ready to bake.)

Bake 8 to 10 minutes or until edges are golden brown. Transfer to wire racks to cool.

Dip plain cookies in melted chocolate or drizzle chocolate over cookies with fork or spoon, if desired. Set cookies on wire racks until chocolate is set. Store in airtight container.

Makes about 48 cookies

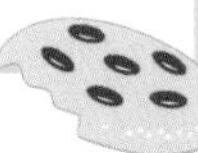

Classic Refrigerator Sugar Cookies

Peanut Butter and Chocolate Spirals

1 package (20 ounces) refrigerated sugar cookie dough
1 package (20 ounces) refrigerated peanut butter cookie dough
¼ cup unsweetened cocoa powder
⅓ cup peanut butter-flavored chips, chopped
¼ cup all-purpose flour
⅓ cup miniature chocolate chips

1. Remove each dough from wrapper according to package directions.

2. Place sugar cookie dough and cocoa in large bowl; mix with fork to blend. Stir in peanut butter chips.

3. Place peanut butter cookie dough and flour in another large bowl; mix with fork to blend. Stir in chocolate chips. Divide each dough in half; refrigerate 1 hour.

4. Roll each dough on floured surface to 12×6-inch rectangle. Layer each half of peanut butter dough onto each half of chocolate dough. Roll up dough, starting at long end to form 2 (12-inch) rolls. Refrigerate 1 hour.

5. Preheat oven to 375°F. Cut dough into ½-inch-thick slices. Place cookies 2 inches apart on ungreased cookie sheets.

6. Bake 10 to 12 minutes or until lightly browned. Remove to wire racks; cool completely. *Makes 4 dozen cookies*

Peanut Butter and Chocolate Spirals

Reese's® Chewy Chocolate Cookies

1¼ cups butter or margarine, softened
2 cups sugar
2 eggs
2 teaspoons vanilla extract
2 cups all-purpose flour
¾ cup HERSHEY'S® Cocoa
1 teaspoon baking soda
½ teaspoon salt
1⅔ cups (10-ounce package) REESE'S® Peanut Butter Chips
½ cup finely chopped nuts (optional)

1. Heat oven to 350°F. Beat butter and sugar in large bowl until light and fluffy. Add eggs and vanilla; beat well. In medium bowl, combine flour, cocoa, baking soda and salt; gradually blend into butter mixture. Stir in peanut butter chips and nuts, if desired. Drop by rounded teaspoonfuls onto ungreased cookie sheets.

2. Bake 8 to 9 minutes. (Do not overbake; cookies will be soft. They will puff while baking and flatten while cooling). Cool slightly; remove from cookie sheets to wire racks. Cool completely. *Makes about 4½ dozen cookies*

Reese's® Chewy Chocolate Pan Cookies: Spread dough into greased 15½×10½×1-inch jelly-roll pan. Bake at 350°F for 20 minutes or until set. Cool completely in pan on wire rack; cut into bars. Makes about 4 dozen bars.

Reese's® Chewy Chocolate Cookie Ice Cream Sandwiches: Prepare Reese's® Chewy Chocolate Cookies as directed; cool. Place small scoop of slightly softened vanilla ice cream between flat sides of two cookies. Gently press together. Serve immediately or wrap and freeze.

High Altitude Directions: Decrease sugar to 1⅔ cups. Increase flour to 2 cups plus 2 tablespoons. Decrease baking soda to ¾ teaspoon. Add 2 teaspoons water with flour mixture. Bake at 350°F 7 to 8 minutes. Makes about 6 dozen cookies.

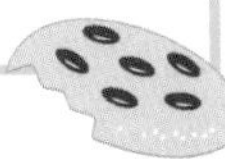

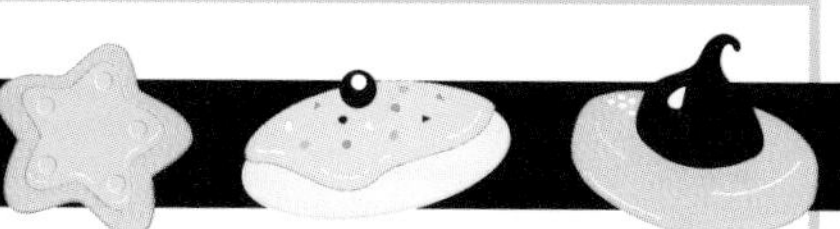

Granola Apple Cookies

- 1 cup packed brown sugar
- ¾ cup margarine or butter, softened
- 1 egg
- ¾ cup MOTT'S® Natural Apple Sauce
- 1 teaspoon vanilla
- 3 cups granola with dates and raisins
- 1½ cups all-purpose flour
- 1 teaspoon baking powder
- ½ teaspoon baking soda
- 1 teaspoon ground cinnamon
- ½ teaspoon allspice
- ½ teaspoon salt
- 1 cup flaked coconut
- 1 cup unsalted sunflower nuts

In large bowl, combine brown sugar, margarine, egg, apple sauce and vanilla; beat well. Stir in remaining ingredients; mix well. Refrigerate 1 to 2 hours or until firm enough to handle.

Preheat oven to 375°F. Grease cookie sheets. Drop dough by teaspoonfuls 2 inches apart onto prepared cookie sheets. Bake 11 to 13 minutes or until edges are light golden brown. Immediately remove from cookie sheets. Cool on wire racks. Store cookies in airtight container to retain their soft, chewy texture.

Makes about 5 dozen cookies

Note: *For larger cookies, press ¼ cup dough for each cookie 3 inches apart onto greased cookie sheets. Bake at 375°F for 13 to 15 minutes.*

Tip

Don't grease your cookie sheets too heavily; it can cause cookies to spread and overbrown on the bottom.

Lip-Smacking Lemon Cookies

½ cup butter, softened
1 cup sugar
1 egg
2 tablespoons lemon juice
2 teaspoons grated lemon peel
2 cups all-purpose flour
1 teaspoon baking powder
⅛ teaspoon salt
Dash ground nutmeg

Tip

One medium lemon will yield about 3 tablespoons juice and 2 to 3 teaspoons grated peel.

Beat butter in large bowl with electric mixer at medium speed until smooth. Add sugar; beat until well blended. Add egg, lemon juice and peel; beat until well blended.

Combine flour, baking powder, salt and nutmeg in large bowl. Gradually add flour mixture to butter mixture at low speed, blending well after each addition.

Shape dough into 2 logs, each about 1½ inches in diameter and 6½ inches long. Wrap each log in plastic wrap. Refrigerate 2 to 3 hours or up to 3 days.

Preheat oven to 350°F. Grease cookie sheets. Cut logs into ¼-inch-thick slices; place 1 inch apart on cookie sheets.

Bake about 15 minutes or until edges are light brown. Transfer to wire rack to cool. Store in airtight container.

Makes about 48 cookies

Lip-Smacking Lemon Cookies

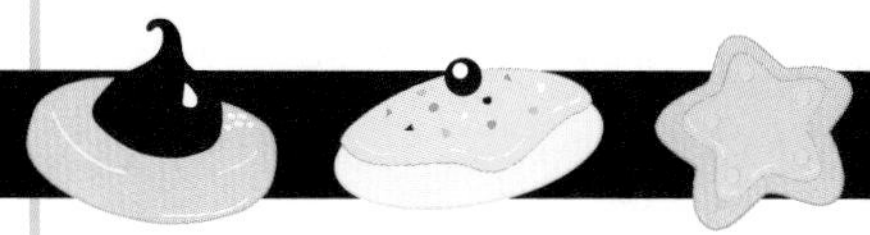

Peanut Butter Chewies

- **1 Butter Flavor* CRISCO® Stick or 1 cup Butter Flavor* CRISCO® all-vegetable shortening**
- **1½ cups creamy peanut butter**
- **1½ cups firmly packed brown sugar**
- **2 eggs**
- **1 can (14 ounces) sweetened condensed milk**
- **2 teaspoons vanilla**
- **2 cups all-purpose flour**
- **1 teaspoon baking soda**
- **1 teaspoon salt**
- **1½ cups chopped pecans**

**Butter Flavor Crisco® is artificially flavored.*

1. Heat oven to 350°F. Place sheets of foil on countertop for cooling cookies.

2. Combine 1 cup shortening, peanut butter and sugar in large bowl. Beat at medium speed of electric mixer until well blended. Beat in eggs, sweetened condensed milk and vanilla.

3. Combine flour, baking soda and salt. Mix into shortening mixture at low speed until just blended. Stir in pecans.

4. Drop rounded tablespoonfuls of dough 2 inches apart onto ungreased baking sheets.

5. Bake one baking sheet at a time at 350°F for 10 to 11 minutes or until lightly browned on bottom. *Do not overbake.* Cool 2 minutes on baking sheets. Remove cookies to foil to cool completely. *Makes about 4 dozen cookies*

Peanut Butter Chewies

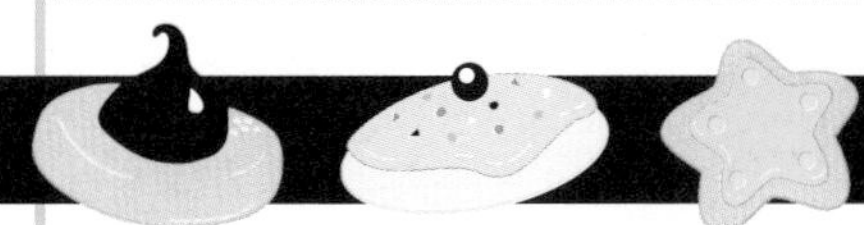

Oatmeal Butterscotch Cookies

- **¾ cup (1½ sticks) butter or margarine, softened**
- **¾ cup granulated sugar**
- **¾ cup packed light brown sugar**
- **2 eggs**
- **1 teaspoon vanilla extract**
- **1¼ cups all-purpose flour**
- **1 teaspoon baking soda**
- **½ teaspoon ground cinnamon**
- **½ teaspoon salt**
- **3 cups quick-cooking or regular rolled oats**
- **1⅔ cups (10-ounce package) HERSHEY®S Butterscotch Chips**

1. Heat oven to 375°F.

2. Beat butter, granulated sugar and brown sugar in large bowl until well blended. Add eggs and vanilla; blend thoroughly. Stir together flour, baking soda, cinnamon and salt; gradually add to butter mixture, beating until well blended. Stir in oats and butterscotch chips; mix well. Drop by teaspoons onto ungreased cookie sheet.

3. Bake 8 to 10 minutes or until golden brown. Cool slightly; remove from cookie sheet to wire rack. Cool completely.

Makes about 4 dozen cookies

Tip

To soften cold butter, cut a stick into ½-inch slices and place on a microwavable plate. Heat at MEDIUM-LOW (30% power) about 30 seconds.

Oatmeal Butterscotch Cookies

Mexican Wedding Cookies

1 cup pecan pieces or halves
1 cup butter, softened
2 cups powdered sugar, divided
2 cups all-purpose flour, divided
2 teaspoons vanilla
⅛ teaspoon salt

Place pecans in food processor. Process using on/off pulsing action until pecans are ground, but not pasty.

Beat butter and ½ cup powdered sugar in large bowl with electric mixer at medium speed until light and fluffy. Gradually add 1 cup flour, vanilla and salt. Beat at low speed until well blended. Stir in remaining 1 cup flour and ground nuts with spoon.

Shape dough into a ball; wrap in plastic wrap and refrigerate 1 hour or until firm.

Preheat oven to 350°F. Shape tablespoons of dough into 1-inch balls. Place 1 inch apart on ungreased cookie sheets.

Bake 12 to 15 minutes or until pale golden brown. Let cookies stand on cookie sheets 2 minutes.

Meanwhile, place 1 cup powdered sugar in 13×9-inch glass dish. Transfer hot cookies to powdered sugar. Roll cookies in powdered sugar, coating well. Let cookies cool in sugar.

Sift remaining ½ cup powdered sugar over sugar-coated cookies before serving. Store tightly covered at room temperature or freeze up to 1 month.

Makes about 48 cookies

Mexican Wedding Cookies

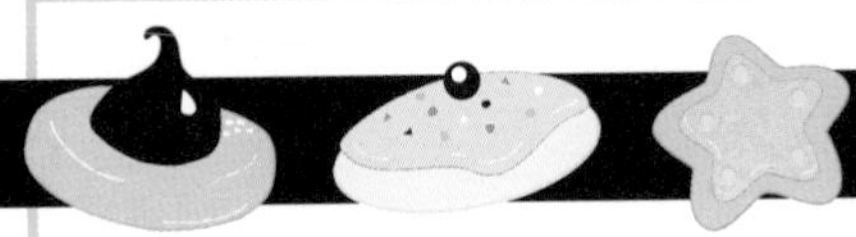

Smucker's® Grandmother's Jelly Cookies

- **1½ cups sugar**
- **1 cup butter or margarine, softened**
- **1 egg**
- **1½ teaspoons vanilla extract**
- **3½ cups all-purpose flour**
- **1 teaspoon salt**
- **¾ cup SMUCKER'S® Red Raspberry, Strawberry or Peach Preserves**

In large bowl, cream together sugar and butter until light and fluffy. Add egg and vanilla; beat well. Stir in flour and salt; mix well. Stir to make smooth dough. (If batter gets too hard to handle, mix with hands.) Cover and refrigerate about 2 hours.

Preheat oven to 375°F. Lightly grease baking sheets. On lightly floured board, roll out half of dough to about ⅛-inch thickness. Cut out cookies with 2½-inch round cookie cutter. Roll out remaining dough; cut with 2½-inch cutter with hole in center. Place on baking sheets. Bake 8 to 10 minutes or until lightly browned. Cool about 30 minutes.

To serve, spread preserves on plain cookies; top with cookies with holes. *Makes approximately 3 dozen cookies*

Classic Peanut Butter Cookies

- **1 cup unsalted butter, softened**
- **1 cup crunchy peanut butter**
- **1 cup granulated sugar**
- **1 cup light brown sugar, firmly packed**
- **2 eggs**
- **2½ cups all-purpose flour**
- **1 teaspoon baking powder**
- **1½ teaspoons baking soda**
- **½ teaspoon salt**

Beat butter, peanut butter and sugars until creamy. Beat in eggs. In separate bowl, sift flour, baking powder, baking soda and salt. Stir into batter until blended. Refrigerate 1 hour. Roll dough into 1-inch balls and place on baking sheets. Flatten each ball with fork, making criss-cross pattern. Bake in preheated 375°F oven about 10 minutes or until cookies begin to brown. Do not overbake.

Makes 4 dozen cookies

Favorite recipe from Peanut Advisory Board

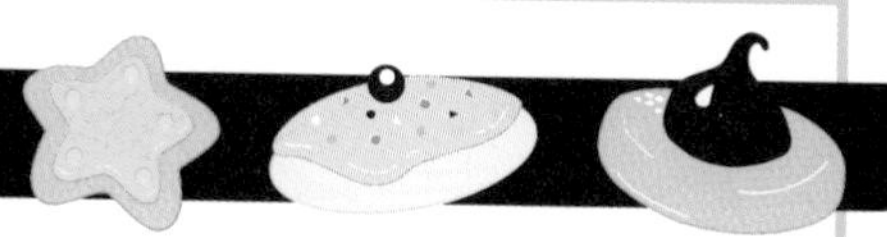

Baker's® One Bowl® Coconut Macaroons

1 package (14 ounces) BAKER'S® ANGEL FLAKE® Coconut (5⅓ cups)
⅔ cup sugar
6 tablespoons flour
¼ teaspoon salt
4 egg whites
1 teaspoon almond extract

HEAT oven to 325°F.

MIX coconut, sugar, flour and salt in large bowl. Stir in egg whites and almond extract until well blended.

DROP by teaspoonfuls onto greased and floured cookie sheets. Press 1 whole candied cherry or whole natural almond into center of each cookie, if desired.

BAKE 20 minutes or until edges of cookies are golden brown. Immediately remove from cookie sheets. Cool on wire racks.

Makes about 3 dozen cookies

Chocolate Dipped Macaroons: Prepare Coconut Macaroons as directed. Cool. Melt 1 package (8 squares) Baker's® Semi-Sweet Baking Chocolate as directed on package. Dip cookies halfway into chocolate or drizzle tops of cookies with chocolate; let excess chocolate drip off. Let stand at room temperature or refrigerate on wax paper-lined tray 30 minutes or until chocolate is firm.

White Chocolate Coconut Macaroons: Prepare Coconut Macaroons as directed, adding 3 squares Baker's® Premium White Baking Chocolate, chopped, to coconut mixture.

Chocolate Macaroons: Prepare Coconut Macaroons as directed, adding 2 squares Baker's® Semi-Sweet Baking Chocolate, melted, to coconut mixture.

Prep Time: 15 minutes
Bake Time: 20 minutes

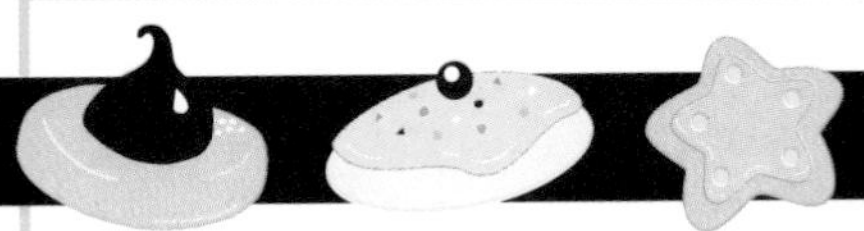

Chocolate Crackletops

2 cups all-purpose flour
2 teaspoons baking powder
2 cups granulated sugar
½ cup (1 stick) butter or margarine
4 squares (1 ounce each) unsweetened baking chocolate, chopped
4 large eggs, lightly beaten
2 teaspoons vanilla extract
1¾ cups "M&M's"® Chocolate Mini Baking Bits
Additional granulated sugar

Combine flour and baking powder; set aside. In 2-quart saucepan over medium heat combine 2 cups sugar, butter and chocolate, stirring until butter and chocolate are melted; remove from heat. Gradually stir in eggs and vanilla. Stir in flour mixture until well blended. Chill mixture 1 hour. Stir in "M&M's"® Chocolate Mini Baking Bits; chill mixture an additional 1 hour.

Preheat oven to 350°F. Line cookie sheets with foil. With sugar-dusted hands, roll dough into 1-inch balls; roll balls in additional granulated sugar. Place about 2 inches apart onto prepared cookie sheets. Bake 10 to 12 minutes. Do not overbake. Cool completely on wire racks. Store in tightly covered container. *Makes about 5 dozen cookies*

Oatmeal Pecan Scotchies

½ cup margarine or butter, softened
½ cup packed light brown sugar
1 egg
1¼ cups all-purpose flour
1 cup old-fashioned rolled oats
1 teaspoon DAVIS® Baking Powder
¼ cup milk
½ cup PLANTERS® Pecan Pieces
½ cup butterscotch chips

1. Beat margarine or butter and sugar in large bowl with mixer at medium speed until creamy. Blend in egg.

2. Mix flour, oats and baking powder in small bowl. Alternately stir flour mixture and milk into egg mixture. Stir in pecans and butterscotch chips.

3. Drop batter by rounded teaspoonfuls onto ungreased baking sheets. Bake at 350°F for 12 to 15 minutes or until lightly golden. Remove from pan; cool on wire rack. Store in airtight container. *Makes 4 dozen cookies*

Chocolate Crackletops

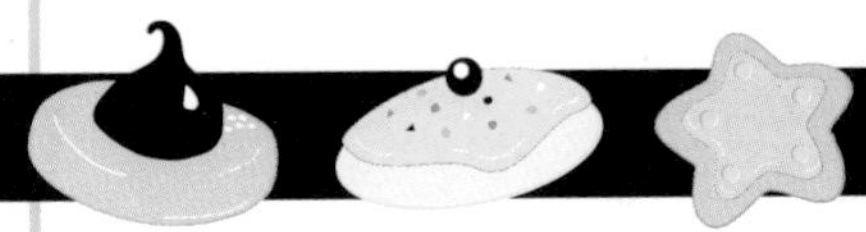

Spicy Oatmeal Raisin Cookies

- **1 package DUNCAN HINES® Moist Deluxe Spice Cake Mix**
- **4 egg whites**
- **1 cup uncooked quick-cooking oats (not instant or old-fashioned)**
- **½ cup vegetable oil**
- **½ cup raisins**

Preheat oven to 350°F. Grease cookie sheets.

Combine cake mix, egg whites, oats and oil in large mixing bowl. Beat at low speed with electric mixer until blended. Stir in raisins. Drop by rounded teaspoons onto prepared cookie sheets.

Bake 7 to 9 minutes or until lightly browned. Cool 1 minute on cookie sheets. Remove to cooling racks; cool completely.

Makes about 4 dozen cookies

Chocolate & Peanut-Butter Tweed Cookies

- **1 cup butter, softened**
- **½ cup packed light brown sugar**
- **¼ cup granulated sugar**
- **1 egg**
- **¼ teaspoon baking soda**
- **2½ cups all-purpose flour**
- **½ cup each semisweet chocolate chips and peanut butter chips, chopped***

**Chips can be chopped in a food processor.*

Beat butter and sugars in large bowl with electric mixer until smooth. Add egg and baking soda; beat until light and fluffy. Stir in flour until dough is smooth. Blend in chopped chips. Divide dough into 4 parts. Shape each part into a roll, about 1½ inches in diameter. Wrap in plastic wrap; refrigerate until firm, at least 1 hour or up to 2 weeks. (For longer storage, freeze up to 6 weeks.)

Preheat oven to 375°F. Lightly grease cookie sheets or line with parchment paper. Cut rolls into ⅛-inch-thick slices; place 2 inches apart on prepared cookie sheets. Bake 10 to 12 minutes or until lightly browned. Remove to wire racks to cool.

Makes about 6 dozen cookies

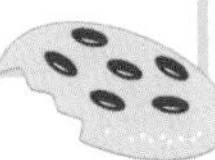

Spicy Oatmeal Raisin Cookies

Peanut Butter Brickle Cookies

1½ cups all-purpose flour
1 cup granulated sugar
1 cup butter or margarine, softened
½ cup peanut butter
1 egg
2 tablespoons packed light brown sugar
½ teaspoon baking soda
1 teaspoon vanilla
1 package (6 ounces) almond brickle bits

Preheat oven to 350°F. Grease cookie sheets. Combine flour, granulated sugar, butter, peanut butter, egg, brown sugar, baking soda and vanilla in large bowl. Beat at medium speed of electric mixer 2 to 3 minutes until well blended, scraping bowl often. Stir in almond brickle bits.

Shape rounded teaspoonfuls of dough into 1-inch balls. Place 2 inches apart on prepared cookie sheets. Flatten cookies to ⅛-inch thickness with bottom of glass covered with waxed paper. Bake 7 to 9 minutes or until edges are very lightly browned. *Makes about 4 dozen cookies*

Hershey®s Classic Milk Chocolate Chip Cookies

1 cup (2 sticks) butter, softened
¾ cup granulated sugar
¾ cup packed light brown sugar
1 teaspoon vanilla extract
2 eggs
2¼ cups all-purpose flour
1 teaspoon baking soda
½ teaspoon salt
2 cups (11.5-ounce package) HERSHEY®S Milk Chocolate Chips
1 cup chopped nuts (optional)

1. Heat oven to 375°F.

2. Beat butter, granulated sugar, brown sugar and vanilla in large bowl. Add eggs; beat well. Stir together flour, baking soda and salt; gradually add to butter mixture, beating until well blended. Stir in chocolate chips and nuts, if desired. Drop by teaspoons onto ungreased cookie sheet.

3. Bake 8 to 10 minutes or until lightly browned. Cool slightly; remove from cookie sheet to wire rack. Cool completely.
Makes about 5 dozen cookies

Pan Recipe: Spread batter into greased 15½×10½×1-inch jelly-roll pan. Bake at 375°F 20 minutes or until lightly browned. Cool completely. Cut into bars. Makes about 48 bars.

Peanut Butter Brickle Cookies

Jammy Pinwheels

1¼ cups granulated sugar
1 Butter Flavor* CRISCO® Stick or 1 cup Butter Flavor* CRISCO® all-vegetable shortening plus additional for greasing
2 eggs
¼ cup light corn syrup or regular pancake syrup
1 tablespoon vanilla
3 cups all-purpose flour (plus 2 tablespoons), divided
¾ teaspoon baking powder
½ teaspoon baking soda
½ teaspoon salt
1 cup apricot, strawberry or seedless raspberry jam

**Butter Flavor Crisco® is artificially flavored.*

1. Place sugar and 1 cup shortening in large bowl. Beat at medium speed of electric mixer until well blended. Add eggs, syrup and vanilla; beat until well blended and fluffy.

2. Combine 3 cups flour, baking powder, baking soda and salt. Add gradually to shortening mixture, beating at low speed until well blended.

3. Divide dough in half. Pat each half into thick rectangle. Sprinkle about 1 tablespoon flour on large sheet of waxed paper. Place rectangle of dough on floured paper. Turn dough over; cover with another large sheet of waxed paper. Roll dough into 12×8-inch rectangle about ⅛ inch thick. Trim edges. Slide dough and waxed paper onto ungreased baking sheets. Refrigerate 20 minutes or until firm. Repeat with remaining dough.

4. Heat oven to 375°F. Grease baking sheets. Place sheets of foil on counter for cooling cookies.

5. Place chilled dough rectangle on work surface. Remove top sheet of waxed paper. Cut dough into 2-inch squares. Place squares 2 inches apart on prepared baking sheets. Make a 1-inch diagonal cut from each corner of square almost to center. Place 1 teaspoon jam in center. Lift every other corner and bring together in center of cookie. Repeat with remaining dough.

6. Bake at 375°F for 7 to 10 minutes or until edges of cookies are golden brown. *Do not overbake.* Cool 2 minutes on baking sheet. Remove cookies to foil to cool completely.

Makes about 4 dozen cookies

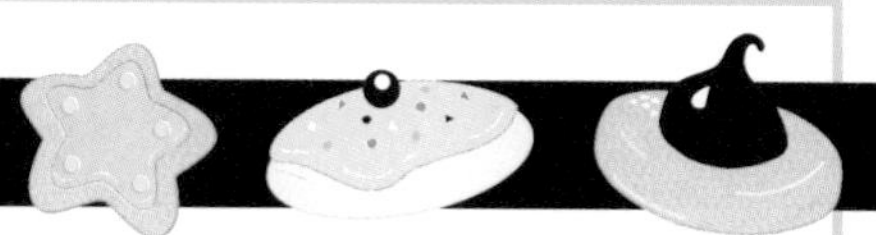

Soft Spicy Molasses Cookies

2 cups all-purpose flour
1 cup sugar
¾ cup butter, softened
⅓ cup light molasses
3 tablespoons milk
1 egg
½ teaspoon baking soda
½ teaspoon ground ginger
½ teaspoon ground cinnamon
½ teaspoon ground cloves
⅛ teaspoon salt
Sugar for rolling

Combine flour, 1 cup sugar, butter, molasses, milk, egg, baking soda, ginger, cinnamon, cloves and salt in large bowl. Beat at low speed of electric mixer 2 to 3 minutes until well blended. Cover; refrigerate until firm enough to handle, at least 4 hours or overnight.

Preheat oven to 350°F. Shape rounded teaspoonfuls of dough into 1-inch balls. Roll in sugar. Place 2 inches apart on ungreased cookie sheets. Bake 10 to 12 minutes or until slightly firm to the touch. Remove immediately.

Makes about 4 dozen cookies

Pecan Drops

¾ cup sugar
½ cup margarine or butter, softened
¼ cup egg substitute
1 teaspoon vanilla extract
2 cups all-purpose flour
⅔ cup PLANTERS® Pecans, finely chopped
3 tablespoons jam, jelly or preserves, any flavor

In small bowl, with electric mixer at medium speed, cream sugar and margarine. Add egg substitute and vanilla; beat 1 minute. Stir in flour until blended. Refrigerate dough 1 hour.

Form dough into 36 (1¼-inch) balls; roll in pecans, pressing into dough. Place 2 inches apart on greased cookie sheets. Indent center of each ball with thumb or back of wooden spoon. Bake at 350°F for 10 minutes; remove from oven. Spoon ¼ teaspoon jam into each cookie indentation. Bake 2 to 5 more minutes or until lightly browned. Remove from sheets; cool on wire racks.

Makes about 3 dozen cookies

Crispy Oat Drops

- 1 cup (2 sticks) butter or margarine, softened
- ½ cup granulated sugar
- ½ cup firmly packed light brown sugar
- 1 large egg
- 2 cups all-purpose flour
- ½ cup quick-cooking or old-fashioned oats, uncooked
- 1 teaspoon cream of tartar
- ½ teaspoon baking soda
- ¼ teaspoon salt
- 1¾ cups "M&M's"® Semi-Sweet Chocolate Mini Baking Bits
- 1 cup toasted rice cereal
- ½ cup shredded coconut
- ½ cup coarsely chopped pecans

Preheat oven to 350°F. In large bowl cream butter and sugars until light and fluffy; beat in egg. In medium bowl combine flour, oats, cream of tartar, baking soda and salt; blend flour mixture into creamed mixture. Stir in "M&M's"® Semi-Sweet Chocolate Mini Baking Bits, cereal, coconut and pecans. Drop by heaping tablespoonfuls about 2 inches apart onto ungreased cookie sheets. Bake 10 to 13 minutes or until lightly browned. Cool completely on wire racks. Store in tightly covered container. *Makes about 4 dozen cookies*

Tip

Quick-cooking rolled oats and old-fashioned rolled oats are essentially the same; the quick-cooking oats simply cook faster because they have been rolled into thinner flakes.

Crispy Oat Drops

Hershey's® Soft & Chewy Cookies

- 1 cup (2 sticks) butter (no substitutes)
- ¾ cup packed light brown sugar
- ½ cup granulated sugar
- ¼ cup light corn syrup
- 1 egg
- 2 teaspoons vanilla extract
- 2½ cups all-purpose flour
- 1 teaspoon baking soda
- ¼ teaspoon salt
- 1 package (10 to 12 ounces) HERSHEY'®S Bake Shoppe pieces (any flavor)

1. Heat oven to 350°F.

2. Beat butter, brown sugar and granulated sugar in large bowl until light and fluffy. Add corn syrup, egg and vanilla; beat well. Stir together flour, baking soda and salt; gradually add to butter mixture, beating until well blended. Stir in any flavor Bake Shoppe pieces. Drop by rounded teaspoons onto ungreased cookie sheet.

3. Bake 8 to 10 minutes or until lightly browned and almost set. Cool slightly; remove from cookie sheet to wire rack. Cool completely. Cookies will be softer the second day.

Makes about 3½ dozen cookies

Chocolate Chocolate Cookies: Decrease flour to 2¼ cups and add ¼ cup HERSHEY'®S Cocoa or HERSHEY'®S European Style Cocoa.

Hershey's® Soft & Chewy Cookies

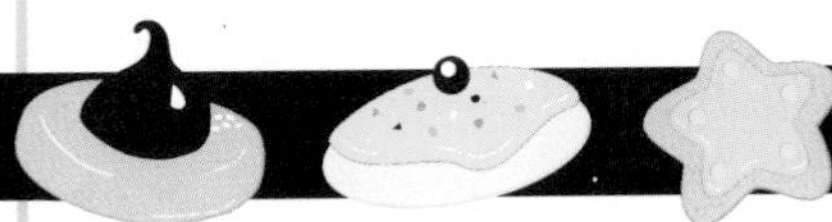

Ranger Cookies

- 1 cup (2 sticks) margarine or butter, softened
- 1 cup granulated sugar
- 1 cup firmly packed brown sugar
- 2 eggs
- 1 teaspoon vanilla
- 2 cups all-purpose flour
- 1 teaspoon baking soda
- ½ teaspoon baking powder
- ½ teaspoon salt (optional)
- 2 cups QUAKER® Oats (quick or old fashioned, uncooked)
- 2 cups corn flakes cereal
- ½ cup flaked or shredded coconut
- ½ cup chopped nuts

Heat oven to 350°F. Beat margarine and sugars until creamy. Add eggs and vanilla; beat well. Add combined flour, baking soda, baking powder and salt; mix well. Stir in oats, corn flakes, coconut and nuts; mix well. Drop dough by heaping tablespoonfuls onto ungreased cookie sheet. Bake 10 to 12 minutes or until light golden brown. Cool 1 minute on cookie sheet; remove to wire rack. Cool completely. Store tightly covered.

Makes 2 dozen large cookies

Tip

Hardened brown sugar can be softened quickly in the microwave. Place one cup sugar in a covered microwavable dish; heat at HIGH 30 to 60 seconds. Repeat if necessary.

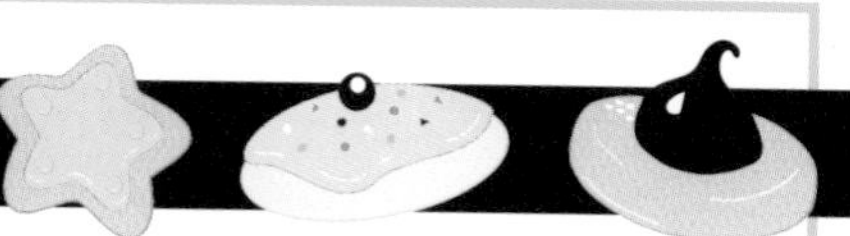

Baker's® One Bowl® Super Chunk Cookies

- 1 package (8 squares) BAKER'S® Semi-Sweet Baking Chocolate
- ½ cup (1 stick) butter *or* margarine
- ½ cup *each* granulated sugar and firmly packed brown sugar
- 1 egg
- 1 teaspoon vanilla
- 1 cup flour
- 1 cup quick-cooking rolled oats
- ½ teaspoon baking soda
- ½ cup chopped nuts (optional)

HEAT oven to 375°F. Break chocolate squares in half; cut each half into 3 chunks.

BEAT butter, sugars, egg and vanilla in large bowl with electric mixer on medium speed 1 minute or until well blended. Beat in flour, oats and baking soda on low speed until combined. Stir in chocolate and nuts.

DROP by rounded tablespoonfuls onto ungreased cookie sheet.

BAKE 10 minutes or until lightly browned. Cool on cookie sheet 2 minutes. Cool completely on wire racks.

Makes about 2 dozen cookies

Variation: Prepare as directed, substituting 1 cup lightly toasted Baker's® Angel Flake® Coconut for the nuts.

Prep Time: 10 minutes
Bake Time: 10 minutes

Chocolate Clouds

- **3 egg whites, at room temperature**
- **⅛ teaspoon cream of tartar**
- **¾ cup sugar**
- **1 teaspoon vanilla extract**
- **2 tablespoons HERSHEY'®S Cocoa**
- **2 cups (12-ounce package) HERSHEY'®S Semi-Sweet Chocolate Chips**

Heat oven to 300°F. Cover cookie sheet with parchment paper or foil.

Beat egg whites and cream of tartar in large bowl at high speed of electric mixer until soft peaks form. Gradually add sugar and vanilla, beating well after each addition until stiff peaks hold, sugar is dissolved and mixture is glossy. Sift cocoa onto egg white mixture; gently fold just until combined. Fold in chocolate chips. Drop by heaping tablespoons onto prepared cookie sheet.

Bake 35 to 45 minutes or just until dry. Cool slightly; peel paper from cookies. Store, covered, at room temperature.

Makes 30 cookies

Peanutty Crisscrosses

- **¾ cup (1½ sticks) margarine or butter, softened**
- **1 cup peanut butter**
- **1½ cups firmly packed brown sugar**
- **⅓ cup water**
- **1 egg**
- **1 teaspoon vanilla**
- **3 cups QUAKER® Oats (quick or old fashioned, uncooked)**
- **1½ cups all-purpose flour**
- **½ teaspoon baking soda**
- **Granulated sugar**

Beat together margarine, peanut butter and sugar until creamy. Add water, egg and vanilla; beat well. Add combined oats, flour and baking soda. Cover; chill about 1 hour.

Heat oven to 350°F. Shape dough into 1-inch balls. Place on ungreased cookie sheet; flatten with tines of fork, dipped in granulated sugar, to form crisscross pattern. Bake 9 to 10 minutes or until edges are golden brown. Cool 2 minutes on cookie sheet; remove to wire rack. Cool completely. Store in tightly covered container.

Makes about 7 dozen cookies

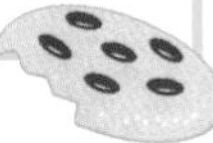

Chocolate Clouds

Molasses Spice Cookies

- 1 cup granulated sugar
- 3/4 cup shortening
- 1/4 cup molasses
- 1 large egg, beaten
- 2 cups all-purpose flour
- 2 teaspoons baking soda
- 1 teaspoon ground cinnamon
- 1 teaspoon ground cloves
- 1 teaspoon ground ginger
- 1/4 teaspoon dry mustard
- 1/4 teaspoon salt
- 1/2 cup granulated brown sugar

1. Preheat oven to 375°F. Grease cookie sheets; set aside.

2. Beat granulated sugar and shortening about 5 minutes in large bowl until light and fluffy. Add molasses and egg; beat until fluffy.

3. Combine flour, baking soda, cinnamon, cloves, ginger, mustard and salt in medium bowl. Add to shortening mixture; mix until just combined.

4. Place brown sugar in shallow dish. Roll tablespoonfuls of dough into 1-inch balls; roll in sugar to coat. Place 2 inches apart on prepared cookie sheets. Bake 15 minutes or until lightly browned. Let cookies stand on cookie sheets 2 minutes. Remove cookies to wire racks; cool completely.

Makes about 6 dozen cookies

Chunky Chocolate Cookies

- 1 cup butter, softened
- 3/4 cup granulated sugar
- 3/4 cup packed light brown sugar
- 2 eggs
- 1 1/2 teaspoons vanilla
- 2 1/4 cups all-purpose flour
- 1 teaspoon baking soda
- 1/2 teaspoon salt
- 1 cup chopped walnuts
- 1 (8-ounce) milk chocolate candy bar, cut into 1/2-inch pieces

Preheat oven to 375°F. Combine butter, granulated sugar, brown sugar, eggs and vanilla in large bowl. Beat at medium speed of electric mixer, scraping bowl often, until well blended, 1 to 2 minutes. Add flour, baking soda and salt. Continue beating until well mixed, 1 to 2 minutes. Stir in walnuts and chocolate. Drop rounded tablespoonfuls of dough 2 inches apart onto ungreased cookie sheets.

Bake 9 to 11 minutes or until lightly browned. Cool 1 minute on cookie sheets; remove immediately to wire racks.

Makes about 3 dozen cookies

Molasses Spice Cookies

Golden Gingersnaps

- 1 package DUNCAN HINES® Golden Sugar Cookie Mix
- 1 egg
- 1 tablespoon water
- 1 tablespoon light molasses
- 1½ teaspoons ground ginger
- 1 teaspoon ground cinnamon
- ½ teaspoon baking soda
- ¼ cup granulated sugar
- 1 tablespoon milk
- ⅓ cup finely chopped pecans

Preheat oven to 375°F. Grease cookie sheets.

Combine cookie mix, egg, water, molasses, ginger, cinnamon and baking soda in large bowl. Stir until thoroughly blended. Drop by level tablespoonfuls into sugar. Roll to completely cover. Place 2 inches apart onto prepared cookie sheets. Flatten slightly with bottom of drinking glass. Brush tops lightly with milk. Sprinkle with pecans. Bake 9 minutes for chewy cookies or 10 minutes for crisp cookies. Cool 2 minutes on cookie sheets. Remove to cooling racks. Cool completely. Store in airtight container.

Makes 3 dozen cookies

Loaded Oatmeal Cookies

- ¾ cup butter, softened
- 1 cup packed brown sugar
- 1 egg
- 1 tablespoon milk
- 1 teaspoon vanilla extract
- 1½ cups uncooked quick oats
- 1 cup all-purpose flour
- ½ teaspoon baking soda
- ½ teaspoon salt
- ½ teaspoon ground cinnamon
- 1 cup (6 ounces) semisweet chocolate chips
- 1 cup (6 ounces) butterscotch chips
- ¾ cup raisins
- ½ cup chopped walnuts

Preheat oven to 350°F. Beat butter and brown sugar in large bowl until creamy. Beat in egg, milk and vanilla until light and fluffy. Mix in oats, flour, baking soda, salt and cinnamon until well blended. Stir in chips, raisins and walnuts. Drop rounded tablespoonfuls of dough 2 inches apart onto ungreased cookie sheets.

Bake 12 to 15 minutes or until lightly browned around edges. Cool 2 minutes on cookie sheets. Remove to wire racks; cool completely. Store in airtight container.

Makes about 3 dozen cookies

Golden Gingersnaps

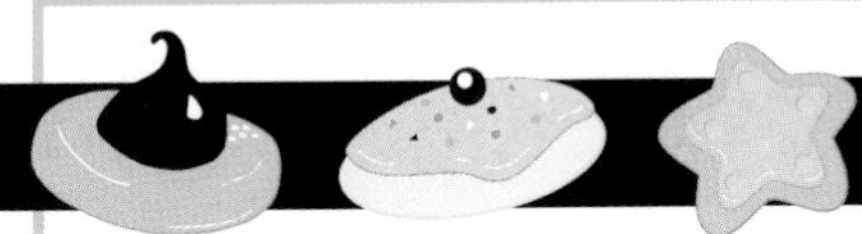

Baker's® Chocolate Sugar Cookies

2 cups all-purpose flour
1 teaspoon baking soda
¼ teaspoon salt
3 squares BAKER'S® Unsweetened Baking Chocolate
1 cup (2 sticks) butter *or* margarine
1 cup sugar
1 egg
1 teaspoon vanilla
Additional sugar

HEAT oven to 375°F. Mix flour, baking soda and salt in medium bowl.

MICROWAVE chocolate and butter in large microwavable bowl on HIGH 2 minutes or until butter is melted. Stir until chocolate is completely melted.

STIR 1 cup sugar into melted chocolate mixture until well blended. Mix in egg and vanilla until completely blended. Stir in flour mixture until well blended. Refrigerate dough about 15 minutes or until easy to handle.

SHAPE dough into 1-inch balls; roll in additional sugar. Place on ungreased cookie sheets.

BAKE 8 to 10 minutes or until set. (If flatter, crisper cookies are desired, flatten with bottom of glass before baking.) Remove from cookie sheets. Cool on wire racks. Store in tightly covered container. *Makes about 3½ dozen cookies*

Melting Chocolate on Top of Stove: Melt chocolate and butter in 3-quart heavy saucepan on low heat; stir constantly until chocolate is just melted. Remove from heat. Continue as directed.

Jam-Filled Chocolate Sugar Cookies: Prepare Baker's® Chocolate Sugar Cookie dough as directed. Roll in finely chopped nuts in place of sugar. Make indentation in each ball; fill center with your favorite jam. Bake as directed.

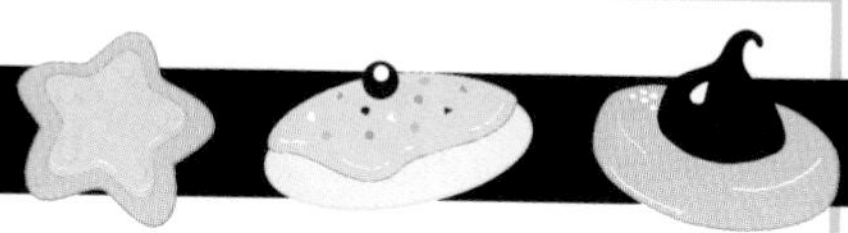

Chocolate-Caramel Sugar Cookies: *Prepare Baker's® Chocolate Sugar Cookie dough as directed. Roll in finely chopped nuts in place of sugar. Make indentation in each ball; bake as directed. Microwave 1 package (14 ounces) KRAFT® Caramels with 2 tablespoons milk in microwavable bowl on HIGH 3 minutes or until melted, stirring after 2 minutes. Fill centers of cookies with caramel mixture. Drizzle with melted Baker's® Semi-Sweet Baking Chocolate.*

Prep Time: 20 minutes plus refrigerating
Bake Time: 10 minutes

Simpler Than Sin Peanut Chocolate Cookies

- **1 cup PETER PAN® Extra Crunchy Peanut Butter**
- **1 cup sugar**
- **1 egg, room temperature and beaten**
- **2 teaspoons vanilla**
- **1 (6-ounce) dark or milk chocolate candy bar, broken into squares**

Preheat oven to 350°F. In medium bowl, combine Peter Pan® Peanut Butter, sugar, egg and vanilla; mix well. Roll dough into 1-inch balls. Place on ungreased cookie sheet 2 inches apart. Bake 12 minutes. Remove from oven and place chocolate squares in center of each cookie. Bake an additional 5 to 7 minutes or until cookies are lightly golden around edges. Cool 5 minutes. Remove to wire rack. Cool.

Makes about 24 cookies

Prep Time: 10 minutes
Bake Time: 19 minutes

Date-Nut Macaroons

1 (8-ounce) package pitted dates, chopped
1½ cups flaked coconut
1 cup PLANTERS® Pecan Halves, chopped
¾ cup sweetened condensed milk (not evaporated milk)
½ teaspoon vanilla extract

Preheat oven to 350°F.

In medium bowl, combine dates, coconut and nuts; blend in sweetened condensed milk and vanilla. Drop by rounded tablespoonfuls onto greased and floured cookie sheets. Bake 10 to 12 minutes or until light golden brown. Carefully remove from cookie sheets; cool completely on wire racks. Store in airtight container.

Makes about 2 dozen cookies

Double Chocolate Cookies

2¼ cups all-purpose flour
1 teaspoon baking soda
1 teaspoon salt
1 cup (2 sticks) butter or margarine, softened
¾ cup granulated sugar
¾ cup firmly packed brown sugar
1 teaspoon vanilla extract
2 eggs
2 (2-ounce) envelopes NESTLÉ® Choco-Bake® Unsweetened Chocolate Flavor
2 cups (12-ounce package) NESTLÉ® TOLL HOUSE® Semi-Sweet Chocolate Morsels
1 cup chopped walnuts

COMBINE flour, baking soda and salt in small bowl. Beat butter, granulated sugar, brown sugar and vanilla in large mixer bowl. Beat in eggs and Choco-Bake. Gradually beat in flour mixture. Stir in morsels and nuts. Drop by rounded tablespoons onto ungreased baking sheets.

BAKE in preheated 375°F. oven for 8 to 10 minutes or until edges are set but centers are still slightly soft. Let stand for 2 minutes; remove to wire racks to cool completely.

Makes about 6 dozen 2½-inch cookies

Date-Nut Macaroons

Chocolate Malted Cookies

½ cup butter, softened
½ cup shortening
1¾ cups powdered sugar, divided
1 teaspoon vanilla
2 cups all-purpose flour
1 cup malted milk powder, divided
¼ cup unsweetened cocoa powder

1. Beat butter, shortening, ¾ cup powdered sugar and vanilla in large bowl with electric mixer at high speed.

2. Add flour, ½ cup malted milk powder and cocoa; beat at low speed until well blended. Refrigerate several hours or overnight.

3. Preheat oven to 350°F. Shape slightly mounded teaspoonfuls of dough into balls.

4. Place dough balls about 2 inches apart on ungreased cookie sheets.

5. Bake 14 to 16 minutes or until lightly browned.

6. Meanwhile, combine remaining 1 cup powdered sugar and ½ cup malted milk powder in medium bowl.

7. Remove cookies to wire racks; cool 5 minutes. Roll cookies in powdered sugar mixture.

Makes about 4 dozen cookies

Tip: Substitute 6 ounces melted semisweet chocolate for the 1 cup powdered sugar and ½ cup malted milk powder used to roll the cookies. Instead, dip cookies in melted chocolate and let dry on wire racks until coating is set.

Chocolate Malted Cookies

Original Nestlé® Toll House® Chocolate Chip Cookies

2¼ cups all-purpose flour
1 teaspoon baking soda
1 teaspoon salt
1 cup (2 sticks) butter, softened
¾ cup granulated sugar
¾ cup packed brown sugar
1 teaspoon vanilla extract
2 eggs
2 cups (12-ounce package) NESTLÉ® TOLL HOUSE® Semi-Sweet Chocolate Morsels
1 cup chopped nuts

COMBINE flour, baking soda and salt in small bowl. Beat butter, granulated sugar, brown sugar and vanilla in large mixer bowl. Add eggs, one at a time, beating well after each addition. Gradually beat in flour mixture. Stir in morsels and nuts. Drop by rounded tablespoons onto ungreased baking sheets.

BAKE in preheated 375°F. oven for 9 to 11 minutes or until golden brown. Cool on baking sheets for 2 minutes; remove to wire racks to cool completely.

Makes about 5 dozen cookies

Pan Cookie Variation: PREPARE dough as directed. Spread into greased 15½×10½-inch jelly-roll pan. Bake in preheated 375°F. oven for 20 to 25 minutes or until golden brown. Cool in pan on wire rack. Makes 4 dozen bars.

Slice and Bake Cookie Variation: PREPARE dough as directed. Divide in half; wrap in wax paper. Chill for 1 hour or until firm. Shape each half into 15-inch log; wrap in wax paper. Chill for 30 minutes. Cut into ½-inch-thick slices; place on ungreased baking sheets. Bake in preheated 375°F. oven for 8 to 10 minutes or until golden brown. Cool on baking sheets for 2 minutes; remove to wire racks to cool completely. Makes about 5 dozen cookies.*

**May be stored in refrigerator for up to 1 week or in freezer for up to 8 weeks.*

Original Nestlé® Toll House® Chocolate Chip Cookies

Lemon Pecan Cookies

1⅔ cups (10-ounce package) HERSHEY®'S Premier White Chips, divided
2¼ cups all-purpose flour
¾ cup sugar
2 eggs
¾ teaspoon baking soda
½ teaspoon freshly grated lemon peel
¼ teaspoon lemon extract
½ cup (1 stick) butter or margarine
¾ cup chopped pecans
Lemon Drizzle (recipe follows)

1. Heat oven to 350°F. Reserve 2 tablespoons white chips for drizzle.

2. Combine flour, sugar, eggs, baking soda, lemon peel and lemon extract in large bowl. Place remaining white chips and butter in medium microwave-safe bowl. Microwave at HIGH (100%) 1 minute; stir. If necessary, microwave at HIGH an additional 15 seconds at a time, stirring after each heating, just until chips and butter are melted when stirred. Add chip mixture to flour mixture; beat until blended. Stir in pecans. Drop dough by rounded teaspoons onto ungreased cookie sheet.

3. Bake 9 to 11 minutes or until very slightly golden around edges. Remove from cookie sheet to wire rack. Cool completely. Prepare Lemon Drizzle; lightly drizzle over cookies.

Makes about 3½ dozen cookies

Lemon Drizzle: *Place reserved 2 tablespoons white chips and ½ teaspoon shortening (do not use butter, margarine, spread or oil) in microwave-safe bowl. Microwave at HIGH (100%) 30 seconds; stir. If necessary, microwave at HIGH an additional 15 seconds at a time, stirring after each heating, just until chips are melted when smooth. Stir in a few drops food color and a few drops lemon extract, if desired.*

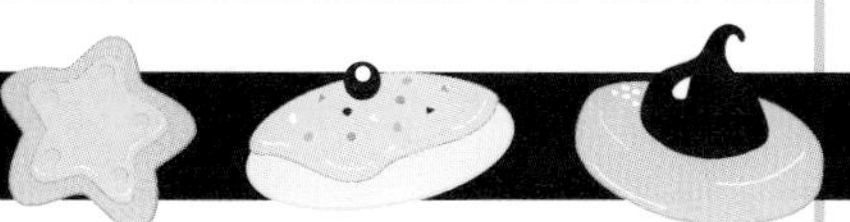

Fudge Cookies

- 1 cup (6 ounces) semisweet chocolate chips
- ½ cup butter or margarine, softened
- 1 cup granulated sugar
- 2 eggs
- 1½ cups all-purpose flour
- Dash salt
- 1½ cups coarsely chopped pecans or walnuts
- Fudge Frosting (recipe follows)

Preheat oven to 375°F. Lightly grease cookie sheets or line with parchment paper. Melt chocolate chips in top of double boiler over hot, not boiling, water. Remove from heat; cool. Beat butter, granulated sugar and eggs in large bowl until smooth. Beat in melted chocolate. Gradually add flour and salt, mixing until smooth. Stir in nuts. Drop dough by rounded teaspoonfuls 2 inches apart onto prepared cookie sheets. Bake 10 to 12 minutes or until slightly firm. Cool 5 minutes on cookie sheet, then remove to wire racks. While cookies bake, prepare Fudge Frosting. Frost cookies while still warm. Cool until frosting is set. *Makes about 5 dozen cookies*

Fudge Frosting

- 1 square (1 ounce) semisweet chocolate
- 3 tablespoons heavy cream
- 1 cup powdered sugar
- 1 teaspoon vanilla

Melt chocolate with cream in small heavy saucepan over medium heat, stirring until chocolate melts completely. Remove from heat; beat in powdered sugar and vanilla. Spread over cookies while frosting is still warm.

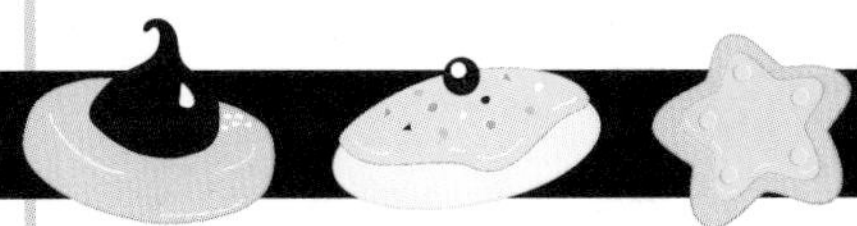

Tiny Mini Kisses™ Peanut Blossoms

- **¾ cup REESE'S® Creamy Peanut Butter**
- **½ cup shortening**
- **⅓ cup granulated sugar**
- **⅓ cup packed light brown sugar**
- **1 egg**
- **3 tablespoons milk**
- **1 teaspoon vanilla extract**
- **1½ cups all-purpose flour**
- **½ teaspoon baking soda**
- **½ teaspoon salt**
- **Granulated sugar**
- **HERSHEY'S MINI KISSES™ Semi-Sweet *or* Milk Chocolate Baking Pieces**

1. Heat oven to 350°F.

2. Beat peanut butter and shortening in large bowl with electric mixer until well mixed. Add ⅓ cup granulated sugar and brown sugar; beat well. Add egg, milk and vanilla; beat until fluffy. Stir together flour, baking soda and salt; gradually add to peanut butter mixture, beating until blended. Shape into ½-inch balls. Roll in granulated sugar; place on ungreased cookie sheet.

3. Bake 5 to 6 minutes or until set. Immediately press MINI KISS™ into center of each cookie. Remove from cookie sheet to wire rack.

Makes about 14 dozen cookies

Variation: For larger cookies, shape dough into 1-inch balls. Roll in granulated sugar. Place on ungreased cookie sheet. Bake 10 minutes or until set. Immediately place 3 MINI KISSES™ in center of each cookie, pressing down slightly. Remove from cookie sheet to wire rack. Cool completely.

Tiny Mini Kisses™ Peanut Blossoms

Chockful of Chips

Oatmeal Scotch Chippers

1¼ Butter Flavor* CRISCO® Sticks or 1¼ cups Butter Flavor* CRISCO® all-vegetable shortening
1½ cups firmly packed brown sugar
1 cup granulated sugar
3 eggs
1¼ cups crunchy peanut butter
4½ cups rolled oats
2 teaspoons baking soda
1 cup semisweet chocolate chips
1 cup butterscotch-flavored chips
1 cup chopped walnuts

**Butter Flavor Crisco is artificially flavored.*

1. Heat oven to 350°F. Place sheets of foil on countertop for cooling cookies.

2. Combine 1¼ cups shortening, brown sugar and granulated sugar in large bowl. Beat at medium speed of electric mixer until well blended. Beat in eggs. Add peanut butter. Beat until blended.

3. Combine oats and baking soda. Stir into shortening mixture with spoon. Stir in chocolate chips, butterscotch chips and nuts until blended.

4. Drop by rounded teaspoonfuls 2 inches apart onto ungreased baking sheets.

5. Bake one baking sheet at a time at 350°F for 10 to 11 minutes or until lightly browned. *Do not overbake.* Cool 2 minutes on baking sheet. Remove cookies to foil to cool completely.

Makes about 6 dozen cookies

Oatmeal Scotch Chippers

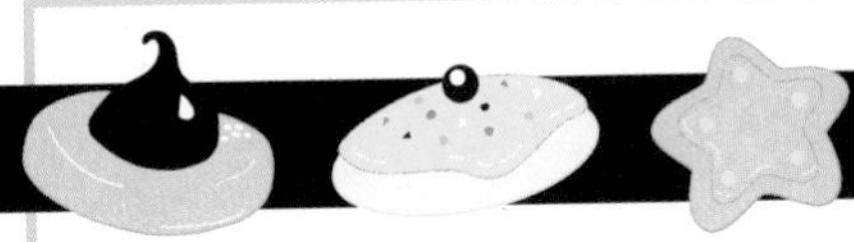

Three-in-One Chocolate Chip Cookies

- **6 tablespoons butter or margarine, softened**
- **½ cup packed light brown sugar**
- **¼ cup granulated sugar**
- **1 egg**
- **1 teaspoon vanilla extract**
- **1½ cups all-purpose flour**
- **½ teaspoon baking soda**
- **¼ teaspoon salt**
- **2 cups (12-ounce package) HERSHEY®S Semi-Sweet Chocolate Chips**

Beat butter, brown sugar and granulated sugar in large bowl until light and fluffy. Add egg and vanilla; beat well. Stir together flour, baking soda and salt; gradually blend into butter mixture. Stir in chocolate chips. Shape and bake cookies into one of the three versions below.

Giant Cookies: Prepare dough. Heat oven to 350°F. Line 12×⅝-inch round pizza pan with foil. Pat dough evenly into prepared pan to within ¾ inch of edge. Bake 15 to 18 minutes or until lightly browned. Cool completely; cut into wedges. Decorate or garnish as desired. Makes about 8 servings (one 12-inch cookie).

Medium-Size Refrigerator Cookies: Prepare dough. On wax paper, shape into 2 rolls, 1½ inches in diameter. Wrap in wax paper; cover with plastic wrap. Refrigerate several hours, or until firm enough to slice. Heat oven to 350°F. Remove rolls from refrigerator; remove wrapping. With sharp knife, cut into ¼-inch-wide slices. Place on ungreased cookie sheet, about 3 inches apart. Bake 8 to 10 minutes or until lightly browned. Cool slightly; remove from cookie sheet to wire rack. Cool completely. Makes about 2½ dozen (2½-inch) cookies.

Miniature Cookies: Prepare dough. Heat oven to 350°F. Drop dough by ¼ teaspoons onto ungreased cookie sheet, about 1½ inches apart. (Or, spoon dough into disposable plastic frosting bag; cut about ¼ inch off tip. Squeeze batter by ¼ teaspoons onto ungreased cookie sheet.) Bake 5 to 7 minutes or just until set. Cool slightly; remove from cookie sheet to wire rack. Cool completely. Makes about 18½ dozen (¾-inch) cookies.

Three-in-One Chocolate Chip Cookies

Banana Chocolate Chip Softies

1¼ cups all-purpose flour
1 teaspoon baking powder
½ teaspoon salt
⅓ cup butter or margarine, softened
⅓ cup granulated sugar
⅓ cup firmly packed light brown sugar
1 ripe, medium banana, mashed
1 large egg
1 teaspoon vanilla
1 cup milk chocolate chips
½ cup coarsely chopped walnuts (optional)

Preheat oven to 375°F. Lightly grease cookie sheets.

Place flour, baking powder and salt in small bowl; stir to combine.

Beat butter, granulated sugar and brown sugar in large bowl with electric mixer at medium speed until light and fluffy. Beat in banana, egg and vanilla. Add flour mixture. Beat at low speed until well blended. Stir in chips and walnuts with mixing spoon. (Dough will be soft.)

Drop rounded teaspoonfuls of dough 2 inches apart onto prepared cookie sheets.

Bake 9 to 11 minutes or until edges are golden brown. Let cookies stand on cookie sheets 2 minutes. Remove cookies with spatula to wire racks; cool completely. Store tightly covered at room temperature. These cookies do not freeze well.

Makes about 3 dozen cookies

Banana Chocolate Chip Softies

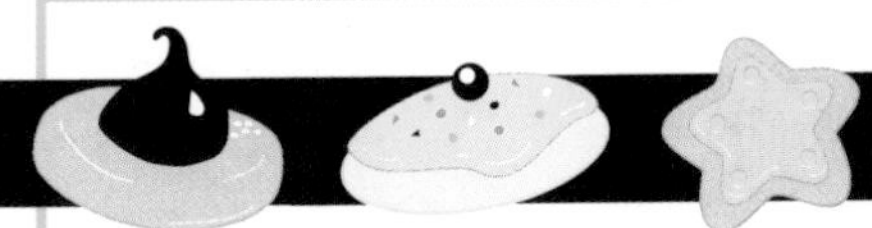

Mrs. J's Chip Cookies

4 cups crispy rice cereal
1 milk chocolate crunch bar (5 ounces), broken into squares
2 cups all-purpose flour
1 teaspoon baking powder
1 teaspoon baking soda
¼ teaspoon salt
1 cup butter or margarine, softened
1 cup granulated sugar
1 cup packed light brown sugar
2 eggs
1 teaspoon vanilla
1 package (12 ounces) semisweet chocolate chips
1½ cups chopped walnuts

Preheat oven to 375°F. Line cookie sheets with parchment paper or leave ungreased. Process cereal in blender or food processor until pulverized. Add chocolate bar; continue processing until both chocolate and cereal are completely ground. Add flour, baking powder, baking soda and salt; process until blended. Beat butter and sugars in large bowl until well blended. Add eggs; beat until light. Blend in vanilla. Add flour mixture; blend until smooth. Stir in chocolate chips and walnuts until blended. Shape dough into walnut-sized balls. Place 2 inches apart on cookie sheets. Bake 10 to 12 minutes or until firm in center. *Do not overbake.* Remove to wire racks to cool. *Makes about 8 dozen cookies*

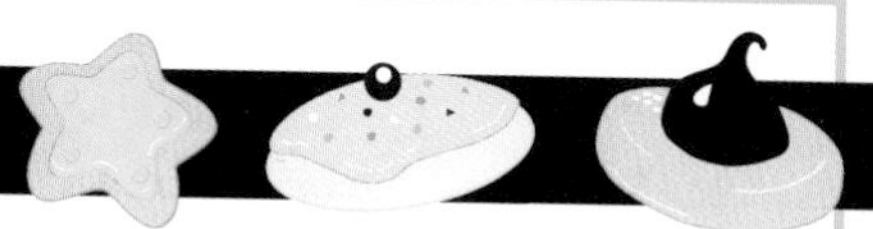

Crunchy Chocolate Chip Cookies

- 2¼ cups unsifted all-purpose flour
- 1 teaspoon ARM & HAMMER® Baking Soda
- 1 teaspoon salt
- 1 cup softened margarine or butter
- ¾ cup granulated sugar
- ¾ cup packed brown sugar
- 1 teaspoon vanilla extract
- 2 eggs
- 2 cups (12 ounces) semisweet chocolate chips
- 1 cup chopped nuts (peanuts, walnuts or pecans)

Preheat oven to 375°F. Sift together flour, Baking Soda and salt in small bowl. Beat margarine, sugars and vanilla in large bowl with electric mixer until creamy. Beat in eggs. Gradually add flour mixture; mix well. Stir in chocolate chips and nuts. Drop by rounded teaspoons onto ungreased cookie sheets. Bake 8 minutes or until lightly browned.

Makes about 8 dozen (2-inch) cookies

Tip

Don't store crisp and soft cookies in the same container--it will cause the crisp cookies to soften quickly.

Chocolate Chip Almond Biscotti

2¾ cups all-purpose flour
1½ teaspoons baking powder
¼ teaspoon salt
½ cup butter, softened
1 cup sugar
3 eggs
3 tablespoons almond-flavored liqueur
1 tablespoon water
1 cup mini semisweet chocolate chips
1 cup sliced almonds, toasted and chopped

1. Place flour, baking powder and salt in medium bowl; stir to combine.

2. Beat butter and sugar in large bowl with electric mixer at medium speed until light and fluffy. Beat in eggs, 1 at a time. Beat in liqueur and water. Gradually add flour mixture. Beat at low speed just until blended. Stir in chips and almonds.

3. Divide dough into fourths. Spread each quarter evenly down center of waxed paper. Using waxed paper to hold dough, roll it back and forth to form a 15-inch log. Wrap in plastic wrap. Refrigerate until firm, about 2 hours.

4. Preheat oven to 375°F. Lightly grease cookie sheet. Unwrap and place each log on prepared cookie sheet. With floured hands, shape each log 2 inches wide and ½ inch thick.

5. Bake 15 minutes. Remove cookie sheet from oven. Cut each log with serrated knife into 1-inch-thick diagonal slices. Place slices, cut side up, on cookie sheet; bake 7 minutes. Turn cookies over; bake 7 minutes or until cut surfaces are golden brown and cookies are dry. Remove cookies with spatula to wire racks; cool completely. Store tightly covered at room temperature or freeze up to 3 months.

Makes about 4 dozen cookies

Chocolate Chip Almond Biscotti

Hershey®s "Perfectly Chocolate" Chocolate Chip Cookies

2¼ cups all-purpose flour
⅓ cup HERSHEY®S Cocoa
1 teaspoon baking soda
½ teaspoon salt
1 cup (2 sticks) butter or margarine, softened
¾ cup granulated sugar
¾ cup packed light brown sugar
1 teaspoon vanilla extract
2 eggs
2 cups (12-ounce package) HERSHEY®S Semi-Sweet Chocolate Chips
1 cup chopped nuts (optional)

1. Heat oven to 375°F.

2. Stir together flour, cocoa, baking soda and salt. Beat butter, granulated sugar, brown sugar and vanilla in large bowl on medium speed of electric mixer until creamy. Add eggs; beat well. Gradually add flour mixture, beating until well blended. Stir in chocolate chips and nuts, if desired. Drop by rounded teaspoons onto ungreased cookie sheet.

3. Bake 8 to 10 minutes or until set. Cool slightly; remove from cookie sheet to wire rack.

Makes about 5 dozen cookies

Tip

Use shiny cookie sheets for the best cookie baking results. Dark cookie sheets can cause the bottoms of the cookies to be dark.

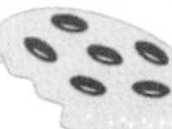

Hershey's® "Perfectly Chocolate" Chocolate Chip Cookies

Chocolate-Pecan Angels

1 cup mini semisweet chocolate chips
1 cup chopped pecans, toasted
1 cup sifted powdered sugar
1 egg white

Preheat oven to 350°F. Grease cookie sheets. Combine chips, pecans and powdered sugar in medium bowl. Add egg white; mix well. Drop batter by teaspoonfuls 2 inches apart onto prepared cookie sheets.

Bake 11 to 12 minutes until edges are light golden brown. Let cookies stand on cookie sheets 1 minute. Remove cookies to wire racks; cool completely.

Makes about 3 dozen cookies

Mini Chip Snowball Cookies

1½ cups (3 sticks) butter, softened
¾ cup powdered sugar
1 tablespoon vanilla extract
½ teaspoon salt
3 cups all-purpose flour
2 cups (12-ounce package) NESTLÉ® TOLL HOUSE® Semi-Sweet Chocolate Mini Morsels
½ cup finely chopped nuts
Powdered sugar

BEAT butter, sugar, vanilla and salt in large mixer bowl until creamy. Gradually beat in flour; stir in morsels and nuts. Shape level tablespoonfuls of dough into 1¼-inch balls. Place on ungreased baking sheets.

BAKE in preheated 375°F. oven for 10 to 12 minutes or until cookies are set and lightly browned. Remove from oven. Sift powdered sugar over hot cookies on baking sheet. Let stand for 10 minutes; remove to wire racks to cool completely. Sprinkle with additional powdered sugar if desired. Store in airtight containers.

Makes 5 dozen cookies

Chocolate-Pecan Angels

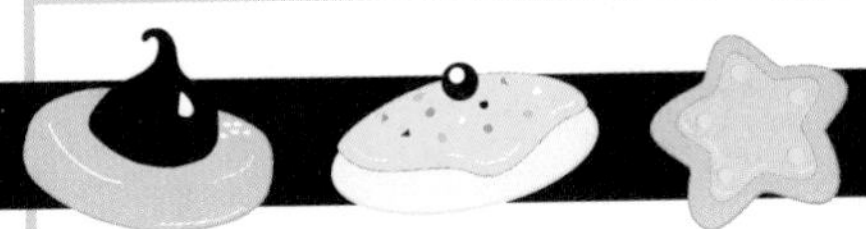

Double Chocolate Banana Cookies

- 3 to 4 extra-ripe, medium DOLE® Bananas, peeled
- 2 cups rolled oats
- 2 cups sugar
- 1¾ cups all-purpose flour
- ½ cup unsweetened cocoa powder
- 1 teaspoon baking soda
- ½ teaspoon salt
- 2 eggs, slightly beaten
- 1¼ cups margarine, melted
- 1 cup DOLE® Chopped Natural Almonds, toasted
- 2 cups semisweet chocolate chips

• Purée bananas in blender; measure 2 cups for recipe.

• Combine oats, sugar, flour, cocoa, baking soda and salt until well mixed. Stir in bananas, eggs and margarine until blended. Stir in almonds and chocolate chips.

• Refrigerate batter 1 hour or until mixture becomes partially firm (batter runs during baking if too soft).

• Measure ¼ cup batter for each cookie; drop onto greased cookie sheet. Flatten slightly with spatula.

• Bake in 350°F oven 15 to 17 minutes until cookies are golden brown. Remove to wire rack to cool.

Makes about 2½ dozen (3-inch) cookies

Prep Time: 15 minutes
Chill Time: 1 hour
Bake Time: 17 minutes/batch

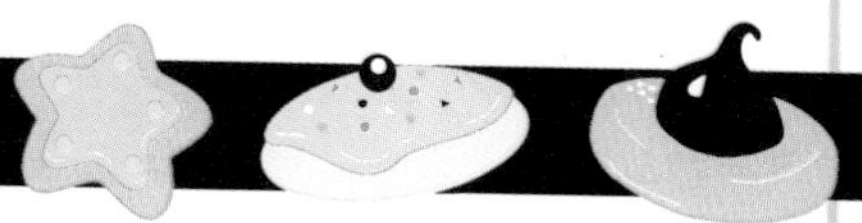

Giant Raisin-Chip Frisbees

- 1 cup butter or margarine, softened
- 1 cup packed brown sugar
- ½ cup granulated sugar
- 2 eggs
- 1 teaspoon vanilla
- 1½ cups all-purpose flour
- ¼ cup unsweetened cocoa powder
- 1 teaspoon baking soda
- 1 cup (6 ounces) semisweet chocolate chips
- ¾ cup raisins
- ¾ cup chopped walnuts

Preheat oven to 350°F. Line cookie sheets with parchment paper or lightly grease and dust with flour.

Beat butter with both sugars in large bowl. Add eggs and vanilla; beat until light. Combine flour, cocoa and baking soda in small bowl. Add to butter mixture with chocolate chips, raisins and walnuts; stir until well blended.

Scoop out about ½ cupful of dough for each cookie. Place on prepared cookie sheets, spacing about 5 inches apart. Using knife dipped in water, smooth balls of dough out to about 3½ inches in diameter. Bake 10 to 12 minutes or until golden. Remove to wire racks to cool.

Makes about 16 cookies

Forgotten Chips Cookies

- 2 egg whites
- ⅛ teaspoon cream of tartar
- ⅛ teaspoon salt
- ⅔ cup sugar
- 1 teaspoon vanilla extract
- 1 cup HERSHEY®'S Semi-Sweet Chocolate Chips or Milk Chocolate Chips

1. Heat oven to 375°F. Lightly grease cookie sheets.

2. Beat egg whites with cream of tartar and salt in small bowl until soft peaks form. Gradually add sugar, beating until stiff peaks form. Carefully fold in vanilla extract and chocolate chips. Drop by teaspoonfuls onto prepared cookie sheets.

3. Place cookie sheets in heated oven; immediately turn off oven and allow cookies to remain in oven six hours or overnight without opening door. Remove cookies from cookie sheets. Store in airtight container in cool, dry place.

Makes about 2½ dozen cookies

Almond Milk Chocolate Chippers

½ cup slivered almonds
1¼ cups all-purpose flour
½ teaspoon baking soda
½ teaspoon salt
½ cup butter, softened
½ cup firmly packed light brown sugar
⅓ cup granulated sugar
1 large egg
2 tablespoons almond-flavored liqueur
1 cup milk chocolate chips

1. Preheat oven to 350°F. To toast almonds, spread on baking sheet. Bake 8 to 10 minutes or until golden brown, stirring frequently. Remove almonds from pan and cool; set aside.

2. *Increase oven temperature to 375°F.* Combine flour, baking soda and salt in small bowl.

3. Beat butter, brown sugar and granulated sugar in large bowl until light and fluffy. Beat in egg until well blended. Beat in liqueur. Gradually add flour mixture. Beat until well blended. Stir in chips and almonds.

4. Drop dough by rounded teaspoonfuls 2 inches apart onto ungreased cookie sheets.

5. Bake 9 to 10 minutes or until edges are golden brown. Let cookies stand on cookie sheets 2 minutes. Remove cookies to wire racks; cool completely. Store tightly covered at room temperature or freeze up to 3 months.

Makes about 3 dozen cookies

Almond Milk Chocolate Chippers

Chocolate Chip Shortbread

- ½ cup butter, softened
- ½ cup sugar
- 1 teaspoon vanilla
- 1 cup all-purpose flour
- ¼ teaspoon salt
- ½ cup mini semisweet chocolate chips

Preheat oven to 375°F.

Beat butter and sugar in large bowl with electric mixer at medium speed until light and fluffy. Beat in vanilla. Add flour and salt; beat at low speed. Stir in chips.

Divide dough in half. Press each half into ungreased 8-inch round cake pan.

Bake 12 minutes or until edges are golden brown. Score shortbread with sharp knife, taking care not to cut completely through shortbread. Make 8 wedges per pan.

Let pans stand on wire racks 10 minutes. Invert shortbread onto wire racks; cool completely. Break into triangles.

Makes 16 cookies

Hershey®s White Chip Chocolate Cookies

- 1 cup (2 sticks) butter or margarine, softened
- 2 cups sugar
- 2 eggs
- 2 teaspoons vanilla extract
- 2 cups all-purpose flour
- ¾ cup HERSHEY®S Cocoa
- 1 teaspoon baking soda
- ½ teaspoon salt
- 1⅔ cups (10-ounce package) HERSHEY®S Premier White Chips

1. Heat oven to 350°F.

2. Beat butter and sugar in large bowl until creamy. Add eggs and vanilla extract; beat until light and fluffy. Stir together flour, cocoa, baking soda and salt; gradually blend into butter mixture. Stir in white chips. Drop by rounded teaspoons onto ungreased cookie sheet.

3. Bake 8 to 9 minutes. (Do not overbake; cookies will be soft. They will puff while baking and flatten upon cooling.) Cool slightly; remove from cookie sheet to wire racks. Cool completely.

Makes about 4½ dozen cookies

Chocolate Chip Shortbread

Oatmeal Candied Chippers

- **¾ cup butter, softened**
- **¾ cup granulated sugar**
- **¾ cup packed light brown sugar**
- **3 tablespoons milk**
- **1 egg**
- **2 teaspoons vanilla**
- **¾ cup all-purpose flour**
- **¾ teaspoon salt**
- **½ teaspoon baking soda**
- **3 cups uncooked rolled oats**
- **1⅓ cups (10-ounce package) candy-coated semisweet chocolate chips or candy-coated chocolate pieces**

Preheat oven to 375°F. Grease cookie sheets; set aside. Beat butter, granulated sugar and brown sugar in large bowl until light and fluffy. Add milk, egg and vanilla; beat well. Add flour, salt and baking soda. Beat until well combined. Stir in oats and chocolate chips.

Drop by rounded tablespoonfuls 2 inches apart on prepared cookie sheets. Bake 10 to 12 minutes until edges are golden brown. Let cookies stand 2 minutes on cookie sheets. Remove cookies to wire racks; cool completely.

Makes about 4 dozen cookies

Tip 

For a delicious change of pace, substitute your favorite candy bars, chopped, for the candy-coated chips.

Oatmeal Candied Chippers

Hershey®s Great American Chocolate Chip Cookies

1 cup (2 sticks) butter, softened
¾ cup granulated sugar
¾ cup packed light brown sugar
1 teaspoon vanilla extract
2 eggs
2¼ cups all-purpose flour
1 teaspoon baking soda
½ teaspoon salt
2 cups (12-ounce package) HERSHEY®S Semi-Sweet Chocolate Chips
1 cup chopped nuts (optional)

1. Heat oven to 375°F.

2. Beat butter, granulated sugar, brown sugar and vanilla in large mixer bowl until creamy. Add eggs; beat well. Stir together flour, baking soda and salt; gradually add to butter mixture, beating well. Stir in chocolate chips and nuts, if desired. Drop dough by rounded teaspoons onto ungreased cookie sheet.

3. Bake 8 to 10 minutes or until lightly browned. Cool slightly; remove from cookie sheet to wire rack. Cool completely.

Makes about 6 dozen cookies

Hershey®s Great American Chocolate Chip Pan Cookies: Spread dough into greased 15½×10½×1-inch jelly-roll pan. Bake at 375°F for 20 minutes or until lightly browned. Cool completely in pan on wire rack. Cut into bars. Makes about 48 bars.

Skor® & Chocolate Chip Cookies: Omit 1 cup HERSHEY®S Semi-Sweet Chocolate Chips and nuts; replace with 1 cup finely chopped SKOR® bars. Drop onto cookie sheets and bake as directed.

Great American Ice Cream Sandwiches: Prepare cookies as directed. Place one small scoop slightly softened vanilla ice cream between flat sides of two cookies. Gently press together. Wrap and freeze.

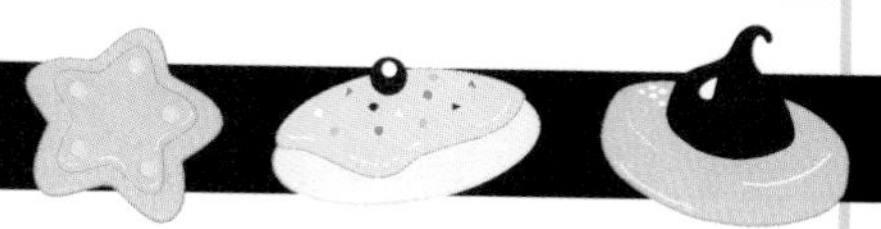

Peanutty Double Chip Cookies

- ½ cup butter or margarine, softened
- ¾ cup packed light brown sugar
- ¾ cup granulated sugar
- 2 eggs
- 1 teaspoon baking soda
- 1 teaspoon vanilla
- 2 cups all-purpose flour
- 1 cup chunky peanut butter
- 1 cup (6 ounces) semisweet or milk chocolate chips
- 1 cup (6 ounces) peanut butter chips

Preheat oven to 350°F. Lightly grease cookie sheets or line with parchment paper. Beat butter and sugars in large bowl until blended. Add eggs, baking soda and vanilla; beat until light. Blend in flour and peanut butter until dough is stiff and smooth. Stir in chocolate and peanut butter chips. Drop dough by teaspoonfuls 2 inches apart onto prepared cookie sheets. Press cookies down with tines of fork to flatten slightly. Bake 12 minutes or until just barely done. *Do not overbake.* Remove to wire racks to cool.

Makes about 5 dozen cookies

Chocolate Chip Macaroons

- 2½ cups flaked coconut
- ⅔ cup mini semisweet chocolate chips
- ⅔ cup sweetened condensed milk
- 1 teaspoon vanilla

Preheat oven to 350°F. Grease cookie sheets. Combine coconut, chocolate chips, milk and vanilla in medium bowl; mix until well blended. Drop dough by rounded teaspoonfuls 2 inches apart onto greased cookie sheets. Press dough gently with back of spoon to flatten slightly. Bake 10 to 12 minutes or until light golden brown. Let cookies stand on cookie sheets 1 minute. Remove cookies to wire racks; cool completely.

Makes about 3½ dozen cookies

Oatmeal Chocolate Chip Cookies

- 1 can (20 ounces) DOLE® Crushed Pineapple
- 1½ cups brown sugar, packed
- 1 cup margarine, softened
- 1 egg
- ¼ teaspoon almond extract
- 4 cups rolled oats, uncooked
- 2 cups flour
- 1 teaspoon baking powder
- 1 teaspoon salt
- 1 teaspoon ground cinnamon
- ½ teaspoon ground nutmeg
- 1 package (12 ounces) semisweet chocolate chips
- ¾ cup DOLE® Slivered Almonds, toasted
- 2 cups flaked coconut

• Preheat oven to 350°F. Grease cookie sheets. Drain pineapple well, reserving ½ cup syrup.

• In large bowl, beat brown sugar and margarine until light and fluffy. Beat in egg. Beat in pineapple, reserved ½ cup liquid and almond extract.

• In small bowl, combine oats, flour, baking powder, salt, cinnamon and nutmeg. Add to margarine mixture; beat until blended. Stir in chocolate chips, almonds and coconut.

• Drop by heaping tablespoonfuls onto prepared cookie sheets. Flatten cookies slightly with back of spoon. Bake 20 to 25 minutes or until golden. Cool on wire racks.

Makes about 5 dozen cookies

Chocolate Chip Macaroons

Peanut Butter Chocolate Chippers

1 cup creamy or chunky peanut butter
1 cup firmly packed light brown sugar
1 large egg
¾ cup milk chocolate chips
Granulated sugar

1. Preheat oven to 350°F.

2. Combine peanut butter, brown sugar and egg in medium bowl; mix until well blended. Add chips; mix well.

3. Roll heaping tablespoonfuls of dough into 1½-inch balls. Place balls 2 inches apart on ungreased cookie sheets.

4. Dip table fork into granulated sugar; press criss-cross fashion onto each ball, flattening to ½-inch thickness.

5. Bake 12 minutes or until set. Let cookies stand on cookie sheets 2 minutes. Remove cookies to wire racks; cool completely.

Makes about 2 dozen cookies

Tip

This simple recipe is unusual because it doesn't contain any flour--but it still makes great cookies!

Peanut Butter Chocolate Chippers

Chocolate Macadamia Chewies

- ¾ cup (1½ sticks) butter or margarine, softened
- ⅔ cup firmly packed light brown sugar
- 1 large egg
- 1 teaspoon vanilla extract
- 1¾ cups all-purpose flour
- ¾ teaspoon baking soda
- ¼ teaspoon salt
- ¾ cup (3½ ounces) coarsely chopped macadamia nuts
- ½ cup shredded coconut
- 1¾ cups "M&M's"® Chocolate Mini Baking Bits

Preheat oven to 350°F. In large bowl cream butter and sugar until light and fluffy; beat in egg and vanilla. In medium bowl combine flour, baking soda and salt; blend into creamed mixture. Blend in nuts and coconut. Stir in "M&M's"® Chocolate Mini Baking Bits. Drop by heaping teaspoonfuls about 2 inches apart onto ungreased cookie sheets; flatten slightly with back of spoon. Bake 8 to 10 minutes or until set. Do not overbake. Cool 1 minute on cookie sheets; cool completely on wire racks. Store in tightly covered container.

Makes about 4 dozen cookies

Chocolate Macadamia Chewies

Double Chocolate Oat Drops

MAZOLA NO STICK® Cooking Spray
2 cups (12 ounces) semisweet chocolate chips, divided
¼ cup (½ stick) MAZOLA® Margarine
⅔ cup KARO® Light or Dark Corn Syrup
2 eggs
¼ teaspoon salt
4 cups uncooked quick oats
⅔ cup packed brown sugar
1 cup coarsely chopped walnuts
1 cup flaked coconut

1. Preheat oven to 350°F. Spray cookie sheets with cooking spray.

2. In medium heavy saucepan over low heat, combine 1 cup chocolate chips and margarine; stir just until melted. Remove from heat. Stir in corn syrup, eggs and salt.

3. In large bowl combine oats, brown sugar, walnuts and coconut. Add chocolate mixture; mix well. Stir in remaining 1 cup chocolate chips.

4. Drop by tablespoonfuls onto prepared cookie sheets. Bake 15 minutes (cookies will not change much in appearance during baking). Cool 5 minutes on cookie sheet or until firm. Remove; cool completely on wire rack.

Makes about 3 dozen cookies

Chocolate-Dipped Oat Drops: *In medium heavy saucepan over low heat, stir 1½ cups (9 ounces) semisweet chocolate chips until melted and smooth. Dip half of each cookie in melted chocolate. Place on waxed paper to cool.*

Tip: *Use your microwave oven to eliminate the risks of melting chocolate on top of the stove. To melt 1 (1-ounce) square, microwave on HIGH (100%) 1 to 2 minutes. For 2 squares, 1½ to 2½ minutes is sufficient. For chocolate chips, allow 1½ to 2½ minutes for 1 cup (6 ounces). Remember that the chocolate will not lose its shape in the microwave oven, so stir often to avoid overheating.*

Prep Time: 20 minutes
Bake Time: 15 minutes, plus cooling

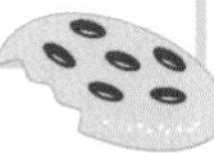

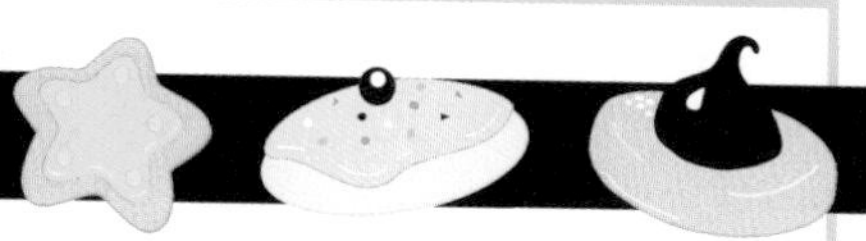

Baker's® Double Chocolate Chunk Cookies

- **1 package (8 squares) BAKER'S® Semi-Sweet Baking Chocolate, divided**
- **½ cup (1 stick) butter *or* margarine**
- **½ cup granulated sugar**
- **¼ cup firmly packed brown sugar**
- **1 egg**
- **1 teaspoon vanilla**
- **1 cup flour**
- **½ teaspoon CALUMET® Baking Powder**
- **¼ teaspoon salt**
- **¾ cup chopped walnuts (optional)**

HEAT oven to 375°F.

MICROWAVE 1 square chocolate in microwavable bowl on HIGH 1 to 2 minutes until almost melted, stirring halfway through heating time. Stir until chocolate is completely melted.

CUT 3 squares chocolate into large (½-inch) chunks; set aside.

BEAT butter until light and fluffy. Gradually beat in sugars. Mix in egg and vanilla. Stir in melted chocolate. Mix in flour, baking powder and salt. Stir in chocolate chunks and walnuts. Refrigerate dough 30 minutes.

DROP dough by rounded tablespoonfuls, about 2 inches apart, onto greased cookie sheets.

BAKE for 8 to 10 minutes or until lightly browned. Cool 2 minutes; remove from cookie sheets.

MICROWAVE remaining 4 squares chocolate in microwavable bowl on HIGH 1½ to 2 minutes until almost melted, stirring halfway through heating time. Stir until completely melted.

DIP ½ of each cookie into melted chocolate. Let stand until chocolate is firm.

Makes about 2 dozen (3-inch) cookies

Melting Chocolate on Top of Stove: Heat chocolate in heavy saucepan on very low heat, stirring constantly, until just melted. Remove from heat. Continue as directed.

Tip: Do not overbake cookies. They will be soft when done and firm up upon cooling.

Prep Time: 20 minutes plus refrigerating
Bake Time: 10 minutes

Tracy's Pizza-Pan Cookies

- **1 cup butter or margarine, softened**
- **¾ cup granulated sugar**
- **¾ cup packed brown sugar**
- **1 package (8 ounces) cream cheese, softened**
- **1 teaspoon vanilla**
- **2 eggs**
- **2¼ cups all-purpose flour**
- **1 teaspoon baking soda**
- **¼ teaspoon salt**
- **1 package (12 ounces) semisweet chocolate chips**
- **1 cup chopped walnuts or pecans**

Preheat oven to 375°F. Lightly grease two 12-inch pizza pans.

Beat butter, sugars, cream cheese and vanilla in large bowl. Add eggs; beat until well blended. Combine flour, baking soda and salt in small bowl. Add to creamed mixture; blend well. Stir in chocolate chips and nuts. Divide dough in half; press each half evenly into prepared pans.

Bake 20 to 25 minutes or until lightly browned around edges. Cool completely in pans on wire racks. To serve, cut into slim wedges or break into pieces. *Makes two (12-inch) cookies*

Tip 

To soften cream cheese for recipes, remove from the wrapper and place in a microwavable bowl. Microwave at MEDIUM (50%) 1½ to 2 minutes or until slightly softened, turning the bowl after 1 minute.

Tracy's Pizza-Pan Cookie

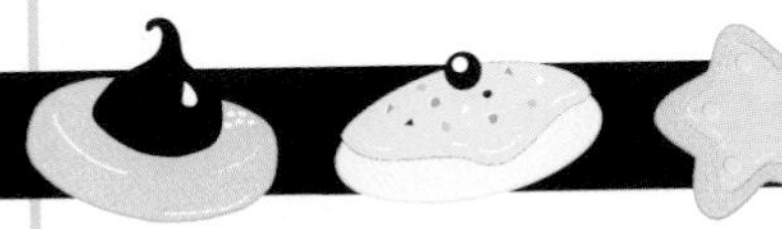

Chocolate Chip 'n Oatmeal Cookies

1 package (18.25 or 18.5 ounces) yellow cake mix
1 cup quick-cooking rolled oats, uncooked
¾ cup butter or margarine, softened
2 eggs
1 cup HERSHEY®S Semi-Sweet Chocolate Chips

1. Heat oven to 350°F.

2. Combine cake mix, oats, butter and eggs in large bowl; mix well. Stir in chocolate chips. Drop by rounded teaspoons onto ungreased cookie sheets.

3. Bake 10 to 12 minutes or until very lightly browned. Cool slightly; remove from cookie sheets to wire racks. Cool completely. *Makes about 4 dozen cookies*

San Francisco Cookies

2 extra-ripe, medium DOLE® Bananas, cut into chunks
2 cups granola
1½ cups all-purpose flour
1 cup packed brown sugar
1 teaspoon baking powder
1 teaspoon ground cinnamon
2 eggs
½ cup margarine, melted
¼ cup vegetable oil
1 cup chocolate chips

• Preheat oven to 350°F. Lightly grease cookie sheets. In food processor or blender, process bananas until puréed (1 cup).

• Combine granola, flour, sugar, baking powder and cinnamon in large bowl. Beat in puréed bananas, eggs, margarine and oil. Stir in chocolate chips.

• Drop by ¼ cupfuls onto prepared cookie sheets. Spread dough into 2½- to 3-inch circles. Bake about 16 minutes or until golden. Remove to wire racks to cool.
Makes about 16 cookies

Chocolate Chip 'n Oatmeal Cookies

Orange-Walnut Chippers

- **1 cup packed light brown sugar**
- **½ cup butter or margarine, softened**
- **1 large egg**
- **1 tablespoon grated orange peel**
- **½ cup all-purpose flour**
- **¼ teaspoon baking soda**
- **¼ teaspoon salt**
- **1½ cups uncooked rolled oats**
- **1 cup semisweet chocolate chips**
- **½ cup coarsely chopped walnuts**

Preheat oven to 375°F. Lightly grease cookie sheets; set aside.

Beat sugar and butter in large bowl until light and fluffy. Beat in egg and orange peel. Add flour, baking soda and salt to butter mixture. Beat until well blended. Stir in oats, chips and nuts. Drop by rounded teaspoonfuls 2 inches apart onto prepared cookie sheets.

Bake 10 to 12 minutes or until golden brown. Let cookies stand on cookie sheets 2 minutes. Remove cookies to wire racks; cool completely. *Makes about 3 dozen cookies*

Tip

One medium orange yields 1 to 2 tablespoons grated peel, which can be frozen for up to six months.

Orange-Walnut Chippers

Peanut Butter Chip Oatmeal Cookies

- 1 cup (2 sticks) butter or margarine, softened
- ¼ cup shortening
- 2 cups packed light brown sugar
- 1 tablespoon milk
- 2 teaspoons vanilla extract
- 1 egg
- 2 cups all-purpose flour
- 1⅔ cups (10-ounce package) REESE'S® Peanut Butter Chips
- 1½ cups quick-cooking or regular rolled oats
- ½ cup chopped walnuts
- ½ teaspoon baking soda
- ½ teaspoon salt

1. Heat oven to 375°F.

2. Beat butter, shortening, brown sugar, milk, vanilla and egg in large mixer bowl until light and fluffy. Add remaining ingredients; mix until well blended. Drop dough by rounded teaspoonfuls about 2 inches apart onto ungreased cookie sheet.

3. Bake until light brown, 10 to 12 minutes for soft cookies or 12 to 14 minutes for crisp cookies. Remove from cookie sheet to wire rack. Cool completely.

Makes about 6 dozen cookies

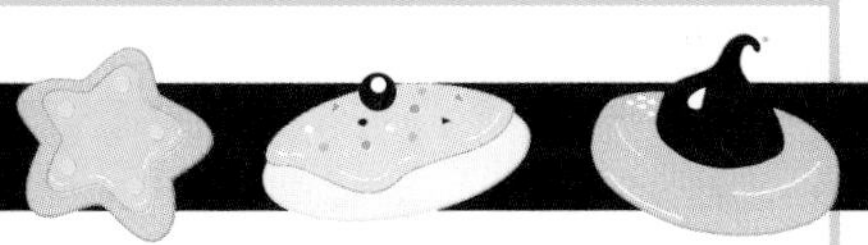

Oatmeal Treasures

COOKIES

- **¾ Butter Flavor* CRISCO® Stick or ¾ cup Butter Flavor* CRISCO® all-vegetable shortening plus additional for greasing**
- **1¼ cups firmly packed light brown sugar**
- **1 egg**
- **⅓ cup milk**
- **1½ teaspoons vanilla**
- **3 cups quick oats, uncooked**
- **1 cup all-purpose flour**
- **½ teaspoon baking soda**
- **½ teaspoon salt**
- **1 cup milk chocolate chips**
- **½ cup flake coconut**

DRIZZLE

- **⅓ cup white chocolate baking pieces**
- **1 tablespoon plus 2 teaspoons Butter Flavor* CRISCO® Stick or 1 tablespoon plus 2 teaspoons Butter Flavor* CRISCO®, divided**
- **⅓ cup semi-sweet chocolate chips**

**Butter Flavor Crisco® is artificially flavored.*

1. Heat oven to 375°F. Grease baking sheets with shortening. Place sheets of foil on countertop for cooling cookies.

2. For cookies, combine ¾ cup shortening, brown sugar, egg, milk and vanilla in large bowl. Beat at medium speed of electric mixer until well blended.

3. Combine oats, flour, baking soda and salt. Mix into creamed mixture at low speed just until blended. Stir in milk chocolate chips and coconut.

4. Drop rounded tablespoonfuls of dough 2 inches apart onto ungreased baking sheet.

5. Bake one baking sheet at a time at 375°F for 10 to 12 minutes or until lightly browned. *Do not overbake.* Cool 2 minutes on baking sheet. Remove cookies to foil to cool completely.

6. For drizzle, place white chocolate pieces and 1 tablespoon shortening in heavy resealable plastic bag or microwave-safe bowl. Microwave at 50% (MEDIUM) for 1 minute. Knead or stir and repeat, if necessary, until completely smooth. Cut tiny tip off corner of bag. Drizzle over top of each cookie. Melt semi-sweet chocolate chips and remaining 2 teaspoons shortening as directed for white chocolate. Drizzle again over top of each cookie.

Makes about 2½ dozen cookies

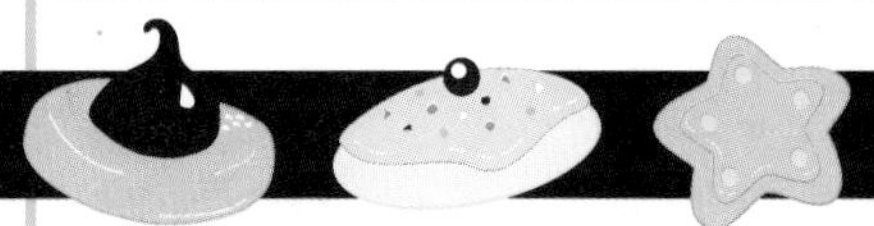

Cowboy Cookies

- ½ cup butter or margarine, softened
- ½ cup packed light brown sugar
- ¼ cup granulated sugar
- 1 egg
- 1 teaspoon vanilla
- 1 cup all-purpose flour
- 2 tablespoons unsweetened cocoa powder
- ½ teaspoon baking powder
- ¼ teaspoon baking soda
- 1 cup uncooked rolled oats
- 1 cup (6 ounces) semisweet chocolate chips
- ½ cup raisins
- ½ cup chopped nuts

Preheat oven to 375°F. Lightly grease cookie sheets or line with parchment paper.

Beat butter with sugars in large bowl until blended. Add egg and vanilla; beat until fluffy. Combine flour, cocoa, baking powder and baking soda in small bowl; stir into butter mixture. Add oats, chocolate chips, raisins and nuts. Drop by rounded teaspoonfuls 2 inches apart onto prepared cookie sheets.

Bake 10 to 12 minutes or until lightly browned around edges. Remove to wire racks to cool.

Makes about 4 dozen cookies

Tip

Using parchment paper on your cookie sheets makes kitchen cleanup a breeze. It is available at gourmet kitchenware stores and at many supermarkets.

Cowboy Cookies

Out of the Ordinary

Chocolate Macadamia Cookies

1 package DUNCAN HINES® Chocolate Chip Cookie Mix
¼ cup unsweetened cocoa powder
⅓ cup vegetable oil
1 egg
3 tablespoons water
⅔ cup coarsely chopped macadamia nuts

Preheat oven to 375°F.

Combine cookie mix and cocoa in large bowl. Add oil, egg and water. Stir until thoroughly blended. Stir in macadamia nuts. Drop by rounded teaspoonfuls 2 inches apart onto *ungreased* cookie sheets.

Bake 8 to 10 minutes or until set. Cool 1 minute on cookie sheets. Remove to cooling racks. Cool completely.

Makes 3 dozen cookies

Chocolate Macadamia Cookies

Peanut Butter Chip Orange Cookies

- ½ cup (1 stick) butter or margarine, softened
- ½ cup shortening
- ¾ cup granulated sugar
- ¾ cup packed light brown sugar
- 2 eggs
- 1 tablespoon freshly grated orange peel
- 1 teaspoon vanilla extract
- 2¼ cups all-purpose flour
- 1 teaspoon baking soda
- 1 teaspoon salt
- ¼ cup orange juice
- 1⅔ cups (10-ounce package) REESE'S® Peanut Butter Chips

1. Heat oven to 350°F.

2. Beat butter, shortening, granulated sugar and brown sugar in large bowl until light and fluffy. Add eggs, orange peel and vanilla; beat until blended. Stir together flour, baking soda and salt; add alternately with orange juice to butter mixture, beating until well blended. Stir in peanut butter chips. Drop by teaspoons onto ungreased cookie sheet.

3. Bake 8 to 10 minutes or until lightly browned. Cool slightly; remove from cookie sheet to wire rack. Cool completely.

Makes about 6 dozen cookies

Tip: Cool cookie sheets completely before putting more cookie dough on them. Dropping cookie dough on warm cookie sheets causes excess spread.

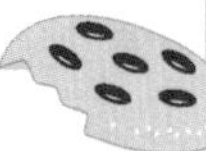

Peanut Butter Chip Orange Cookies

Jam-Up Oatmeal Cookies

1 Butter Flavor* CRISCO® Stick or 1 cup Butter Flavor* CRISCO® all-vegetable shortening plus additional for greasing
1½ cups firmly packed brown sugar
2 eggs
2 teaspoons almond extract
2 cups all-purpose flour
1 teaspoon baking powder
1 teaspoon salt
½ teaspoon baking soda
2½ cups quick oats (not instant or old fashioned), uncooked
1 cup finely chopped pecans
1 jar (12 ounces) strawberry jam
Sugar for sprinkling

**Butter Flavor Crisco® is artificially flavored.*

1. Combine 1 cup shortening and brown sugar in large bowl. Beat at medium speed of electric mixer until well blended. Beat in eggs and almond extract.

2. Combine flour, baking powder, salt and baking soda. Mix into shortening mixture at low speed until just blended. Stir in oats and chopped nuts with spoon. Cover and refrigerate at least 1 hour.

3. Heat oven to 350°F. Grease baking sheets with shortening. Place sheets of foil on countertop for cooling cookies.

4. Roll out dough, half at a time, to about ¼-inch thickness on floured surface. Cut out with 2½-inch round cookie cutter. Place 1 teaspoonful of jam in center of half of the rounds. Top with remaining rounds. Press edges to seal. Prick centers; sprinkle with sugar. Place 1 inch apart on baking sheets.

5. Bake one baking sheet at a time at 350°F for 12 to 15 minutes or until lightly browned. *Do not overbake.* Cool 2 minutes on baking sheets. Remove cookies to foil to cool completely.

Makes about 2 dozen cookies

Jam-Up Oatmeal Cookies

Chocolate Edged Lace Cookies

⅔ cup ground almonds
½ cup butter
½ cup sugar
2 tablespoons milk
1 tablespoon flour
4 ounces dark sweet or bittersweet chocolate candy bar, broken into pieces

Preheat oven to 325°F. Grease cookie sheets very lightly. Combine almonds, butter, sugar, milk and flour in large skillet. Cook and stir over low heat until well blended. Keep mixture warm over very low heat while forming and baking cookies.

Drop tablespoonfuls of batter 2 inches apart on prepared cookie sheets. Bake 6 minutes or until cookies are golden brown. Let cookies stand on cookie sheets 30 seconds to 1 minute before loosening with thin spatula. (If cookies become too brittle to remove, warm them briefly in oven.) Remove cookies to wire rack;* cool.

Melt chocolate in small, heavy saucepan over low heat, stirring constantly. Tilt saucepan to pool chocolate at one end; dip edge of each cookie in chocolate, turning cookie slowly so entire edge is tinged with chocolate. Let cookies stand on waxed paper until chocolate is set.

Makes about 2 dozen cookies

**For tuile-shaped cookies, balance a wooden spoon over two cans of the same height. Working quickly while cookies are still hot, drape the cookies (bottom side down) over the handle of the spoon so that both sides hang down and form a taco shape. When firm, transfer to wire rack to cool completely. Dip both edges of cooled cookies into chocolate.*

Chocolate Edged Lace Cookies

Peanut Butter Knockouts

1 package DUNCAN HINES® Peanut Butter Cookie Mix
1 whole egg
1 (3-ounce) package cream cheese, softened
¼ cup creamy peanut butter
1 egg yolk
2½ tablespoons granulated sugar
Dash salt (optional)
½ cup semisweet mini chocolate chips (optional)
½ cup semisweet chocolate chips
2 teaspoons shortening

Preheat oven to 375°F.

Combine cookie mix, contents of peanut butter packet from mix and whole egg in large bowl. Stir until thoroughly blended. Shape dough into 36 (about 1-inch) balls. Place 2 inches apart onto *ungreased* cookie sheets. Press thumb gently in center of each cookie.

Combine cream cheese, peanut butter, egg yolk, sugar and salt in medium bowl. Beat at medium speed with electric mixer until blended. Stir in mini chocolate chips, if desired. Fill center of each cookie with rounded teaspoonful of filling. Bake 8 to 10 minutes or until light golden brown. Cool 2 minutes on cookie sheets. Remove to cooling racks. Cool completely.

Place chocolate chips and shortening in small resealable plastic bag; seal. Place bag in bowl of hot water for several minutes. Dry bag with towel. Knead bag until contents are blended and chocolate is smooth. Snip tiny hole in corner of bag. Drizzle contents over cookies. Allow drizzle to set before storing cookies between layers of waxed paper in airtight container. *Makes 3 dozen cookies*

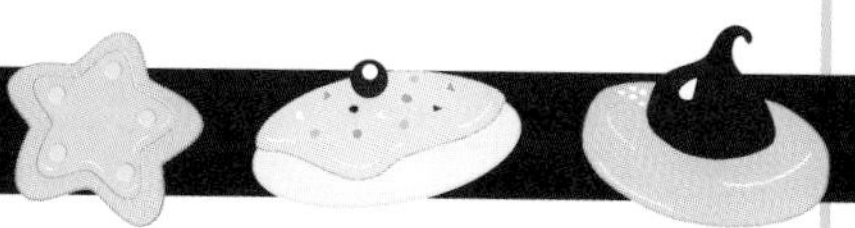

Snow Caps

- 3 egg whites, room temperature
- ¼ teaspoon cream of tartar
- ¾ cup sugar
- ½ teaspoon vanilla extract
- 1 cup (6 ounces) semisweet chocolate chips
- 4 ounces white chocolate, grated

Preheat oven to 200°F. Line baking sheets with plain ungreased brown paper such as heavy brown paper bags (not recycled). Combine egg whites and cream of tartar in large bowl of electric mixer. Beat at highest speed until mixture is just frothy. Add sugar, 1 tablespoon at a time, beating well after each addition. Beat until stiff peaks form. Add vanilla; beat 1 minute. Fold in chocolate chips. Drop mixture by teaspoonfuls onto prepared baking sheets. Bake 2 hours or until meringues are thoroughly dry to touch but not browned, rotating baking sheets halfway through baking. Turn off heat and leave in closed oven 3 to 4 hours or until completely dry. Remove from oven and cool completely. Carefully remove meringues from paper.

Bring water in bottom of double boiler to a boil; turn off heat. Place white chocolate in top of double boiler; place over hot water. Stir constantly until chocolate melts. Dip top of each meringue into melted chocolate. Place on waxed paper to dry. Store at room temperature in a tightly covered container.

Makes about 6 dozen cookies

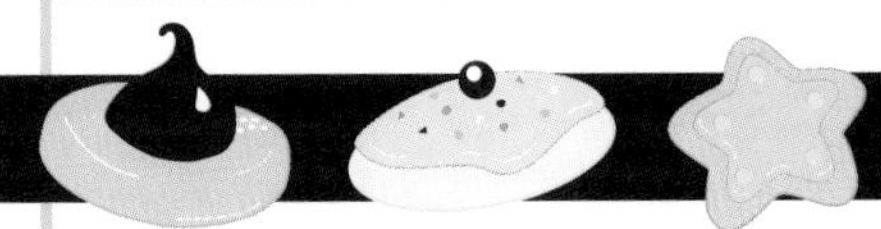

Apple Pie Wedges

- 1 cup butter, softened
- ⅔ cup sugar
- 1 egg yolk
- ⅓ cup apple butter
- 2⅓ cups all-purpose flour
- 1 teaspoon ground cinnamon
- ½ teaspoon apple pie spice
- ½ teaspoon vanilla

1. Beat butter and sugar in medium bowl at medium speed of electric mixer until fluffy.

2. Add egg yolk and apple butter; mix well. Add flour, cinnamon, apple pie spice and vanilla; beat at low speed until well blended.

3. Divide dough in half. Shape each half into 6-inch disc and wrap in plastic wrap. Refrigerate 30 minutes.

4. Preheat oven to 325°F. Invert 1 disc of dough into ungreased 9-inch round pie plate.

5. Press dough into plate with lightly floured hand, covering plate completely.

6. Flute edge using handle of wooden spoon. Deeply score into 8 wedges.

7. Prick surface using tines of fork. Repeat steps with remaining disc of dough and another pie plate.

8. Bake 35 minutes or until golden brown. Remove to wire rack; cool completely. Cut into wedges.

Makes 16 wedges

Tip: Serve these tasty cookies warm with a big scoop of vanilla or cinnamon-flavored ice cream.

Apple Pie Wedges

Cocoa Crinkle Sandwiches

1¾ cups all-purpose flour
½ cup unsweetened cocoa
1 teaspoon baking soda
¼ teaspoon salt
½ cup butter
1¾ cups sugar, divided
2 eggs
2 teaspoons vanilla
1 can (16 ounces) chocolate or favorite flavor frosting
½ cup crushed candy canes* (optional)

**To crush candy canes, place candy in sealed heavy-duty plastic food storage bag. Break into pieces with heavy object (such as meat mallet or can of vegetables); crush pieces with rolling pin.*

Combine flour, cocoa, baking soda and salt in medium bowl.

Melt butter in large saucepan over medium heat; cool slightly. Add 1¼ cups sugar; whisk until smooth. Whisk in eggs, 1 at a time, until blended. Stir in vanilla until smooth. Stir in flour mixture just until combined. Wrap dough in plastic wrap; refrigerate 2 hours.

Preheat oven to 350°F. Grease cookie sheets. Shape dough into 1-inch balls. Place remaining ½ cup sugar in shallow bowl; roll balls in sugar. Place 1½ inches apart on cookie sheets.

Bake12 minutes or until cookies feel set to the touch. Let cookies stand on cookie sheets 5 minutes; transfer to wire racks to cool completely.

Stir frosting until soft and smooth. Place crushed candy canes on piece of waxed paper. Spread about 2 teaspoons frosting over flat side of one cookie. Place second cookie, flat side down, over frosting, pressing down to allow frosting to squeeze out slightly between cookies. Press exposed frosting into crushed candy canes. Repeat with remaining cookies. Store in airtight container.

Makes about 20 sandwich cookies (about 40 unfilled cookies)

Cocoa Crinkle Sandwiches

Spicy Lemon Crescents

1 cup (2 sticks) butter or margarine, softened
1½ cups powdered sugar, divided
½ teaspoon lemon extract
½ teaspoon grated lemon zest
2 cups cake flour
½ cup finely chopped almonds, walnuts or pecans
1 teaspoon ground cinnamon
½ teaspoon ground cardamom
½ teaspoon ground nutmeg
1¾ cups "M&M's"® Chocolate Mini Baking Bits

Preheat oven to 375°F. Lightly grease cookie sheets; set aside. In large bowl cream butter and ½ cup sugar; add lemon extract and zest until well blended. In medium bowl combine flour, nuts, cinnamon, cardamom and nutmeg; add to creamed mixture until well blended. Stir in "M&M's"® Chocolate Mini Baking Bits. Using 1 tablespoon of dough at a time, form into crescent shapes; place about 2 inches apart onto prepared cookie sheets. Bake 12 to 14 minutes or until edges are golden. Cool 2 minutes on cookie sheets. Gently roll warm crescents in remaining 1 cup sugar. Cool completely on wire racks. Store in tightly covered container.

Makes about 2 dozen cookies

Spicy Lemon Crescents

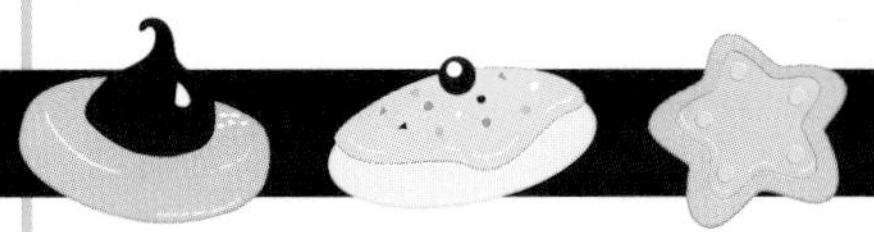

Mocha Cookies

- 2 tablespoons plus 1½ teaspoons instant coffee granules
- 1½ tablespoons skim milk
- ⅓ cup packed light brown sugar
- ¼ cup granulated sugar
- ¼ cup margarine
- 1 egg
- ½ teaspoon almond extract
- 2 cups all-purpose flour, sifted
- ¼ cup wheat flakes
- ½ teaspoon ground cinnamon
- ¼ teaspoon baking powder

Preheat oven to 350°F. Spray cookie sheets with nonstick cooking spray. Dissolve coffee granules in milk. In large bowl, beat brown sugar, granulated sugar and margarine until smooth and creamy. Beat in egg, almond extract and coffee mixture. Combine flour, wheat flakes, cinnamon and baking powder; gradually beat flour mixture into sugar mixture. Drop by teaspoonfuls onto prepared cookie sheets; flatten with back of fork. Bake 8 to 10 minutes.

Makes about 40 cookies

Favorite recipe from The Sugar Association, Inc.

Tip

Let your cookie sheets cool to room temperature before adding more dough and baking another batch of cookies. Hot cookie sheets will cause the dough to melt and spread, affecting the cookies' final texture.

Mocha Cookies

Date Pinwheel Cookies

1¼ cups dates, pitted and finely chopped
¾ cup orange juice
½ cup granulated sugar
1 tablespoon butter
3 cups plus 1 tablespoon all-purpose flour, divided
2 teaspoons vanilla, divided
4 ounces cream cheese
¼ cup vegetable shortening
1 cup packed brown sugar
2 eggs
1 teaspoon baking soda
½ teaspoon salt

1. Heat dates, orange juice, granulated sugar, butter and 1 tablespoon flour in medium saucepan over medium heat. Cook 10 minutes or until thick, stirring frequently; remove from heat. Stir in 1 teaspoon vanilla; set aside to cool.

2. Beat cream cheese, shortening and brown sugar about 3 minutes in large bowl until light and fluffy. Add eggs and remaining 1 teaspoon vanilla; beat 2 minutes longer.

3. Combine 3 cups flour, baking soda and salt in medium bowl. Add to shortening mixture; stir just until blended. Divide dough in half. Roll one half of dough on lightly floured work surface into 12×9-inch rectangle. Spread half of date mixture over dough. Spread evenly, leaving ¼-inch border on top short edge. Starting at short side, tightly roll up dough jelly-roll style. Wrap in plastic wrap; freeze for at least 1 hour. Repeat with remaining dough.

4. Preheat oven to 350°F. Grease cookie sheets. Unwrap dough. Using heavy thread or dental floss, cut dough into ¼-inch slices. Place slices 1 inch apart on prepared cookie sheets.

5. Bake 12 minutes or until lightly browned. Let cookies stand on cookie sheets 2 minutes. Remove cookies to wire rack; cool completely.

Makes 6 dozen cookies

Date Pinwheel Cookies

Heavenly Oatmeal Hearts

COOKIES

¾ Butter Flavor* CRISCO® Stick or ¾ cup Butter Flavor* CRISCO® all-vegetable shortening plus additional for greasing
1¼ cups packed brown sugar
1 egg
⅓ cup milk
1½ teaspoons vanilla
3 cups quick oats, uncooked
1 cup all-purpose flour
1½ teaspoons cinnamon
½ teaspoon baking soda
½ teaspoon salt
1 cup milk chocolate chips
1 cup white chocolate baking pieces
1 cup honey-roasted peanuts, chopped

DRIZZLE

½ cup milk chocolate chips
½ cup white chocolate baking pieces
1 teaspoon Butter Flavor* CRISCO® Stick or 1 teaspoon Butter Flavor* CRISCO® all-vegetable shortening

**Butter Flavor Crisco® is artificially flavored.*

1. Heat oven to 375°F. Grease baking sheets. Place sheets of foil on countertop for cooling cookies.

2. For cookies, combine ¾ cup shortening, brown sugar, egg, milk and vanilla in large bowl. Beat at medium speed of electric mixer until well blended.

3. Combine oats, flour, cinnamon, baking soda and salt. Mix into creamed mixture at low speed just until blended. Stir in chips, baking pieces and nuts.

4. Place 3-inch heart-shaped cookie cutter on prepared baking sheet. Place ⅓ cup dough inside cutter. Press to edges and level. Remove cutter. Repeat to form remaining cookies, spacing 2½ inches apart.

5. Bake one baking sheet at a time at 375°F for 10 to 12 minutes or until lightly browned. *Do not overbake.* Cool 2 minutes on baking sheet. Remove cookies to foil to cool completely.

6. For drizzle, place both chips in separate heavy resealable sandwich bags. Add ½ teaspoon shortening to each bag. Seal. Microwave 1 bag at 50% power (MEDIUM). Knead bag after 1 minute. Repeat until mixture is smooth. Repeat with remaining bag. Cut tiny piece off corner of each bag. Squeeze out and drizzle both mixtures over cookies. To serve, cut cookies in half, if desired.

Makes 2½ dozen heart cookies

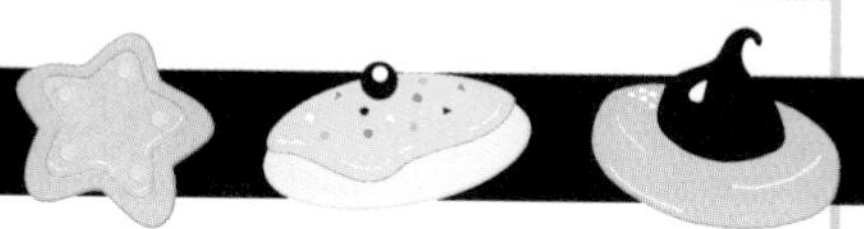

Peppersass Cookies

- 2¼ cups all-purpose flour
- ½ teaspoon baking soda
- ½ teaspoon salt
- 1½ cups sugar, divided
- ⅔ cup butter or margarine, at room temperature
- 1 egg
- 2 teaspoons TABASCO® brand Pepper Sauce
- 1 teaspoon vanilla extract

Combine flour, baking soda and salt in small bowl. Beat 1 cup sugar and butter in large bowl with electric mixer at low speed until well blended. Add egg, TABASCO® Sauce, vanilla and flour mixture; beat until smooth.

Divide dough in half; place halves on plastic wrap. Shape each half into log about 1½ inches in diameter. Cover and refrigerate until firm, 2 to 3 hours or overnight.

Preheat oven to 350°F. Place remaining ½ cup sugar in shallow dish. Cut dough logs into ¼-inch-thick slices; dip each slice in sugar. Place slices 1 inch apart on ungreased cookie sheets. Bake 10 to 12 minutes or until cookies are golden around the edges. Cool on wire racks.

Makes about 5 dozen cookies

Milk Chocolate Florentine Cookies

- ⅔ cup butter
- 2 cups quick oats, uncooked
- 1 cup granulated sugar
- ⅔ cup all-purpose flour
- ¼ cup light or dark corn syrup
- ¼ cup milk
- 1 teaspoon vanilla extract
- ¼ teaspoon salt
- 2 cups (11.5-ounce package) NESTLÉ® TOLL HOUSE® Milk Chocolate Morsels

MELT butter in medium saucepan; remove from heat. Stir in oats, sugar, flour, corn syrup, milk, vanilla and salt; mix well. Drop by level teaspoonfuls, about 3 inches apart, onto foil-lined baking sheets. Spread thinly with rubber spatula.

BAKE in preheated 375°F. oven for 6 to 8 minutes, until golden brown; cool on baking sheets on wire racks. Peel foil from cookies.

MICROWAVE morsels in medium microwave-safe bowl on MEDIUM-HIGH (70%) power for 1 minute; stir. Microwave at additional 10- to 20-second intervals, stirring until smooth. Spread thin layer of melted chocolate on flat side of *half* the cookies. Top with remaining cookies.

Makes about 3½ dozen sandwich cookies

Cashew-Lemon Shortbread Cookies

- ½ cup roasted cashews
- 1 cup butter, softened
- ½ cup sugar
- 2 teaspoons lemon extract
- 1 teaspoon vanilla
- 2 cups all-purpose flour
- Additional sugar

1. Preheat oven to 325°F. Place cashews in food processor; process until finely ground. Add butter, sugar, lemon extract and vanilla; process until well blended. Add flour; process using on/off pulsing action until dough is well blended and begins to form a ball.

2. Shape dough into 1½-inch balls; roll in additional sugar. Place about 2 inches apart onto ungreased baking sheets; flatten with bottom of glass.

3. Bake cookies 17 to 19 minutes or just until set and edges are lightly browned. Remove cookies from baking sheets to wire rack to cool. *Makes 2 to 2½ dozen cookies*

Chocolate Sugar Drops

- ½ cup butter or margarine, softened
- ½ cup vegetable oil
- ½ cup powdered sugar
- ½ cup granulated sugar
- 1 egg
- 2 cups all-purpose flour
- ¼ cup unsweetened cocoa
- ½ teaspoon baking soda
- ½ teaspoon cream of tartar
- ¼ teaspoon salt
- 1 teaspoon vanilla
- Additional granulated sugar

Beat butter, oil, powdered sugar, ½ cup granulated sugar and egg in large bowl until light and fluffy. Combine flour, cocoa, baking soda, cream of tartar and salt in small bowl. Add to butter mixture with vanilla, stirring until dough is smooth. Cover; refrigerate 30 minutes or overnight, if desired.

Preheat oven to 350°F. Lightly grease cookie sheets or line with parchment paper. Shape dough into marble-sized balls. Place 2 inches apart on prepared cookie sheets. Flatten each cookie to about ⅓-inch thickness with bottom of greased glass dipped in additional granulated sugar.

Bake 10 minutes or until firm. *Do not overbake.* Remove to wire racks to cool. *Makes about 5 dozen cookies*

Cashew-Lemon Shortbread Cookies

Marbled Biscotti

½ cup (1 stick) butter or margarine, softened
1 cup granulated sugar
2 large eggs
1 teaspoon vanilla extract
2½ cups all-purpose flour
1 teaspoon baking powder
1 teaspoon baking soda
1¾ cups "M&M's"® Chocolate Mini Baking Bits, divided
1 cup slivered almonds, toasted*
¼ cup unsweetened cocoa powder
2 tablespoons instant coffee granules

**To toast almonds, spread in single layer on baking sheet. Bake at 350°F for 7 to 10 minutes until light golden, stirring occasionally. Remove almonds from pan and cool completely before using.*

Preheat oven to 350°F. Lightly grease cookie sheets; set aside. In large bowl cream butter and sugar until light and fluffy; beat in eggs and vanilla. In medium bowl combine flour, baking powder and baking soda; blend into creamed mixture. Dough will be stiff. Stir in 1¼ cups "M&M's"® Chocolate Mini Baking Bits and nuts. Divide dough in half. Add cocoa powder and coffee granules to half of the dough, mixing to blend. On well-floured surface, gently knead doughs together just enough to marble. Divide dough in half and gently roll each half into 12×2-inch log; place on prepared cookie sheets at least 4 inches apart. Press remaining ½ cup "M&M's"® Chocolate Mini Baking Bits onto outside of both logs. Bake 25 minutes. Dough will spread. Cool logs 15 to 20 minutes. Slice each log into 12 slices; arrange on cookie sheet cut-side down. Bake an additional 10 minutes. (For softer biscotti, omit second baking.) Cool completely. Store in tightly covered container.

Makes 24 pieces

Marbled Biscotti

Chocolate Peanut Butter Cup Cookies

COOKIES

1 cup semi-sweet chocolate chips
2 squares (1 ounce each) unsweetened baking chocolate
1 cup sugar
½ Butter Flavor* CRISCO® Stick or ½ cup Butter Flavor* CRISCO® all-vegetable shortening
2 eggs
1 teaspoon salt
1 teaspoon vanilla
1½ cups plus 2 tablespoons all-purpose flour
½ teaspoon baking soda
¾ cup finely chopped peanuts
36 miniature peanut butter cups, unwrapped

DRIZZLE

1 cup peanut butter chips

**Butter Flavor Crisco® is artificially flavored.*

1. Heat oven to 350°F. Place sheets of foil on countertop for cooling cookies.

2. For cookies, combine chocolate chips and chocolate squares in microwave-safe measuring cup or bowl. Microwave at 50% (MEDIUM). Stir after 2 minutes. Repeat until smooth (or melt on rangetop in small saucepan on very low heat). Cool slightly.

3. Combine sugar and ½ cup shortening in large bowl. Beat at medium speed of electric mixer until blended and crumbly. Beat in eggs, one at a time, then salt and vanilla. Reduce speed to low. Add chocolate slowly. Mix until well blended. Stir in flour and baking soda with spoon until well blended. Shape dough into 1¼-inch balls. Roll in nuts. Place 2 inches apart on ungreased baking sheet.

4. Bake at 350°F for 8 to 10 minutes or until set. *Do not overbake.* Press peanut butter cup into center of each cookie immediately. Press cookie against cup. Cool 2 minutes on baking sheet before removing to cooling rack. Cool completely.

5. For drizzle, place peanut butter chips in heavy resealable sandwich bag. Seal. Microwave at 50% (MEDIUM). Knead bag after 1 minute. Repeat until smooth (or melt by placing bag in hot water). Cut tiny tip off corner of bag. Squeeze out and drizzle over cookies. *Makes 3 dozen cookies*

Chocolate Peanut Butter Cup Cookies

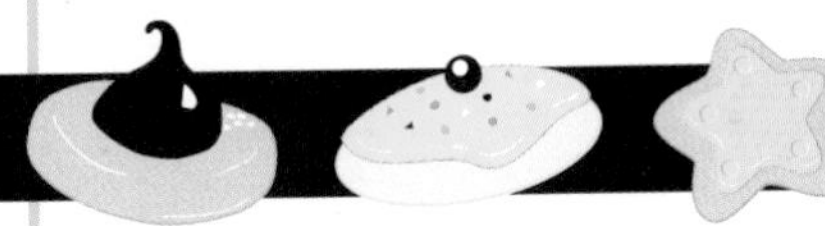

Raspberry Almond Sandwich Cookies

- 1 package DUNCAN HINES® Golden Sugar Cookie Mix
- 1 egg
- ¼ cup vegetable oil
- 1 tablespoon water
- ¾ teaspoon almond extract
- 1⅓ cups sliced natural almonds, broken
- Seedless red raspberry jam

Tip

Sandwich cookies should be stored in layers separated by waxed paper to prevent them from sticking together.

Preheat oven to 375°F.

Combine cookie mix, egg, oil, water and almond extract in large bowl. Stir until thoroughly blended. Drop half of dough by level teaspoonfuls 2 inches apart onto *ungreased* cookie sheets. (Dough will spread during baking to 1½ to 1¾ inches.)

Place almonds on waxed paper. Drop remaining half of dough by level teaspoonfuls onto nuts. Place almond side up 2 inches apart onto *ungreased* cookie sheets.

Bake both plain and almond cookies 6 minutes or until set but not browned. Cool 1 minute on cookie sheets. Remove to cooling racks. Cool completely.

Spread bottoms of plain cookies with jam; top with almond cookies. Press together to make sandwiches. Store in airtight container.

Makes 6 dozen sandwich cookies

Raspberry Almond Sandwich Cookies

Macaroon Kiss Cookies

- ⅓ cup butter or margarine, softened
- 1 package (3 ounces) cream cheese, softened
- ¾ cup sugar
- 1 egg yolk
- 2 teaspoons almond extract
- 2 teaspoons orange juice
- 1¼ cups all-purpose flour
- 2 teaspoons baking powder
- ¼ teaspoon salt
- 5 cups MOUNDS® Sweetened Coconut Flakes, divided
- 1 bag (8 ounces) HERSHEY'S KISSES® Milk Chocolates

1. Beat together butter, cream cheese and sugar in large bowl. Add egg yolk, almond extract and orange juice; beat well. Stir together flour, baking powder and salt; gradually add to butter mixture. Stir in 3 cups coconut. Cover; refrigerate 1 hour or until firm enough to handle.

2. Heat oven to 350°F. Shape dough into 1-inch balls; roll in remaining 2 cups coconut. Place on ungreased cookie sheets.

3. Bake 10 to 12 minutes or until lightly browned. Meanwhile, remove wrappers from chocolate pieces. Remove cookies from oven; immediately press chocolate piece in center of each cookie. Cool 1 minute. Carefully remove from cookie sheets to wire racks. Cool completely.

Makes about 4½ dozen cookies

Snow-Covered Almond Crescents

- 1 cup (2 sticks) margarine or butter, softened
- ¾ cup powdered sugar
- ½ teaspoon almond extract or 2 teaspoons vanilla extract
- 2 cups all-purpose flour
- ¼ teaspoon salt (optional)
- 1 cup QUAKER® Oats (quick or old fashioned, uncooked)
- ½ cup finely chopped almonds
- Additional powdered sugar

Preheat oven to 325°F. Beat margarine, ¾ cup powdered sugar and almond extract until fluffy. Add flour and salt; mix until well blended. Stir in oats and almonds. Shape level measuring tablespoonfuls of dough into crescents. Place on ungreased cookie sheet about 2 inches apart.

Bake 14 to 17 minutes or until bottoms are light golden brown. Remove to wire rack. Sift additional powdered sugar generously over warm cookies. Cool completely. Store tightly covered.

Makes about 4 dozen cookies

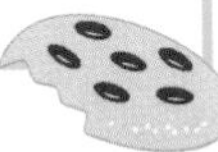

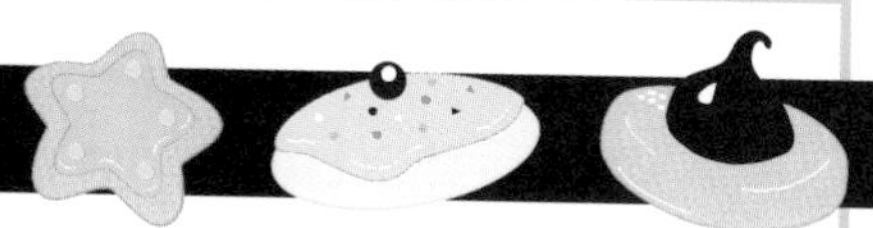

Slice 'n' Bake Ginger Wafers

½ cup butter or margarine, softened
1 cup packed brown sugar
¼ cup light molasses
1 egg
2 teaspoons ground ginger
1 teaspoon grated orange peel
¼ teaspoon salt
¼ teaspoon ground cinnamon
¼ teaspoon ground cloves
2 cups all-purpose flour

1. Beat butter, sugar and molasses in large bowl until light and fluffy. Add egg, ginger, orange peel, salt, cinnamon and cloves; beat until well blended. Stir in flour until well blended. (Dough will be very stiff.)

2. Divide dough in half. Roll each half into 8×1½-inch log. Wrap logs in waxed paper or plastic wrap; refrigerate at least 5 hours or up to 3 days.

3. Preheat oven to 350°F. Cut dough into ¼-inch-thick slices. Place about 2 inches apart onto ungreased baking sheets. Bake 12 to 14 minutes or until set. Remove from baking sheet to wire rack to cool. *Makes about 4½ dozen cookies*

Serving Suggestion: Dip half of each cookie in melted white chocolate or drizzle cookies with a glaze of 1¼ cups powdered sugar and 2 tablespoons orange juice. Or, cut cookie dough into ⅛-inch-thick slices; bake and sandwich melted caramel candy or peanut butter between cookies.

Banana Crescents

- ½ cup DOLE® Chopped Almonds, toasted
- 6 tablespoons sugar, divided
- ½ cup margarine, cut into pieces
- 1½ cups plus 2 tablespoons all-purpose flour
- ⅛ teaspoon salt
- 1 extra-ripe, medium DOLE® Banana, peeled
- 2 to 3 ounces semisweet chocolate chips

• Pulverize almonds with 2 tablespoons sugar.

• Beat margarine, almonds, remaining 4 tablespoons sugar, flour and salt.

• Purée banana; add to almond mixture and mix until well blended.

• Roll tablespoonfuls of dough into logs, then shape into crescents. Place on ungreased cookie sheet. Bake in 375°F oven 25 minutes or until golden. Cool on wire rack.

• Melt chocolate in microwavable dish at MEDIUM (50% power) 1½ to 2 minutes, stirring once. Dip ends of cookies in chocolate. Refrigerate until chocolate is set.

Makes 2 dozen cookies

Triple Chocolate Cookies

- 1 package DUNCAN HINES® Moist Deluxe® Swiss Chocolate Cake Mix
- ½ cup butter or margarine, melted
- 1 egg
- ½ cup semisweet chocolate chips
- ½ cup milk chocolate chips
- ½ cup coarsely chopped white chocolate
- ½ cup chopped pecans

1. Preheat oven to 375°F.

2. Combine cake mix, melted butter and egg in large bowl. Beat at low speed with electric mixer until blended. Stir in all 3 chocolates and pecans.

3. Drop by rounded tablespoonfuls onto ungreased baking sheets. Bake at 375°F 9 to 11 minutes. Cool 1 minute on baking sheet. Remove to cooling racks.

Makes 3½ to 4 dozen cookies

Tip: Cookies may be stored in an airtight container in freezer for up to 6 months.

Banana Crescents

Fudge Meringues

- ⅓ cup unsweetened cocoa powder
- 2 tablespoons all-purpose flour
- 1 square (1 ounce) semisweet chocolate, finely chopped
- 3 egg whites
- ¼ teaspoon cream of tartar
- ¼ teaspoon salt
- 2 cups powdered sugar

1. Preheat oven to 300°F. Combine cocoa, flour and chocolate in small bowl; set aside. Beat egg whites in medium bowl with electric mixer at high speed until foamy. Add cream of tartar and salt; beat until soft peaks form. Gradually beat in powdered sugar; beat until stiff peaks form. Fold in chocolate mixture.

2. Drop mixture by rounded tablespoonfuls onto cookie sheets lined with parchment paper. Bake 20 minutes or until cookies are crisp when lightly touched with fingertip (cookies will crack). Slide parchment paper onto wire racks; cool completely. Carefully remove cookies from parchment paper. Cookies are best when eaten the day they are baked but can be stored in an airtight container for up to 2 days. Cookies will become crispier when stored.

Makes 2 dozen cookies

Honey Carrot Cookies

- 1 cup sugar
- ½ cup butter, softened
- 2 eggs
- 3 tablespoons honey
- 1 teaspoon vanilla
- 2¼ cups all-purpose flour
- 2 teaspoons baking soda
- ½ teaspoon nutmeg
- ¼ teaspoon salt
- ½ cup shredded carrot

Preheat oven to 325°F. Combine sugar and butter in large bowl. Beat well. Add eggs, honey and vanilla; beat until well mixed. Combine flour, baking soda, nutmeg and salt in medium bowl. Stir dry ingredients into butter mixture; mix well. Stir in carrot. Using well-floured hands, shape rounded teaspoonfuls of dough into 1-inch balls. Place 2 inches apart on ungreased cookie sheets.

Bake 13 to 18 minutes or until edges are lightly browned. Remove immediately to wire racks to cool.

Makes about 3 dozen cookies

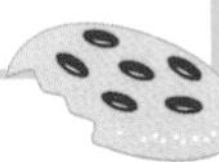

Fudge Meringues

Oatmeal Apple Cookies

1¼ cups firmly packed brown sugar
¾ Butter Flavor* CRISCO® Stick *or* ¾ cup Butter Flavor* CRISCO® all-vegetable shortening plus additional for greasing
¼ cup milk
1 egg
1½ teaspoons vanilla
1 cup all-purpose flour
1¼ teaspoons ground cinnamon
½ teaspoon salt
¼ teaspoon baking soda
¼ teaspoon ground nutmeg
3 cups quick-cooking oats (not instant or old-fashioned), uncooked
1 cup diced, peeled apples
¾ cup raisins (optional)
¾ cup coarsely chopped walnuts (optional)

**Butter Flavor Crisco® is artificially flavored.*

1. Heat oven to 375°F. Grease baking sheet. Place sheets of foil on countertop for cooling cookies.

2. Combine brown sugar, ¾ cup shortening, milk, egg and vanilla in large bowl. Beat at medium speed of electric mixer until well blended and creamy.

3. Combine flour, cinnamon, salt, baking soda and nutmeg. Add gradually to creamed mixture at low speed. Mix just until blended. Stir in, one at a time, oats, apples, raisins and nuts with spoon. Drop by rounded tablespoonfuls 2 inches apart onto prepared baking sheet.

4. Bake at 375°F for 13 minutes or until set. *Do not overbake.* Cool 2 minutes on baking sheet. Remove cookies to foil to cool completely.

Makes about 2½ dozen cookies

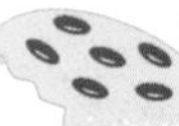

Oatmeal Apple Cookies

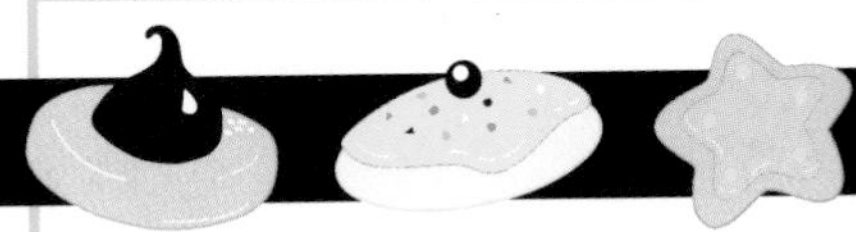

Drizzled Raspberry Crinkles

1⅔ cups (10-ounce package) HERSHEY'®S Raspberry Chips, divided
1 cup (2 sticks) butter or margarine, softened
1 cup packed light brown sugar
¾ cup granulated sugar
2 eggs
1 teaspoon vanilla extract
2½ cups all-purpose flour
⅓ cup HERSHEY'®S Cocoa
1 teaspoon baking powder
1 teaspoon baking soda
1½ teaspoons shortening (do not use butter, margarine, spread or oil)

1. Heat oven to 350°F.

2. Set aside ½ cup raspberry chips. In small microwave-safe bowl, place remaining chips. Microwave at HIGH (100%) 1 minute or until melted when stirred.

3. Beat butter, brown sugar and granulated sugar in large bowl until well blended. Add melted chips; beat until well blended. Beat in eggs and vanilla. Stir together flour, cocoa, baking powder and baking soda. Gradually beat into chocolate mixture. Drop by rounded teaspoons onto ungreased cookie sheet.

4. Bake 8 to 9 minutes for chewy cookies or 10 to 11 minutes for crisp cookies. Cool slightly. Remove from cookie sheet to wire rack. Cool completely.

5. Place reserved chips and shortening in small microwave-safe bowl. Microwave at HIGH 30 seconds or until chips are melted when stirred. Drizzle over cookies.

Makes about 5 dozen cookies

Drizzled Raspberry Crinkles

Chocolate-Flecked Pirouettes

½ cup butter or margarine, softened
½ cup sugar
2 egg whites
1 teaspoon vanilla
½ cup all-purpose flour
⅓ cup coarsely grated bittersweet or dark sweet chocolate bar (about 2 ounces)

1. Preheat oven to 400°F. Grease cookie sheets well; set aside.

2. Beat butter and sugar in small bowl with electric mixer at medium speed until light and fluffy. Beat in egg whites, 1 at a time. Beat in vanilla. Add flour; beat at low speed just until blended. Gently fold in grated chocolate with rubber spatula.

3. Drop teaspoonfuls of batter 4 inches apart onto prepared cookie sheets. Spread dough into 2-inch rounds with small spatula. Make only 3 or 4 rounds per sheet.

4. Bake 1 sheet at a time 4 to 5 minutes until edges are barely golden. *Do not overbake.*

5. Remove from oven and quickly loosen edge of 1 cookie from baking sheet with thin spatula. Quickly roll cookie around clean handle of wooden spoon overlapping edges to form cigar shape. Repeat with remaining cookies. (If cookies become too firm to shape, return to oven for a few seconds to soften.) Slide cookie off handle to wire rack; cool completely.

6. Store tightly covered at room temperature or freeze up to 3 months. *Makes about 3 dozen cookies*

Chocolate-Flecked Pirouettes

Almond Crescents

1 cup butter, softened
⅓ cup granulated sugar
1¾ cups all-purpose flour
¼ cup cornstarch
1 teaspoon vanilla extract
1½ cups ground toasted almonds*
Chocolate Glaze (recipe follows) or powdered sugar

**To toast almonds, spread on cookie sheet. Bake at 325°F for 4 minutes or until fragrant and golden.*

Preheat oven to 325°F. Beat butter and granulated sugar in large bowl until creamy. Mix in flour, cornstarch and vanilla. Stir in almonds. Shape tablespoonfuls of dough into crescents. Place 2 inches apart on ungreased cookie sheets. Bake 22 to 25 minutes or until light brown. Cool 1 minute. Remove to wire racks; cool completely. Prepare Chocolate Glaze; drizzle over cookies. Allow chocolate to set, then store in airtight container. Or, before serving, sprinkle with powdered sugar.

Makes about 3 dozen cookies

Chocolate Glaze: Place ½ cup semisweet chocolate chips and 1 tablespoon butter or margarine in small resealable plastic bag. Place bag in bowl of hot water for 2 to 3 minutes or until chocolate is softened. Dry with paper towel. Knead until chocolate mixture is smooth. Cut off very tiny corner of bag. Drizzle chocolate mixture over cookies.

Almond Crescents

Chocolate-Raspberry Kolachy

2 squares (1 ounce each) semisweet chocolate, coarsely chopped
1½ cups all-purpose flour
¼ teaspoon baking soda
¼ teaspoon salt
½ cup butter or margarine, softened
3 ounces cream cheese or light cream cheese, softened
⅓ cup granulated sugar
1 teaspoon vanilla
Seedless raspberry jam
Powdered sugar

Place chocolate in 1-cup glass measure. Microwave at HIGH (100% power) 1 to 2 minutes or until chocolate is melted, stirring after 1 minute.

Combine flour, baking soda and salt in small bowl; stir well. Beat butter and cream cheese in large bowl with electric mixer at medium speed until well blended. Beat in granulated sugar until light and fluffy. Beat in vanilla and chocolate. Gradually add flour mixture. Beat at low speed just until blended. Divide dough in half; flatten each half into a disc. Wrap separately in plastic wrap. Refrigerate 1 to 2 hours or until firm.

Preheat oven to 375°F. Lightly grease cookie sheets. Roll each dough disc of dough on well-floured surface to ¼- to ⅛-inch thickness. Cut out with 3-inch round cookie cutter. Place 2 inches apart on prepared cookie sheets. Place rounded ½ teaspoon jam in center of each circle. Bring three edges of dough circles up over jam; pinch edges together to seal, leaving center of triangle slightly open.

Bake 10 minutes or until set. Let cookies stand on cookie sheets 2 minutes. Remove cookies with spatula to wire racks; cool completely. Just before serving, sprinkle with powdered sugar. Store tightly covered in refrigerator; let stand for 30 minutes at room temperature before serving.

Makes about 1½ dozen cookies

Note: *These cookies do not freeze well.*

Chocolate-Raspberry Kolachy Cups: *Fit dough circles into greased mini-muffin cups; fill with heaping teaspoon of jam. Bake 10 minutes or until set. Let pans stand on wire racks; cool completely. Dust with powdered sugar before serving.*

Chocolate-Raspberry Kolachy

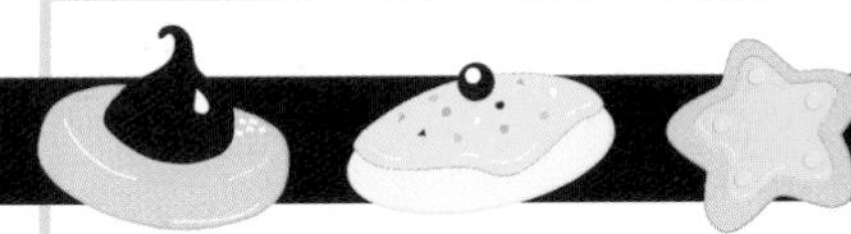

Peanut Butter and Chocolate Cookie Sandwich Cookies

- **½ cup REESE'S® Peanut Butter Chips**
- **3 tablespoons plus ½ cup (1 stick) butter or margarine, softened and divided**
- **1¼ cups sugar, divided**
- **¼ cup light corn syrup**
- **1 egg**
- **1 teaspoon vanilla extract**
- **2 cups plus 2 tablespoons all-purpose flour, divided**
- **2 teaspoons baking soda**
- **¼ teaspoon salt**
- **½ cup HERSHEY'S® Cocoa**
- **5 tablespoons butter or margarine, melted**
- **Additional sugar**
- **About 2 dozen large marshmallows**

1. Heat oven to 350°F. Melt peanut butter chips and 3 tablespoons softened butter in small saucepan over very low heat. Remove from heat; cool slightly.

2. Beat remaining ½ cup softened butter and 1 cup sugar in large bowl until light and fluffy. Add corn syrup, egg and vanilla; blend thoroughly. Stir together 2 cups flour, baking soda and salt; add to butter mixture, blending well. Remove 1¼ cups batter and place in small bowl; with wooden spoon stir in the remaining 2 tablespoons flour and peanut butter chip mixture.

3. Blend cocoa, remaining ¼ cup sugar and 5 tablespoons melted butter into remaining batter. Refrigerate both batters 5 to 10 minutes or until firm enough to handle. Roll each dough into 1-inch balls; roll in sugar. Place on ungreased cookie sheets.

4. Bake 10 to 11 minutes or until set. Cool slightly; remove from cookie sheets to wire racks. Cool completely. Place 1 marshmallow on flat side of 1 chocolate cookie. Microwave at MEDIUM (50%) 10 seconds or until marshmallow is softened; place a peanut butter cookie over marshmallow, pressing down slightly. Repeat for remaining cookies. Serve immediately. *Makes about 2 dozen cookie sandwiches*

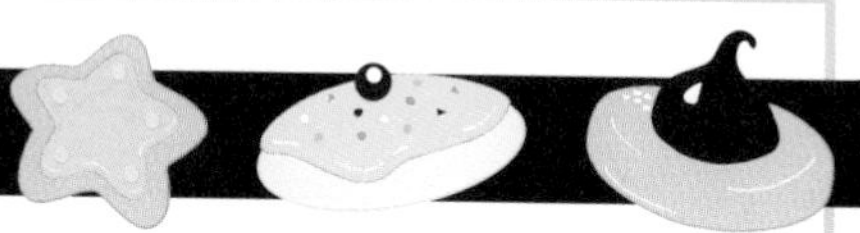

Pineapple Raisin Jumbles

- 2 cans (8 ounces each) DOLE® Crushed Pineapple
- ½ cup margarine, softened
- ½ cup sugar
- 1 teaspoon vanilla extract
- 1 cup all-purpose flour
- 4 teaspoons grated orange peel
- 1 cup DOLE® Blanched Slivered Almonds, toasted
- 1 cup DOLE® Seedless Raisins

• Preheat oven to 350°F. Drain pineapple well, pressing out excess liquid with back of spoon.

• In large bowl, beat margarine and sugar until light and fluffy. Stir in pineapple and vanilla. Beat in flour and orange peel. Stir in almonds and raisins.

• Drop heaping tablespoons of dough 2 inches apart onto greased cookie sheets.

• Bake 20 to 22 minutes or until firm. Cool on wire racks.

Makes 2 to 2½ dozen cookies

Walnut Crescents

- 3¾ cups flour
- ½ teaspoon cinnamon
- 1½ cups (3 sticks) MAZOLA® Margarine or butter
- ¾ cup KARO® Light or Dark Corn Syrup
- 1 tablespoon vanilla
- 2¼ cups ground walnuts
- 1½ cups confectioners sugar

1. In medium bowl combine flour and cinnamon; set aside.
2. In large bowl with mixer at medium speed, beat margarine until creamy. Gradually beat in corn syrup and vanilla until well blended. Stir in flour mixture and walnuts.
3. Cover; refrigerate several hours or until easy to handle.
4. Preheat oven to 350°F. Shape rounded teaspoonfuls of dough into 2-inch-long rolls. Place 2 inches apart on ungreased cookie sheets, curving to form crescents.
5. Bake 15 to 18 minutes or until bottoms are lightly browned. Remove from cookie sheets; cool completely on wire racks. Roll in confectioners sugar.

Makes about 8 dozen cookies

Chocolate-Dipped Cinnamon Thins

1¼ cups all-purpose flour
1½ teaspoons ground cinnamon
¼ teaspoon salt
1 cup unsalted butter, softened
1 cup powdered sugar
1 large egg
1 teaspoon vanilla
4 ounces broken bittersweet chocolate candy bar, melted

1. Place flour, cinnamon, and salt in small bowl; stir to combine.

2. Beat butter in large bowl with electric mixer at medium speed until light and fluffy. Add sugar; beat well. Add egg and vanilla. Gradually add flour mixture. Beat at low speed just until blended.

3. Place dough on sheet of waxed paper. Using waxed paper to hold dough, roll it back and forth to form a log about 12 inches long and 2½ inches wide.

4. Securely wrap log in plastic wrap. Refrigerate at least 2 hours or until firm. (Log may be frozen up to 3 months; thaw in refrigerator before baking.)

5. Preheat oven to 350°F. Cut dough with long, sharp knife into ¼-inch-thick slices. Place 2 inches apart on ungreased cookie sheets.

6. Bake 10 minutes or until set. Let cookies stand on cookie sheets 2 minutes. Remove cookies with spatula to wire racks; cool completely.

7. Dip each cookie into chocolate, coating 1 inch up sides. Transfer to wire racks or waxed paper; let stand at cool room temperature about 40 minutes until chocolate is set.

8. Store cookies between sheets of waxed paper at cool room temperature or in refrigerator. These cookies do not freeze well.

Makes about 2 dozen cookies

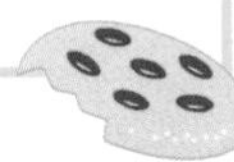

Chocolate-Dipped Cinnamon Thins

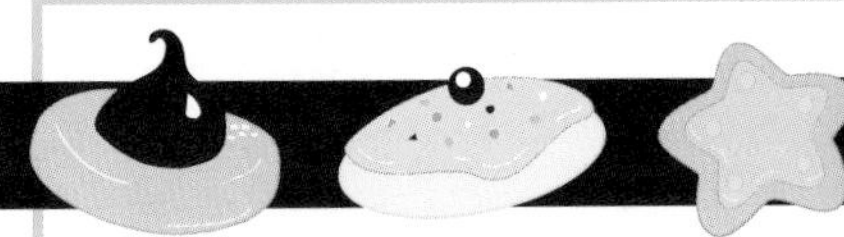

Choco-Caramel Delights

- ½ cup (1 stick) butter or margarine, softened
- ⅔ cup sugar
- 1 egg, separated
- 2 tablespoons milk
- 1 teaspoon vanilla extract
- 1 cup all-purpose flour
- ⅓ cup HERSHEY'S® Cocoa
- ¼ teaspoon salt
- 1 cup finely chopped pecans
- Caramel Filling (recipe follows)
- ½ cup HERSHEY'S® Semi-Sweet Chocolate Chips
- 1 teaspoon shortening (do not use butter, margarine, spread or oil)

1. Beat butter, sugar, egg yolk, milk and vanilla in medium bowl until blended. Stir together flour, cocoa and salt; blend into butter mixture. Refrigerate dough at least 1 hour or until firm enough to handle.

2. Heat oven to 350°F. Lightly grease cookie sheet.

3. Beat egg white slightly. Shape dough into 1-inch balls. Dip each ball into egg white; roll in pecans to coat. Place on prepared cookie sheet. Press thumb gently in center of each ball. Bake 10 to 12 minutes or until set.

4. Meanwhile, prepare Caramel Filling. Remove cookies from oven; press center of each cookie again with thumb to make indentation. Immediately spoon about ½ teaspoon Caramel Filling in center of each cookie. Carefully remove from cookie sheets; cool on wire racks.

5. Place chocolate chips and shortening in small microwave-safe bowl. Microwave at HIGH (100%) 1 minute or until softened; stir. Allow to stand several minutes to finish melting; stir until smooth. Place wax paper under wire rack with cookies. Drizzle chocolate mixture over top of cookies.

Makes about 2 dozen cookies

Caramel Filling: *In small saucepan, combine 14 unwrapped light caramels and 3 tablespoons whipping cream. Cook over low heat, stirring frequently, until caramels are melted and mixture is smooth.*

Choco-Caramel Delights

Chocolate Biscotti Nuggets

¾ cup old-fashioned or quick oats
2¼ cups all-purpose flour
1½ teaspoons baking powder
½ teaspoon salt
¾ cup chopped dates
½ cup coarsely chopped toasted pecans
½ cup honey
2 large eggs
1 teaspoon vanilla
½ cup (1 stick) butter, melted
Grated peel of 2 oranges

CHOCOLATE COATING
1¾ cups semisweet dark chocolate or white chocolate chips
4 teaspoons shortening

1. Grease baking sheet; set aside. Preheat oven to 350°F.

2. Place oats in food processor; process until oats resemble coarse flour. Combine oats, flour, baking powder and salt in large bowl. Stir in dates and pecans.

3. Whisk together honey, eggs and vanilla in medium bowl. Add melted butter and orange peel. Stir egg mixture into oat mixture just until blended. Turn out dough onto lightly floured surface; flatten slightly. Knead until dough holds together, adding flour if necessary to prevent sticking. Divide dough into 3 equal pieces; roll each into 9×½-inch log. Carefully transfer logs to prepared baking sheet, spacing about 2 inches apart. If dough cracks, pat back into shape.

4. Bake logs 25 to 30 minutes or until lightly golden but still soft. Remove from oven. Reduce oven temperature to 275°F. Let logs cool on baking sheet 10 minutes. Trim ends using serrated knife. Slice logs on slight diagonal about ¾ inch thick. Arrange biscotti on their sides on baking sheet. Return to oven and bake 15 to 20 minutes or until lightly golden. Turn biscotti over and bake 10 to 15 minutes longer. Remove biscotti to wire rack to cool completely.

5. Brush individual biscotti with dry pastry brush to remove any loose crumbs. Heat chocolate chips and shortening in small heavy saucepan over very low heat until melted and smooth. Dip half of each biscotti slice into melted chocolate, letting any excess run off. Place on prepared baking sheet. Let stand until set. Store in waxed paper-lined tin at room temperature.

Makes about 36 biscotti slices

Chocolate Biscotti Nuggets

Mexican Chocolate Macaroons

1 package (8 ounces) semisweet baking chocolate, divided
1¾ cups plus ⅓ cup whole almonds, divided
¾ cup sugar
1 teaspoon ground cinnamon
1 teaspoon vanilla
2 egg whites

Tip

To handle sticky doughs more easily, flour your hands before shaping the cookies. Or, wet your hands with water and keep them wet as long as you are working with the dough.

1. Preheat oven to 400°F. Grease baking sheets; set aside.

2. Place 5 squares of chocolate in food processor; process until coarsely chopped. Add 1¾ cups almonds and sugar; process using on/off pulsing action until mixture is finely ground. Add cinnamon, vanilla and egg whites; process just until mixture forms moist dough.

3. Form dough into 1-inch balls (dough will be sticky). Place about 2 inches apart onto prepared baking sheets. Press 1 almond on top of each cookie.

4. Bake 8 to 10 minutes or just until set. Cool 2 minutes on baking sheets. Remove cookies from baking sheets to wire rack to cool.

5. Heat remaining 3 squares chocolate in small saucepan over very low heat until melted. Spoon chocolate into small resealable plastic food storage bag. Cut small corner off bottom of bag with scissors. Drizzle chocolate over cookies.

Makes 3 dozen cookies

Tip: For longer storage, allow cookies to stand until chocolate drizzle is set. Store in airtight containers.

Greeting Card Cookies

Brownie Bonanza

Derby Brownies

1 package DUNCAN HINES® Walnut Brownie Mix
½ cup (1 stick) butter or margarine, softened
1 pound confectioners' sugar (about 3½ to 4 cups)
2 tablespoons bourbon or milk
1 container DUNCAN HINES® Dark Chocolate Frosting

Preheat oven to 350°F. Grease bottom only of 13×9-inch pan.

Prepare brownie mix as directed on package for cake-like brownies. Pour into prepared pan. Bake 24 to 27 minutes or until set. Cool completely in pan. Beat butter until smooth in large mixing bowl; stir in sugar and bourbon. Beat until smooth and of spreading consistency. Spread over brownies; chill. Top with frosting. Chill 2 to 4 hours. Cut into bars and serve at room temperature. *Makes 24 brownies*

Derby Brownies

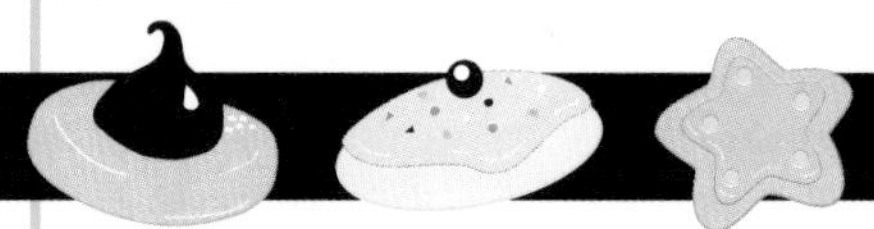

Fabulous Blonde Brownies

- 1¾ cups all-purpose flour
- 1 teaspoon baking powder
- ¼ teaspoon salt
- 1 cup (6 ounces) white chocolate chips
- 1 cup (4 ounces) blanched whole almonds, coarsely chopped
- 1 cup English toffee bits
- ⅔ cup margarine or butter, softened
- 1½ cups packed light brown sugar
- 2 eggs
- 2 teaspoons vanilla

Preheat oven to 350°F. Lightly grease 13×9-inch baking pan.

Combine flour, baking powder and salt in small bowl; mix well. Combine white chocolate, almonds and toffee in medium bowl; mix well.

Beat margarine and brown sugar in large bowl with electric mixer at medium speed until light and fluffy. Beat in eggs and vanilla. Add flour mixture; beat at low speed until well blended. Stir in ¾ cup of white chocolate mixture. Spread evenly into prepared pan.

Bake 20 minutes. Immediately after removing brownies from oven, sprinkle remaining white chocolate mixture evenly over brownies. Press down lightly. Bake 15 to 20 minutes or until wooden pick inserted into center comes out clean. Cool brownies completely in pan on wire rack. Cut into 2×1½-inch bars. *Makes 3 dozen brownies*

Fabulous Blonde Brownies

Brownie Turtle Cookies

2 squares (1 ounce each) unsweetened baking chocolate
⅓ cup solid vegetable shortening
1 cup granulated sugar
½ teaspoon vanilla extract
2 large eggs
1¼ cups all-purpose flour
½ teaspoon baking powder
½ teaspoon salt
1 cup "M&M's"® Milk Chocolate Mini Baking Bits, divided
1 cup pecan halves
⅓ cup caramel ice cream topping
⅓ cup shredded coconut
⅓ cup finely chopped pecans

Preheat oven to 350°F. Lightly grease cookie sheets; set aside. Heat chocolate and shortening in 2-quart saucepan over low heat, stirring constantly until melted; remove from heat. Mix in sugar, vanilla and eggs. Blend in flour, baking powder and salt. Stir in ⅔ cup "M&M's"® Milk Chocolate Mini Baking Bits. For each cookie, arrange 3 pecan halves, with ends almost touching at center, on prepared cookie sheets. Drop dough by rounded teaspoonfuls onto center of each group of pecans; mound the dough slightly. Bake 8 to 10 minutes just until set. Do not overbake. Cool completely on wire racks. In small bowl combine ice cream topping, coconut and chopped nuts; top each cookie with about 1½ teaspoons mixture. Press remaining ⅓ cup "M&M's"® Milk Chocolate Mini Baking Bits into topping.

Makes about 2½ dozen cookies

Brownie Turtle Cookies

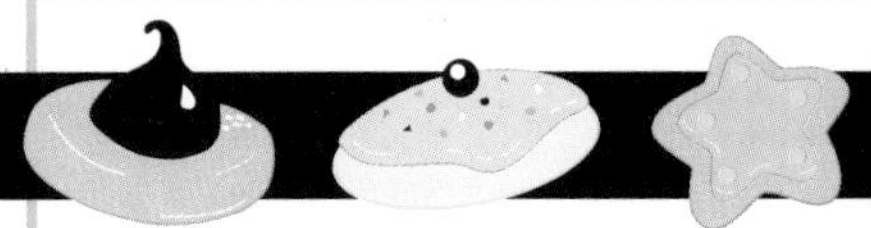

Orange Cappuccino Brownies

- ¾ cup butter
- 2 squares (1 ounce each) semisweet chocolate, coarsely chopped
- 2 squares (1 ounce each) unsweetened chocolate, coarsely chopped
- 1¾ cups granulated sugar
- 1 tablespoon instant espresso powder or instant coffee granules
- 3 eggs
- ¼ cup orange-flavored liqueur
- 2 teaspoons grated orange peel
- 1 cup all-purpose flour
- 1 package (12 ounces) semisweet chocolate chips
- 2 tablespoons shortening

Preheat oven to 350°F. Grease 13×9-inch baking pan.

Melt butter and chopped chocolates in large, heavy saucepan over low heat, stirring constantly. Stir in granulated sugar and espresso powder. Remove from heat. Cool slightly. Beat in eggs, 1 at a time. Whisk in liqueur and orange peel. Beat flour into chocolate mixture just until blended. Spread batter evenly in prepared pan.

Bake 25 to 30 minutes or until center is just set. Remove pan to wire rack. Meanwhile, melt chocolate chips and shortening in small, heavy saucepan over low heat, stirring constantly. Immediately, spread hot chocolate mixture over warm brownies. Cool completely in pan on wire rack. Cut into 2-inch squares. *Makes about 2 dozen brownies*

Tip

One medium orange yields 1 to 2 tablespoons grated peel, which can be frozen for up to six months.

Orange Cappuccino Brownies

Sensational Peppermint Pattie Brownies

24 small (1½-inch) YORK® Peppermint Patties
1½ cups (3 sticks) butter or margarine, melted
3 cups sugar
1 tablespoon vanilla extract
5 eggs
2 cups all-purpose flour
1 cup HERSHEY'S Cocoa
1 teaspoon baking powder
1 teaspoon salt

1. Heat oven to 350°F. Remove wrappers from peppermint patties. Grease 13×9×2-inch baking pan.

2. Stir together butter, sugar and vanilla in large bowl. Add eggs; beat until well blended. Stir together flour, cocoa, baking powder and salt; gradually add to butter mixture, blending well. Reserve 2 cups batter. Spread remaining batter into prepared pan. Arrange peppermint patties about ½ inch apart in single layer over batter. Spread reserved batter over patties.

3. Bake 50 to 55 minutes or until brownies pull away from sides of pan. Cool completely in pan on wire rack.

Makes about 36 brownies

Peanut Butter Chip Brownies

½ cup butter or margarine
4 squares (1 ounce each) semisweet chocolate
½ cup sugar
2 eggs
1 teaspoon vanilla
½ cup all-purpose flour
1 package (12 ounces) peanut butter chips
1 cup (6 ounces) milk chocolate chips

Preheat oven to 350°F. Grease 8-inch square baking pan. Melt butter and semisweet chocolate in small, heavy saucepan over low heat, stirring just until chocolate melts completely. Remove from heat; cool. Beat sugar and eggs in large bowl until light and fluffy. Blend in vanilla and chocolate mixture. Stir in flour until blended; fold in peanut butter chips. Spread batter evenly in prepared pan.

Bake 25 to 30 minutes or just until firm and dry in center. Remove from oven; sprinkle milk chocolate chips over top. Place pan on wire rack. When chocolate chips have melted, spread over brownies. Refrigerate until chocolate topping is set. Cut into 2-inch squares. *Makes 16 brownies*

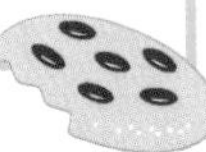

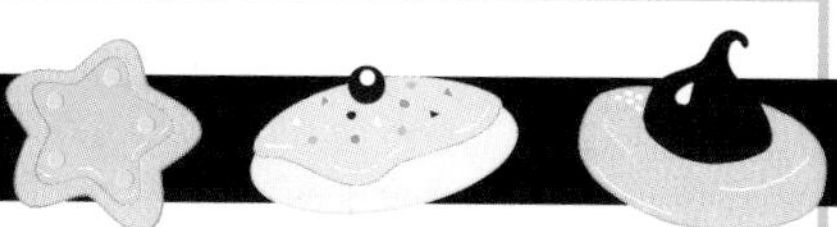

Devil's Fudge Brownies

½ cup (1 stick) butter or margarine, softened
1 cup granulated sugar
2 large eggs
2 tablespoons FRANK'S® REDHOT® Sauce
1 teaspoon vanilla extract
⅔ cup all-purpose flour
½ cup unsweetened cocoa
¼ teaspoon baking soda
1 cup chopped pecans
½ cup mini chocolate chips
Pecan halves
Confectioners' sugar
Ice cream (optional)
Fudge sauce (optional)

Beat butter, granulated sugar, eggs, REDHOT sauce and vanilla in large bowl of electric mixer on medium speed until light and fluffy. Blend in flour, cocoa and baking soda. Beat until smooth. Stir in chopped nuts and mini chips. Spread into greased deep-dish 9-inch microwave-safe pie plate. Arrange pecan halves on top.

Place pie plate on top of inverted custard cup in microwave oven. Microwave, uncovered, on HIGH 6 minutes or until toothpick inserted in center comes out clean, turning once. (Brownie may appear moist on surface. Do not overcook.) Cool completely on wire rack.

Dust top with confectioners' sugar. Cut into wedges. Serve with ice cream and fudge sauce, if desired.

Makes 8 servings

Prep Time: 20 minutes
Cook Time: 6 minutes

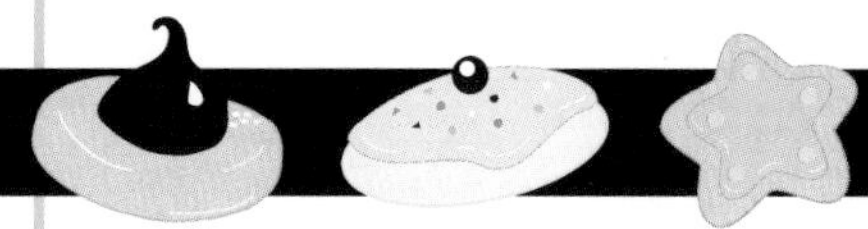

Butterscotch Brownies

- **1 cup butterscotch-flavored chips**
- **½ cup packed light brown sugar**
- **¼ cup butter, softened**
- **2 eggs**
- **½ teaspoon vanilla**
- **1 cup all-purpose flour**
- **½ teaspoon baking powder**
- **¼ teaspoon salt**
- **1 cup semisweet chocolate chips**

Preheat oven to 350°F. Grease 9-inch square baking pan. Melt butterscotch chips in small saucepan over low heat, stirring constantly; set aside.

Beat sugar and butter in large bowl until light and fluffy. Beat in eggs, one at a time, scraping down side of bowl after each addition. Beat in vanilla and melted butterscotch chips. Combine flour, baking powder and salt in small bowl; add to butter mixture. Beat until well blended. Spread batter evenly in prepared pan.

Bake 20 to 25 minutes or until golden brown and center is set. Remove pan from oven and immediately sprinkle with chocolate chips. Let stand about 4 minutes or until chocolate is melted. Spread chocolate evenly over top. Place pan on wire rack; cool completely. Cut into 2¼-inch squares.

Makes about 16 brownies

Nuggets o' Gold Brownies

- **3 ounces unsweetened baking chocolate**
- **¼ cup WESSON® Vegetable Oil**
- **2 eggs**
- **1 cup sugar**
- **¼ teaspoon salt**
- **1 teaspoon vanilla extract**
- **½ cup all-purpose flour**
- **1 (3.8-ounce) BUTTERFINGER® Candy Bar, coarsely chopped**

In microwave-safe measuring cup, heat chocolate 2 minutes on HIGH in microwave oven. Stir and continue heating in 30 second intervals until chocolate is completely melted. Stir in oil and set aside to cool. In mixing bowl, beat eggs until foamy. Whisk in sugar, then add salt and vanilla. Stir in chocolate mixture then mix in flour until all ingredients are moistened. Gently fold in candy. Pour batter into a 9-inch greased baking pan and bake at 350°F for 25 to 30 minutes or until edges begin to leave sides of pan. Cool before cutting.

Makes 20 brownies

Butterscotch Brownies

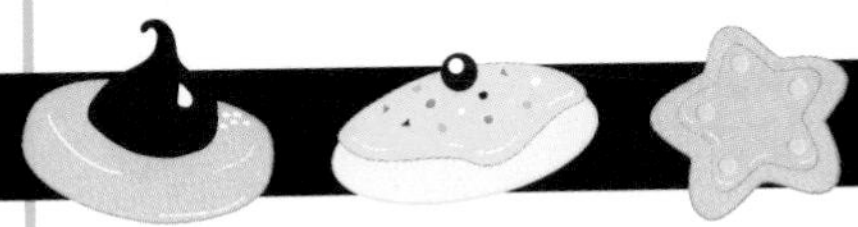

Irish Brownies

- **4 squares (1 ounce each) semisweet baking chocolate, coarsely chopped**
- **½ cup butter or margarine**
- **½ cup sugar**
- **2 eggs**
- **¼ cup Irish cream liqueur**
- **1 cup all-purpose flour**
- **½ teaspoon baking powder**
- **¼ teaspoon salt**
- **Irish Cream Frosting (recipe follows)**

Preheat oven to 350°F. Grease 8-inch square baking pan. Melt chocolate and butter in medium, heavy saucepan over low heat, stirring constantly. Remove from heat. Stir in sugar. Beat in eggs, 1 at a time, with wire whisk. Whisk in Irish cream. Combine flour, baking powder and salt in small bowl; stir into chocolate mixture until just blended. Spread batter evenly in prepared pan.

Bake 22 to 25 minutes or until center is set. Remove pan to wire rack; cool completely before frosting. Spread Irish Cream Frosting over cooled brownies. Chill at least 1 hour or until frosting is set. Cut into 2-inch squares.

Makes about 16 brownies

Irish Cream Frosting

- **2 ounces cream cheese (¼ cup), softened**
- **2 tablespoons butter or margarine, softened**
- **2 tablespoons Irish cream liqueur**
- **1½ cups powdered sugar**

Beat cream cheese and butter in small bowl with electric mixer at medium speed until smooth. Beat in Irish cream. Gradually beat in powdered sugar until smooth.

Makes about ⅔ cup frosting

Irish Brownies

Quick & Easy Fudgey Brownies

- **4 bars (1 ounce each) HERSHEY®S Unsweetened Baking Chocolate, broken into pieces**
- **¾ cup (1½ sticks) butter or margarine**
- **2 cups sugar**
- **3 eggs**
- **1½ teaspoons vanilla extract**
- **1 cup all-purpose flour**
- **1 cup chopped nuts (optional)**
- **Creamy Quick Chocolate Frosting (recipe follows, optional)**

Heat oven to 350°F. Grease 13×9×2-inch baking pan.

Place chocolate and butter in large microwave-safe bowl. Microwave at HIGH 1½ to 2 minutes or until chocolate is melted and mixture is smooth when stirred. Add sugar; stir with spoon until well blended. Add eggs and vanilla; mix well. Add flour and nuts, if desired; stir until well blended. Spread into prepared pan.

Bake 30 to 35 minutes or until wooden pick inserted in center comes out almost clean. Cool in pan on wire rack.

Frost with Quick & Easy Chocolate Frosting, if desired. Cut into squares. *Makes about 24 brownies*

Creamy Quick Chocolate Frosting

- **3 tablespoons butter or margarine**
- **3 bars (1 ounce each) HERSHEY®S Unsweetened Baking Chocolate, broken into pieces**
- **3 cups powdered sugar**
- **½ cup milk**
- **1 teaspoon vanilla extract**
- **⅛ teaspoon salt**

Melt butter and chocolate in saucepan over very low heat. Cook, stirring constantly, until chocolate is melted and mixture is smooth. Pour into large bowl; add powdered sugar, milk, vanilla and salt. Beat on medium speed of electric mixer until well blended. If necessary, refrigerate 10 minutes or until of spreading consistency. *Makes about 2 cups frosting*

Quick & Easy Fudgey Brownies

Heavenly Hash Brownies

- 1 cup butter
- ¼ cup unsweetened cocoa powder
- 4 eggs
- 1¼ cups granulated sugar
- 2 cups chopped walnuts or pecans
- 1½ cups all-purpose flour
- 2 teaspoons vanilla
- Creamy Cocoa Icing (recipe follows)
- 1 package (10 ounces) miniature marshmallows*

For best results, use fresh marshmallows.

Preheat oven to 350°F. Grease 13×9-inch baking pan. Melt butter in 2-quart saucepan; stir in cocoa. Remove from heat; beat in eggs and granulated sugar. Blend in nuts, flour and vanilla. Spread batter evenly in prepared pan.

Bake 20 to 25 minutes or until wooden pick inserted in center comes out clean. Do not overbake. Meanwhile, prepare Creamy Cocoa Icing. Remove brownies from oven. Immediately sprinkle marshmallows over hot brownies. Pour hot icing evenly over marshmallows. Cool in pan on wire rack. Cut into 2-inch squares.

Makes about 2 dozen brownies

Creamy Cocoa Icing

- 6 tablespoons butter or margarine
- ¾ cup undiluted evaporated milk
- 6 cups powdered sugar
- ¾ cup unsweetened cocoa powder

Melt butter in 2-quart saucepan. Add milk, powdered sugar and cocoa. Stir over low heat until smooth and creamy.

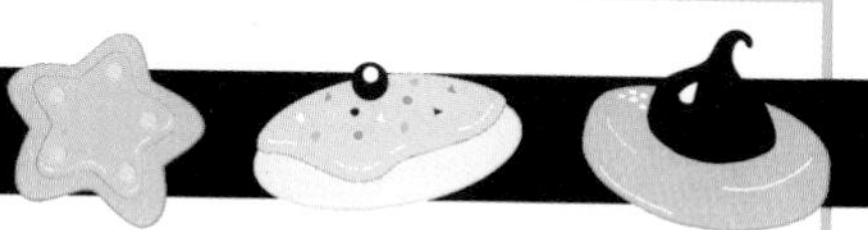

Baker's® Raspberry Truffle Brownies

BROWNIE LAYER:

- **4 squares BAKER'S® Unsweetened Baking Chocolate**
- **¾ cup (1½ sticks) butter *or* margarine**
- **2 cups sugar**
- **3 eggs**
- **1 teaspoon vanilla**
- **1 cup flour**
- **1 cup coarsely chopped macadamia nuts *or* toasted almonds**
- **¼ cup seedless raspberry jam**

GLAZE:

- **1 cup whipping (heavy) cream**
- **6 squares BAKER'S® Semi-Sweet Baking Chocolate, finely chopped**
- **2 squares BAKER'S® Unsweetened Baking Chocolate, finely chopped**
- **3 tablespoons seedless raspberry jam**

BROWNIE LAYER

HEAT oven to 350°F (325°F for glass baking dish). Line 13×9-inch baking pan with foil. Grease foil.

MICROWAVE chocolate and butter in large microwavable bowl on HIGH 2 minutes or until butter is melted. Stir until chocolate is completely melted.

STIR sugar into chocolate mixture until well blended. Mix in eggs and vanilla. Stir in flour and nuts until well blended. Spread in prepared pan.

BAKE 30 to 35 minutes or until toothpick inserted in center comes out with fudgy crumbs. DO NOT OVERBAKE. Cool in pan. Spread jam over brownies.

GLAZE

MICROWAVE cream in medium microwavable bowl on HIGH 45 seconds or until simmering. Stir in chopped chocolates and jam until chocolates are melted and mixture is smooth. Spread glaze over jam layer on brownies.

REFRIGERATE 1 hour or until glaze is set. Lift out of pan onto cutting board. Cut into diamond-shaped bars. Garnish with fresh raspberries, if desired.

Makes about 3 dozen brownies

Prep Time: 20 minutes plus refrigerating
Bake Time: 35 minutes

German Chocolate Brownies

1 package DUNCAN HINES® Milk Chocolate Chunk Brownie Mix
2 eggs
⅓ cup water
⅓ cup vegetable oil
½ cup packed brown sugar
2 tablespoons butter or margarine, softened
1 tablespoon all-purpose flour
½ cup chopped pecans
½ cup flaked coconut

Preheat oven to 350°F. Grease bottom only of 13×9-inch pan.

Combine brownie mix, eggs, water and oil in large bowl. Stir with spoon until well blended, about 50 strokes. Spread into prepared pan.

Combine sugar, butter and flour in small bowl. Mix until well blended. Stir in pecans and coconut. Sprinkle mixture over batter. Bake 25 to 30 minutes or until topping is browned. Cool completely in pan. Cut into bars.

Makes 24 brownies

Tip: *Always mix brownies by hand. Never use an electric mixer.*

Deep Dish Brownies

¾ cup (1½ sticks) butter or margarine, melted
1½ cups sugar
1½ teaspoons vanilla extract
3 eggs
¾ cup all-purpose flour
½ cup HERSHEY'S Cocoa
½ teaspoon baking powder
½ teaspoon salt

1. Heat oven to 350°F. Grease 8-inch square baking pan.

2. Blend butter, sugar and vanilla in medium bowl. Add eggs; using spoon, beat well. Combine flour, cocoa, baking powder and salt; gradually add to egg mixture, beating until well blended. Spread batter into prepared pan.

3. Bake 40 to 45 minutes or until brownies begin to pull away from sides of pan. Cool completely in pan on wire rack. Cut into squares.

Makes about 16 brownies

Variation: *Stir 1 cup REESE'S® Peanut Butter Chips or HERSHEY'S Semi-Sweet Chocolate Chips into batter before spreading into pan. Proceed as directed.*

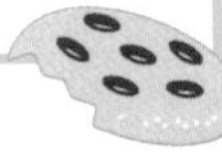

German Chocolate Brownies

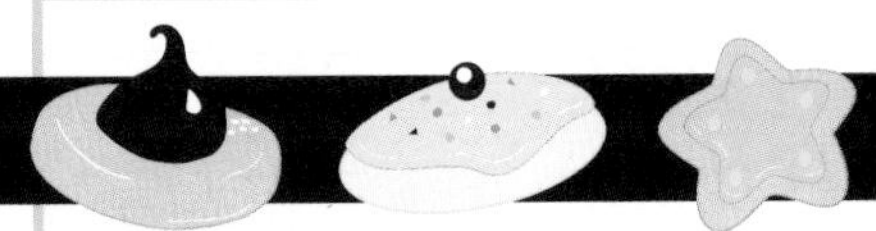

Minted Chocolate Chip Brownies

- ¾ cup granulated sugar
- ½ cup butter
- 2 tablespoons water
- 1 cup semisweet chocolate chips or mini semisweet chocolate chips
- 1½ teaspoons vanilla
- 2 eggs
- 1¼ cups all-purpose flour
- ½ teaspoon baking soda
- ½ teaspoon salt
- 1 cup mint chocolate chips
- Powdered sugar for garnish

Preheat oven to 350°F. Grease 9-inch square baking pan. Combine sugar, butter and water in medium microwavable bowl. Microwave on HIGH 2½ to 3 minutes or until butter is melted. Stir in semisweet chips; stir gently until chips are melted and mixture is well blended. Stir in vanilla; let stand 5 minutes to cool.

Beat eggs into chocolate mixture, 1 at a time. Combine flour, baking soda and salt in small bowl; add to chocolate mixture. Stir in mint chocolate chips. Spread into prepared pan.

Bake 25 minutes for fudgy brownies or 30 minutes for cakelike brownies.

Remove pan to wire rack; cool completely. Cut into 2¼-inch squares. Sprinkle with powdered sugar, if desired.

Makes about 16 brownies

Philadelphia® Marble Brownies

- 1 package (21½ ounces) brownie mix
- 1 package (8 ounces) PHILADELPHIA® Cream Cheese, softened
- ⅓ cup sugar
- ½ teaspoon vanilla
- 1 egg
- 1 cup BAKER'S® Semi-Sweet Real Chocolate Chips

PREPARE brownie mix as directed on package. Spread in greased 13×9-inch baking pan.

MIX cream cheese, sugar and vanilla with electric mixer on medium speed until well blended. Add egg; mix well. Pour over brownie mixture; cut through batter with knife several times for marble effect. Sprinkle with chips.

BAKE at 350°F for 35 to 40 minutes or until cream cheese mixture is lightly browned. Cool in pan on wire rack. Cut into squares.

Makes 24 brownies

Prep Time: 20 minutes plus cooling
Bake Time: 40 minutes

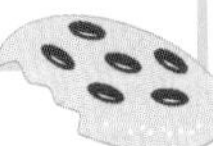

Minted Chocolate Chip Brownies

Peanut Butter Marbled Brownies

- **4 ounces cream cheese, softened**
- **½ cup peanut butter**
- **2 tablespoons sugar**
- **1 egg**
- **1 package (20 to 22 ounces) brownie mix plus ingredients to prepare mix**
- **¾ cup lightly salted cocktail peanuts**

Preheat oven to 350°F. Lightly grease 13×9-inch baking pan. Beat cream cheese, peanut butter, sugar and egg in medium bowl with electric mixer at medium speed until blended.

Prepare brownie mix according to package directions. Spread brownie mixture evenly in prepared pan. Spoon peanut butter mixture in dollops over brownie mixture. Swirl peanut butter mixture into brownie mixture with tip of knife. Sprinkle peanuts on top; lightly press peanuts down.

Bake 30 to 35 minutes or until wooden pick inserted into center comes out almost clean. (Do not overbake.) Cool brownies completely in pan on wire rack. Cut into 2-inch squares.

Makes 2 dozen brownies

Chewy Chocolate Brownies

- **¾ cup granulated sugar**
- **½ cup (1 stick) butter or margarine**
- **2 tablespoons water**
- **4 bars (2 ounces *each*) NESTLÉ® TOLL HOUSE® Semi-Sweet Baking Chocolate, broken into pieces**
- **2 eggs**
- **2 teaspoons vanilla extract**
- **1 cup all-purpose flour**
- **¼ teaspoon baking soda**
- **¼ teaspoon salt**
- **½ cup chopped nuts (optional)**

MICROWAVE sugar, butter and water in large, microwave-safe bowl on HIGH (100%) power for 3 minutes until mixture boils, stirring once. Add baking bars; stir until melted.

STIR in eggs one at a time until well blended. Stir in vanilla. Add flour, baking soda and salt; stir well. Stir in nuts. Pour into greased 13×9-inch baking pan.

BAKE in preheated 350°F. oven for 16 to 20 minutes until wooden pick inserted in center comes out still slightly sticky. Cool in pan on wire rack.

Makes about 2 dozen brownies

Saucepan Method: BRING sugar, butter and water in medium saucepan just to a boil, stirring constantly. Remove from heat. Proceed as directed.

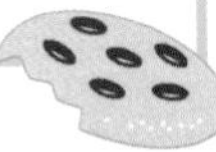

Peanut Butter Marbled Brownies

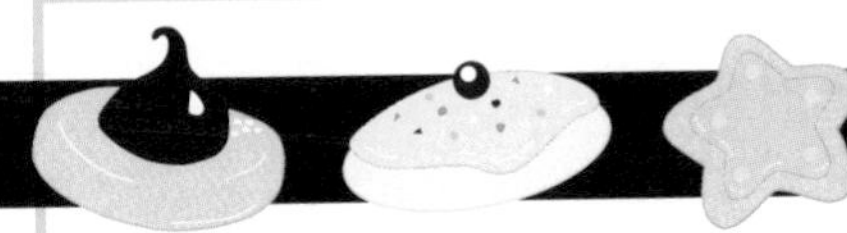

Hershey's® White Chip Brownies

4 eggs
1¼ cups sugar
½ cup (1 stick) butter or margarine, melted
2 teaspoons vanilla extract
1⅓ cups all-purpose flour
⅔ cup HERSHEY'S® Cocoa
1 teaspoon baking powder
½ teaspoon salt
1⅔ cups (10-ounce package) HERSHEY'S® Premier White Chips

1. Heat oven to 350°F. Grease 13×9×2-inch baking pan.

2. Beat eggs in large bowl until foamy; gradually beat in sugar. Add butter and vanilla; beat until blended. Stir together flour, cocoa, baking powder and salt; add to egg mixture, beating until blended. Stir in white chips. Spread batter into prepared pan.

3. Bake 25 to 30 minutes or until brownies begin to pull away from sides of pan. Cool completely in pan on wire rack. Cut into squares. *Makes about 36 brownies*

Tip: Brownies and bar cookies cut into different shapes can add interest to a plate of simple square cookies. Cut cookies into different size rectangles or make triangles by cutting them into 2- to 2½-inch squares; then cut each square in half diagonally. To make diamond shapes, cut straight lines 1 or 1½ inches apart the length of the baking pan, then cut straight lines 1½ inches apart diagonally across the pan.

Prep Time: 15 minutes
Bake Time: 25 minutes
Cool Time: 2 hours

Hershey®s White Chip Brownies

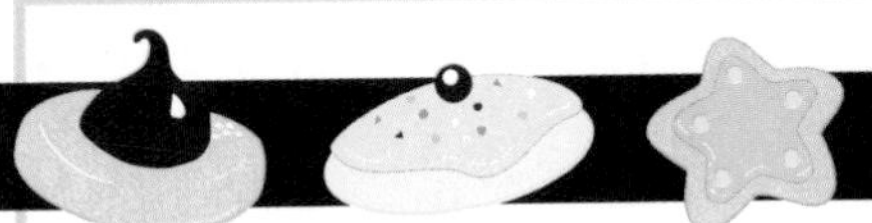

Double-Decker Confetti Brownies

- ¾ cup (1½ sticks) butter or margarine, softened
- 1 cup granulated sugar
- 1 cup firmly packed light brown sugar
- 3 large eggs
- 1 teaspoon vanilla extract
- 2½ cups all-purpose flour, divided
- 2½ teaspoons baking powder
- ½ teaspoon salt
- ⅓ cup unsweetened cocoa powder
- 1 tablespoon butter or margarine, melted
- 1 cup "M&M's"® Semi-Sweet Chocolate Mini Baking Bits, divided

Preheat oven to 350°F. Lightly grease 13×9×2-inch baking pan; set aside. In large bowl cream butter and sugars until light and fluffy; beat in eggs and vanilla. In medium bowl combine 2¼ cups flour, baking powder and salt; blend into creamed mixture. Divide batter in half. Blend together cocoa powder and melted butter; stir into one half of the dough. Spread cocoa dough evenly into prepared baking pan. Stir remaining ¼ cup flour and ½ cup "M&M's"® Semi-Sweet Chocolate Mini Baking Bits into remaining dough; spread evenly over cocoa dough in pan. Sprinkle with remaining ½ cup "M&M's"® Semi-Sweet Chocolate Mini Baking Bits. Bake 25 to 30 minutes or until edges start to pull away from sides of pan. Cool completely. Cut into bars. Store in tightly covered container.

Makes 24 brownies

Double-Decker Confetti Brownies

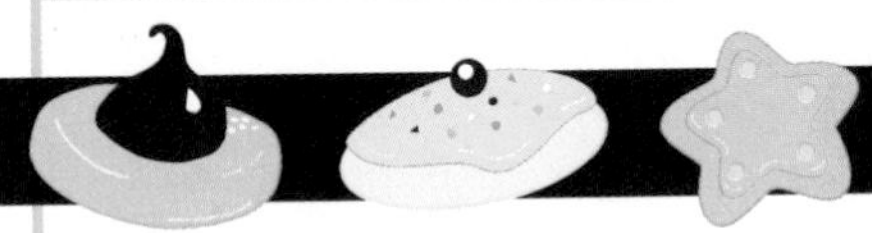

Rich Chocolate Caramel Brownies

- **1 package (18.25 to 18.5 ounces) devil's food or chocolate cake mix**
- **1 cup chopped nuts**
- **½ cup (1 stick) butter or margarine, melted**
- **1 cup undiluted CARNATION® Evaporated Milk, divided**
- **35 (10 ounces) light caramels, unwrapped**
- **1 cup (6 ounces) NESTLÉ® TOLL HOUSE® Semi-Sweet Chocolate Morsels**

COMBINE cake mix and nuts in large bowl; stir in butter. Stir in ⅔ *cup* evaporated milk (batter will be thick). Spread *half* of batter into greased 13×9-inch baking pan. Bake in preheated 350°F. oven for 15 minutes.

COMBINE caramels and *remaining* evaporated milk in small saucepan. Cook over low heat, stirring constantly, for about 10 minutes or until caramels are melted. Sprinkle chocolate morsels over baked layer; drizzle caramel mixture over top. Drop *remaining* batter by heaping teaspoon over caramel mixture. Bake for additional 20 to 25 minutes (top layer will be soft). Cool completely on wire rack.

Makes about 48 brownies

Variation: For Rich Chocolate Butterscotch Brownies, pour 12.25-ounce jar of butterscotch-flavored topping over Nestlé® Toll House® Semi-Sweet Chocolate Morsels, instead of melting caramels with ⅓ cup evaporated milk.

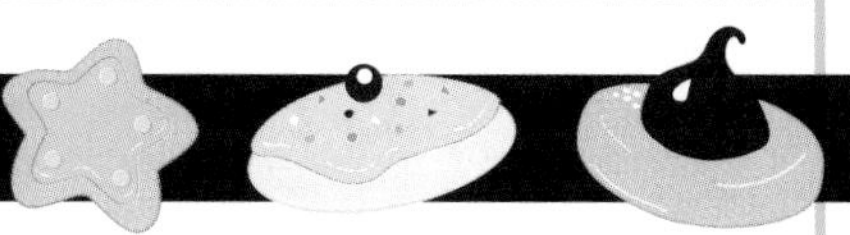

Double Fudge Brownie Bars

- **1 package DUNCAN HINES® Double Fudge Brownie Mix**
- **2 eggs**
- **⅓ cup water**
- **¼ cup vegetable oil**
- **1 (6-ounce) package semisweet chocolate chips**
- **1 cup peanut butter chips**
- **½ cup chopped pecans**
- **1 cup flaked coconut**
- **1 (14-ounce) can sweetened condensed milk**

Preheat oven to 350°F. Grease bottom only of 13×9-inch pan.

Combine brownie mix, contents of fudge packet from mix, eggs, water and oil in large bowl. Stir with spoon until well blended, about 50 strokes. Spread in prepared pan. Bake 18 minutes. Remove from oven. Sprinkle chocolate chips over brownie base, then sprinkle with peanut butter chips, pecans and coconut. Pour milk over top. Bake 22 to 25 minutes or until light golden brown. Cool completely in pan. Cut into bars.

Makes 20 to 24 bars

Tip: For a delicious flavor variation, substitute butterscotch-flavored chips for the peanut butter chips.

Tip

Sweetened condensed milk is a mixture of whole milk and sugar that is heated until about 60 percent of the water evaporates, resulting in a sticky, sweet mixture frequently used in baked goods. Unopened sweetened condensed milk should be stored at room temperature for up to six months. Once opened, store unused milk in an airtight container in the refrigerator for up to five days.

Chocolate Espresso Brownies

- **4 squares (1 ounce each) unsweetened chocolate**
- **1 cup sugar**
- **¼ cup Prune Purée (recipe follows) or prepared prune butter**
- **3 egg whites**
- **1 to 2 tablespoons instant espresso coffee powder**
- **1 teaspoon baking powder**
- **1 teaspoon salt**
- **1 teaspoon vanilla**
- **½ cup all-purpose flour**
- **Powdered sugar (optional)**

Preheat oven to 350°F. Coat 8-inch square baking pan with vegetable cooking spray. In small heavy saucepan, melt chocolate over very low heat, stirring until melted and smooth. Remove from heat; cool. In mixer bowl, beat chocolate and remaining ingredients except flour and powdered sugar at medium speed until well blended; mix in flour. Spread batter evenly in prepared pan. Bake in center of oven about 30 minutes until pick inserted into center comes out clean. Cool completely in pan on wire rack. Dust with powdered sugar. Cut into 1⅓-inch squares. *Makes 36 brownies*

Prune Purée: Combine 1⅓ cups (8 ounces) pitted prunes and 6 tablespoons hot water in container of food processor or blender. Pulse on and off until prunes are finely chopped and smooth. Store leftovers in a covered container in the refrigerator for up to two months. Makes 1 cup.

Favorite recipe from California Prune Board

Chocolate Espresso Brownies

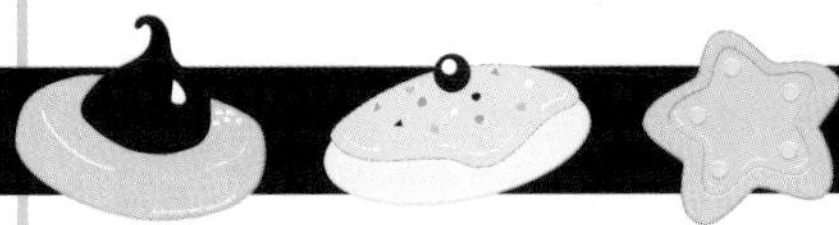

Three Great Tastes Blond Brownies

2 cups packed light brown sugar
1 cup (2 sticks) butter or margarine, melted
2 eggs
2 teaspoons vanilla extract
2 cups all-purpose flour
1 teaspoon salt
⅔ cup (of each) HERSHEY'S Semi-Sweet Chocolate Chips, REESE'S® Peanut Butter Chips, and HERSHEY'S Premier White Chips
Chocolate Chip Drizzle (recipe follows)

1. Heat oven to 350°F. Grease 15½×10½×1-inch jelly-roll pan.

2. Stir together brown sugar and butter in large bowl; beat in eggs and vanilla until smooth. Add flour and salt, beating just until blended; stir in chocolate, peanut butter and white chips. Spread batter into prepared pan.

3. Bake 25 to 30 minutes or until wooden pick inserted in center comes out clean. Cool completely in pan on wire rack. Cut into bars. With tines of fork, drizzle Chocolate Chip Drizzle randomly over bars. *Makes about 72 bars*

Chocolate Chip Drizzle: In small microwave-safe bowl, place ¼ cup HERSHEY'S Semi-Sweet Chocolate Chips and ¼ teaspoon shortening (do not use butter, margarine, spread or oil). Microwave at HIGH (100%) 30 seconds to 1 minute; stir until chips are melted and mixture is smooth.

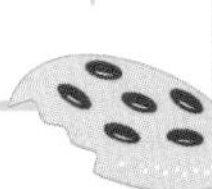

Three Great Tastes Blond Brownies

Triple Chocolate Brownies

- 3 squares (1 ounce each) unsweetened chocolate, coarsely chopped
- 2 squares (1 ounce each) semisweet chocolate, coarsely chopped
- ½ cup butter
- 1 cup all-purpose flour
- ½ teaspoon salt
- ¼ teaspoon baking powder
- 1½ cups sugar
- 3 large eggs
- 1 teaspoon vanilla
- ¼ cup sour cream
- ½ cup milk chocolate chips
- Powdered sugar (optional)

Preheat oven to 350°F. Lightly grease 13×9-inch baking pan.

Place unsweetened chocolate, semisweet chocolate and butter in medium microwavable bowl. Microwave at HIGH 2 minutes or until butter is melted; stir until chocolate is completely melted. Cool to room temperature.

Place flour, salt and baking powder in small bowl; stir to combine.

Beat sugar, eggs and vanilla in large bowl with electric mixer at medium speed until slightly thickened. Beat in chocolate mixture until well combined. Add flour mixture; beat at low speed until blended. Add sour cream; beat at low speed until combined. Stir in milk chocolate chips. Spread mixture evenly into prepared pan.

Bake 20 to 25 minutes or until toothpick inserted into center comes out almost clean. (Do not overbake.) Cool brownies completely in pan on wire rack. Cut into 2-inch squares. Place powdered sugar in fine-mesh strainer; sprinkle over brownies, if desired.

Store tightly covered at room temperature or freeze up to 3 months. *Makes 2 dozen brownies*

Triple Chocolate Brownies

A Bevy of Bars

Rich Chocolate Chip Toffee Bars

2⅓ cups all-purpose flour
⅔ cup packed light brown sugar
¾ cup (1½ sticks) butter or margarine
1 egg, slightly beaten
2 cups (12-ounce package) HERSHEY'S® Semi-Sweet Chocolate Chips, divided
1 cup coarsely chopped nuts
1 can (14 ounces) sweetened condensed milk (not evaporated milk)
1¾ cups (10-ounce package) SKOR® English Toffee Bits, divided

1. Heat oven to 350°F. Grease 13×9×2-inch baking pan.

2. Stir together flour and brown sugar in large bowl. Cut in butter with pastry blender until mixture resembles coarse crumbs. Add egg; mix well. Stir in 1½ cups chocolate chips and nuts. Reserve 1½ cups mixture. Press remaining crumb mixture onto bottom of prepared pan.

3. Bake 10 minutes. Pour sweetened condensed milk evenly over hot crust. Top with 1½ cups toffee bits. Sprinkle reserved crumb mixture and remaining ½ cup chips over top.

4. Bake 25 to 30 minutes or until golden brown. Sprinkle with remaining ¼ cup toffee bits. Cool completely in pan on wire rack. Cut into bars. *Makes about 36 bars*

Rich Chocolate Chip Toffee Bars

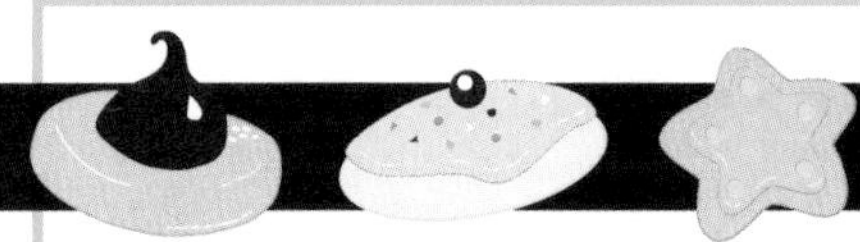

Choco Cheesecake Squares

- 1/3 cup butter, softened
- 1/3 cup packed light brown sugar
- 1 cup plus 1 tablespoon all-purpose flour, divided
- 1/2 cup chopped pecans (optional)
- 1 cup semisweet chocolate chips
- 1 package (8 ounces) cream cheese, softened
- 1/4 cup granulated sugar
- 1 large egg
- 1 teaspoon vanilla

Preheat oven to 350°F. Grease 8-inch square baking pan; set aside. Beat butter and brown sugar in large bowl until light and fluffy. Add 1 cup flour. Beat until well combined. Stir in nuts, if desired. (Mixture will be crumbly.) Press evenly into prepared pan. Bake 15 minutes.

Place chocolate chips in glass measuring cup. Melt in microwave oven at HIGH 2½ to 3 minutes, stirring after 2 minutes. Beat cream cheese and granulated sugar in medium bowl until light and fluffy. Add remaining 1 tablespoon flour, egg and vanilla; beat until smooth. Gradually stir in melted chocolate, mixing well. Pour cream cheese mixture over partially baked crust. Return to oven; bake 15 minutes or until set. Remove pan to wire rack; cool completely. Cut into 2-inch squares. *Makes about 16 squares*

Buttery Lemon Bars

CRUST

- 1¼ cups all-purpose flour
- 1/2 cup butter, softened
- 1/4 cup powdered sugar
- 1/2 teaspoon vanilla

FILLING

- 1 cup granulated sugar
- 2 eggs
- 1/3 cup fresh lemon juice
- 2 tablespoons all-purpose flour
- Grated peel of 1 lemon
- Powdered sugar

1. Preheat oven to 350°F.

2. Combine all crust ingredients in small bowl. Beat at low speed 2 to 3 minutes until mixture is crumbly. Press onto bottom of 8-inch square baking pan. Bake 15 to 20 minutes or until edges are lightly browned.

3. Combine all filling ingredients except powdered sugar in small bowl. Beat at low speed until well mixed.

4. Pour filling over hot crust. Continue baking 15 to 18 minutes or until filling is set. Sprinkle with powdered sugar; cool completely. Cut into bars; sprinkle again with powdered sugar. *Makes about 16 bars*

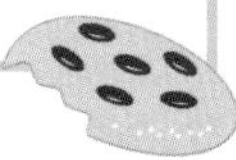

Choco Cheesecake Squares

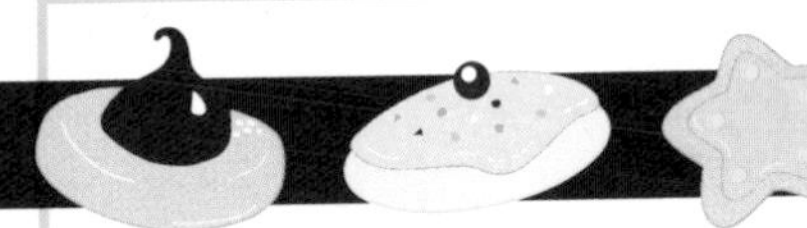

Mini Kisses™ Coconut Macaroon Bars

3¾ cups (10-ounce package) MOUNDS® Sweetened Coconut Flakes
¾ cup sugar
¼ cup all-purpose flour
¼ teaspoon salt
3 egg whites
1 whole egg, slightly beaten
1 teaspoon almond extract
1 cup HERSHEY'S MINI KISSES™ Milk Chocolate Baking Pieces

1. Heat oven to 350°F. Lightly grease 9-inch square baking pan.

2. Stir together coconut, sugar, flour and salt in large bowl. Add egg whites, whole egg and almond extract; stir until well blended. Stir in MINI KISSES. Spread mixture into prepared pan, covering all chocolate pieces with coconut mixture.

3. Bake 35 minutes or until lightly browned. Cool completely in pan on wire rack. Cover with foil; allow to stand at room temperature about 8 hours or overnight. Cut into bars.

Makes about 24 bars

Variation: *Omit MINI KISSES in batter. Immediately after removing pan from oven, place desired number of chocolate pieces on top, pressing down lightly. Cool completely. Cut into bars.*

Prep Time: 15 minutes
Bake Time: 35 minutes
Cool Time: 9 hours

Mini Kisses™ Coconut Macaroon Bars

Chocolate Cheesecake Bars

CRUST

1 cup graham cracker crumbs
¼ cup firmly packed brown sugar
⅓ Butter Flavor* CRISCO® Stick *or* ⅓ cup Butter Flavor* CRISCO® all-vegetable shortening, melted

FILLING

1 package (8 ounces) cream cheese, softened
½ cup granulated sugar
3 tablespoons cocoa
2 eggs
1 tablespoon all-purpose flour
½ teaspoon vanilla

TOPPING

2 tablespoons Butter Flavor* CRISCO® Stick *or* 2 tablespoons Butter Flavor* CRISCO® all-vegetable shortening
1 package (3 ounces) cream cheese, softened
1 cup powdered sugar
½ teaspoon vanilla

**Butter Flavor Crisco® is artificially flavored.*

1. Heat oven to 350°F. Place cooling rack on countertop.

2. For crust, combine graham cracker crumbs and brown sugar. Stir in melted shortening. Press into ungreased 8-inch square baking pan.

3. Bake at 350°F for 10 minutes. *Do not overbake.*

4. For filling, beat 8-ounce package cream cheese in small bowl at medium speed of electric mixer until smooth. Add, one at a time, granulated sugar, cocoa, eggs, flour and vanilla. Mix well after each addition. Pour over baked crust.

5. Bake for 30 minutes. *Do not overbake.* Cool to room temperature on cooling rack.

6. For topping, combine 2 tablespoons shortening and 3-ounce package cream cheese in small bowl. Beat at medium speed until well blended. Add powdered sugar and vanilla. Beat until smooth. Spread over filling. Cut into bars about 2×1½ inches. Refrigerate. *Makes 20 bars*

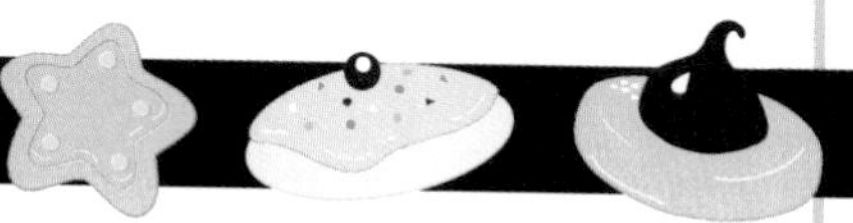

Mott's® Chewy Oatmeal Raisin Squares

- **1 cup raisins**
- **1 cup rolled oats**
- **¾ cup boiling water**
- **1 cup granulated sugar**
- **½ cup MOTT'S® Natural Apple Sauce**
- **¼ cup MOTT'S® Grandma's® Molasses**
- **1 whole egg**
- **2 egg whites, lightly beaten**
- **2 tablespoons vegetable oil**
- **1 teaspoon vanilla extract**
- **2 cups all-purpose flour**
- **1½ teaspoons baking powder**
- **½ teaspoon baking soda**
- **1 teaspoon cinnamon**
- **½ teaspoon ground cloves**
- **½ teaspoon salt**

1. Preheat oven to 400°F. Spray 13×9-inch baking pan with nonstick cooking spray.

2. In medium bowl, combine raisins and rolled oats. Pour boiling water over ingredients; mix until moistened. Set aside.

3. In large bowl, combine sugar, apple sauce, molasses, whole egg, egg whites, oil and vanilla.

4. In separate medium bowl, combine flour, baking powder, baking soda, spices and salt.

5. Add flour mixture to apple sauce mixture; mix until ingredients are combined. Stir in raisin-oatmeal mixture.

6. Spread batter evenly into prepared pan. Bake 12 to 15 minutes. Place pan on cooling rack to cool.

7. Let cool 15 minutes before cutting into squares.

Makes 16 servings

Coconut Pecan Bars

- **1¼ cups granulated sugar, divided**
- **½ cup plus 3 tablespoons all-purpose flour, divided**
- **1½ cups finely chopped pecans, divided**
- **¾ cup (1½ sticks) butter or margarine, softened, divided**
- **2 large eggs**
- **1 tablespoon vanilla extract**
- **1¾ cups "M&M's"® Chocolate Mini Baking Bits, divided**
- **1 cup shredded coconut**

Preheat oven to 350°F. Lightly grease 13×9×2-inch baking pan; set aside. In large bowl combine ¾ cup sugar, ½ cup flour and ½ cup nuts; add ¼ cup melted butter and mix well. Press mixture onto bottom of prepared pan. Bake 10 minutes or until set; cool slightly. In large bowl cream remaining ½ cup butter and ½ cup sugar; beat in eggs and vanilla. Combine 1 cup "M&M's"® Chocolate Mini Baking Bits and remaining 3 tablespoons flour; stir into creamed mixture. Spread mixture over cooled crust. Combine coconut and remaining 1 cup nuts; sprinkle over batter. Sprinkle remaining ¾ cup "M&M's"® Chocolate Mini Baking Bits over coconut and nuts; pat down lightly. Bake 25 to 30 minutes or until set. Cool completely. Cut into bars. Store in tightly covered container.

Makes 24 bars

Tip

Cut brownies and bar cookies into triangles or diamonds for a festive new look. To make serving easy, remove a corner piece first; then remove the rest.

Coconut Pecan Bars

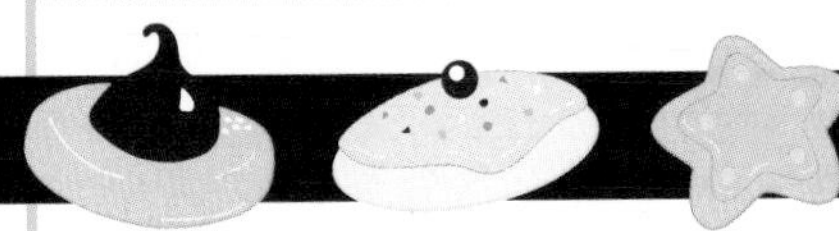

Butterscotch Blondies

- **3/4 cup (1 1/2 sticks) butter or margarine, softened**
- **3/4 cup packed light brown sugar**
- **1/2 cup granulated sugar**
- **2 eggs**
- **2 cups all-purpose flour**
- **1 teaspoon baking soda**
- **1/2 teaspoon salt**
- **1 2/3 cups (10-ounce package) HERSHEY'S® Butterscotch Chips**
- **1 cup chopped nuts (optional)**

1. Heat oven to 350°F. Grease 13×9×2-inch baking pan.

2. Beat butter, brown sugar and granulated sugar in large bowl until creamy. Add eggs; beat well. Stir together flour, baking soda and salt; gradually add to butter mixture, blending well. Stir in butterscotch chips and nuts, if desired. Spread into prepared pan.

3. Bake 30 to 35 minutes or until top is golden brown and center is set. Cool completely in pan on wire rack. Cut into bars. *Makes about 36 bars*

Orange Chess Bars

CRUST

- **1 package DUNCAN HINES® Moist Deluxe Orange Supreme Cake Mix**
- **1/2 cup vegetable oil**
- **1/3 cup chopped pecans**

TOPPING

- **1 pound confectioners sugar (3 1/2 to 4 cups)**
- **1 (8-ounce) package cream cheese, softened**
- **2 eggs**
- **2 teaspoons grated orange peel**

1. Preheat oven to 350°F. Grease 13×9-inch baking pan.

2. For crust, combine cake mix, oil and pecans in large bowl. Stir until blended (mixture will be crumbly). Press in bottom of prepared pan.

3. For topping, combine confectioners sugar and cream cheese in large bowl. Beat at low speed with electric mixer until blended. Add eggs and orange peel. Beat at low speed until blended. Pour over crust. Bake 30 to 35 minutes or until topping is set. Cool. Refrigerate until ready to serve. Cut into bars. *Makes about 24 bars*

Butterscotch Blondies

Fruit and Oat Squares

- **1 cup all-purpose flour**
- **1 cup uncooked quick oats**
- **¾ cup packed light brown sugar**
- **½ teaspoon baking soda**
- **¼ teaspoon salt**
- **¼ teaspoon ground cinnamon**
- **⅓ cup margarine or butter, melted**
- **¾ cup apricot, cherry or other fruit flavor preserves**

1. Preheat oven to 350°F. Spray 9-inch square baking pan with nonstick cooking spray; set aside.

2. Combine flour, oats, brown sugar, baking soda, salt and cinnamon in medium bowl; mix well. Add margarine; stir with fork until mixture is crumbly. Reserve ¾ cup crumb mixture for topping. Press remaining crumb mixture evenly onto bottom of prepared pan. Bake 5 to 7 minutes or until lightly browned. Spread preserves onto crust; sprinkle with reserved crumb mixture.

3. Bake 20 to 25 minutes or until golden brown. Cool completely in pan on wire rack. Cut into 16 squares.

Makes 16 servings

"Everything but the Kitchen Sink" Bar Cookies

- **1 package (18 ounces) refrigerated chocolate chip cookie dough**
- **1 jar (7 ounces) marshmallow creme**
- **½ cup creamy peanut butter**
- **1½ cups toasted corn cereal**
- **½ cup miniature candy-coated chocolate pieces**

1. Preheat oven to 350°F. Grease 13×9-inch baking pan. Remove dough from wrapper according to package directions.

2. Press dough into prepared baking pan. Bake 13 minutes.

3. Remove baking pan from oven. Drop teaspoonfuls of marshmallow creme and peanut butter over hot cookie base.

4. Bake 1 minute. Carefully spread marshmallow creme and peanut butter over cookie base.

5. Sprinkle cereal and chocolate pieces over melted marshmallow and peanut butter mixture.

6. Bake 7 minutes. Cool completely on wire rack. Cut into 2-inch bars.

Makes 3 dozen bar cookies

Fruit and Oat Squares

Chocolate Peppermint Bars

CRUST

1¾ cups all-purpose flour
1½ cups confectioners sugar
½ cup unsweetened cocoa powder
1 Butter Flavor* CRISCO® Stick or 1 cup Butter Flavor* CRISCO® all-vegetable shortening
2 tablespoons milk

TOPPING

1 package (8 ounces) cream cheese, softened
1 can (14 ounces) sweetened condensed milk
1 egg
1 teaspoon peppermint extract
Red food color
½ cup coarsely crushed hard peppermint candies (about 20 to 24)

**Butter Flavor Crisco® is artificially flavored.*

1. Heat oven to 350°F. Place cooling rack on counter for cooling bars.

2. For crust, combine flour, confectioners sugar and cocoa powder in large bowl. Beat in 1 cup shortening and milk on low speed of electric mixer until mixture is crumbly. Reserve 1¾ cups of mixture for topping. Press remainder into ungreased 13×9-inch baking pan.

3. Bake at 350°F for 15 minutes.

4. For topping, beat cream cheese in medium bowl at medium speed. Beat in condensed milk gradually. Beat until mixture is smooth. Beat in egg and peppermint extract. Add food color until desired shade of red is achieved. Mix well. Stir in chopped candies.

5. Pour mixture over baked crust. Sprinkle reserved crumb topping evenly over cream cheese filling.

6. Bake at 350°F for 25 to 30 minutes or until filling is set. *Do not overbake.* Cool in pan. Loosen from sides of pan with knife or spatula. Refrigerate until ready to serve. Cut into bars approximately 2×1½-inches. *Makes 3 dozen bars*

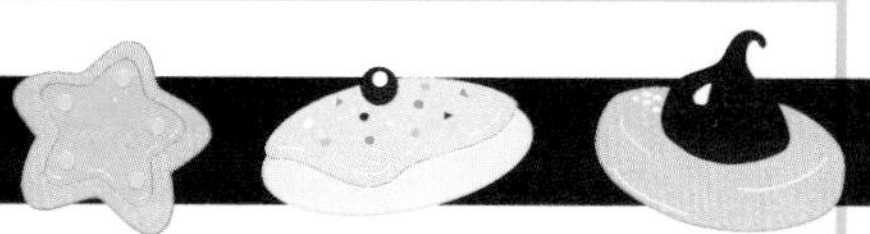

Brownie Caramel Pecan Bars

- **½ cup sugar**
- **2 tablespoons butter or margarine**
- **2 tablespoons water**
- **2 cups (12-ounce package) HERSHEY'S® Semi-Sweet Chocolate Chips, divided**
- **2 eggs**
- **1 teaspoon vanilla extract**
- **⅔ cup all-purpose flour**
- **¼ teaspoon baking soda**
- **¼ teaspoon salt**
- **Caramel Topping (recipe follows)**
- **1 cup pecan pieces**

1. Heat oven to 350°F. Line 9-inch square baking pan with foil, extending foil over edges of pan. Grease and flour foil.

2. In medium saucepan, combine sugar, butter and water; cook over low heat, stirring constantly, until mixture boils. Remove from heat. Immediately add 1 cup chocolate chips; stir until melted. Beat in eggs and vanilla until well blended. Stir together flour, baking soda and salt; stir into chocolate mixture. Spread batter into prepared pan.

3. Bake 15 to 20 minutes or until brownies begin to pull away from sides of pan. Meanwhile, prepare Caramel Topping. Remove brownies from oven; immediately and carefully spread with prepared topping. Sprinkle remaining 1 cup chips and pecans over topping. Cool completely in pan on wire rack, being careful not to disturb chips while soft. Lift out of pan. Cut into bars. *Makes about 16 bars*

Caramel Topping: *Remove wrappers from 25 caramels. In medium microwave-safe bowl, place ¼ cup (½ stick) butter or margarine, caramels and 2 tablespoons milk. Microwave at HIGH (100%) 1 minute; stir. Microwave an additional 1 to 2 minutes, stirring every 30 seconds, or until caramels are melted and mixture is smooth when stirred. Use immediately.*

Oatmeal Toffee Bars

1 cup (2 sticks) butter or margarine, softened
½ cup packed light brown sugar
½ cup granulated sugar
2 eggs
1 teaspoon vanilla extract
1½ cups all-purpose flour
1 teaspoon baking soda
½ teaspoon ground cinnamon
½ teaspoon salt
3 cups quick-cooking or regular rolled oats
1¾ cups (10-ounce package) SKOR® English Toffee Bits or 1¾ cups HEATH® Bits 'O Brickle, divided

1. Heat oven to 350°F. Grease 13×9×2-inch baking pan.

2. Beat butter, brown sugar and granulated sugar in large bowl until well blended. Add eggs and vanilla; beat well. Stir together flour, baking soda, cinnamon and salt; gradually add to butter mixture, beating until well blended. Stir in oats and 1⅓ cups toffee bits (mixture will be stiff). Spread mixture into prepared pan.

3. Bake 25 minutes or until wooden pick inserted in center comes out clean. Immediately sprinkle remaining toffee bits over surface. Cool completely in pan on wire rack. Cut into bars. *Makes about 36 bars*

Tip: Bar cookies can be cut into different shapes for variety. To cut into triangles, cut cookie bars into 2- to 3-inch squares, then diagonally cut each square in half. To make diamond shapes, cut parallel lines 2 inches apart across the length of the pan, then cut diagonal lines 2 inches apart.

Oatmeal Toffee Bars

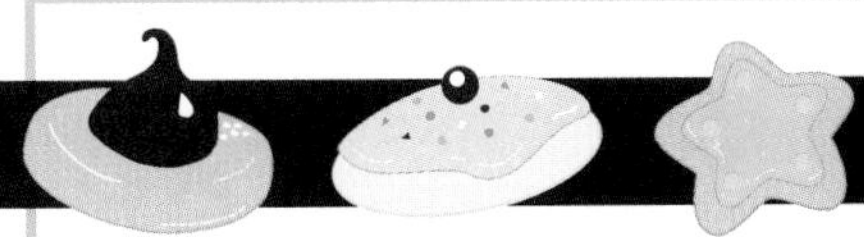

Spiced Chocolate Pecan Squares

COOKIE BASE

- **1 cup all-purpose flour**
- **½ cup packed light brown sugar**
- **½ teaspoon baking soda**
- **¼ cup (½ stick) butter or margarine, softened**

TOPPING

- **1 package (8 ounces) semi-sweet chocolate baking squares**
- **2 large eggs**
- **¼ cup packed light brown sugar**
- **¼ cup light corn syrup**
- **2 tablespoons FRENCH'S® Worcestershire Sauce**
- **1 tablespoon vanilla extract**
- **1½ cups chopped pecans or walnuts, divided**

Preheat oven to 375°F. To prepare cookie base, place flour, ½ cup sugar and baking soda in food processor or bowl of electric mixer. Process or mix 10 seconds. Add butter. Process or beat 30 seconds or until mixture resembles fine crumbs. Press evenly into bottom of greased 9-inch baking pan. Bake 15 minutes.

Meanwhile, to prepare topping, place chocolate in microwave-safe bowl. Microwave, uncovered, on HIGH 2 minutes or until chocolate is melted, stirring until chocolate is smooth; set aside.

Place eggs, ¼ cup sugar, corn syrup, Worcestershire and vanilla in food processor or bowl of electric mixer. Process or beat until well blended. Add melted chocolate. Process or beat until smooth. Stir in 1 cup nuts. Pour chocolate mixture over cookie base. Sprinkle with remaining ½ cup nuts. Bake 40 minutes or until toothpick inserted into center comes out with slightly fudgy crumbs. (Cookie will be slightly puffed along edges.) Cool completely on wire rack. To serve, cut into squares. *Makes 16 servings*

Prep Time: 20 minutes
Cook Time: 55 minutes

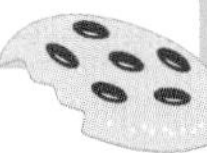

Spiced Chocolate Pecan Squares

Raspberry Coconut Layer Bars

1⅔ cups graham cracker crumbs
½ cup butter or margarine, melted
2⅔ cups (7-ounce package) flaked coconut
1¼ cups (14-ounce can) CARNATION® Sweetened Condensed Milk
1 cup red raspberry jam or preserves
⅓ cup finely chopped walnuts, toasted
½ cup NESTLÉ® TOLL HOUSE® Semi-Sweet Chocolate Morsels, melted
¼ cup (1½ ounces) chopped NESTLÉ® Premier White Baking Bar, melted

COMBINE graham cracker crumbs and butter in medium bowl. Spread evenly over bottom of 13×9-inch baking pan, pressing to make compact crust. Sprinkle with coconut; pour sweetened condensed milk evenly over coconut.

BAKE in preheated 350°F. oven 20 to 25 minutes or until lightly browned; cool.

SPREAD jam over coconut layer; chill for 3 to 4 hours. Sprinkle with walnuts. Drizzle semi-sweet chocolate then white chocolate over top layer to make lacy effect; chill. Cut into 3×1½-inch bars.

Makes 24 bar cookies

Tip

Crush graham crackers quickly and easily by placing them in a sealed plastic food storage bag, then running a rolling pin over the bag several times to pulverize them.

Raspberry Coconut Layer Bars

Caramel Apple Bars

CRUST

¾ Butter Flavor* CRISCO® Stick or ¾ cup Butter Flavor* CRISCO® all-vegetable shortening plus additional for greasing
1 cup firmly packed light brown sugar
1 egg
1½ cups all-purpose flour
½ teaspoon salt
½ teaspoon baking soda
1¾ cups quick oats, uncooked

FILLING

3 to 4 Granny Smith or Golden Delicious apples, peeled and cut into ½-inch dice (about 4 cups)
2 tablespoons all-purpose flour
1 teaspoon lemon juice
1 bag (14 ounces) caramel candy, unwrapped

**Butter Flavor Crisco® is artificially flavored.*

1. Heat oven to 350°F. Grease 13×9×2-inch baking pan with shortening.

2. For crust, combine shortening and brown sugar in large bowl. Beat at medium speed of electric mixer. Add egg to creamed mixture. Beat until well blended.

3. Combine 1½ cups flour, salt and baking soda. Add to creamed mixture gradually. Add in oats. Mix until blended. Reserve 1¼ cups of mixture for topping. Press remaining mixture into prepared pan.

4. Bake at 350°F for 10 minutes.

5. For filling, toss apples with 2 tablespoons flour and lemon juice. Distribute apple mixture evenly over partially baked crust. Press in lightly.

6. Place caramels in microwave-safe bowl. Microwave at HIGH (100%) for 1 minute. Stir. Repeat until caramels are melted. Drizzle melted caramel evenly over apples. Crumble reserved topping evenly over caramel.

7. Bake at 350°F for 30 to 40 minutes, or until apples are tender and top is golden brown. Loosen caramel from sides of pan with knife. Cool completely. *Do not overbake.* Cut into 1½-inch bars. Cover tightly with plastic wrap to store.

Makes about 4 dozen bars

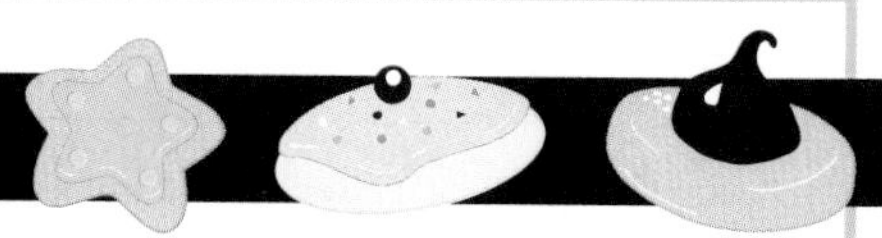

Baker's® Mississippi Mud Bars

½ cup (1 stick) butter or margarine
¾ cup firmly packed brown sugar
1 egg
1 teaspoon vanilla
1 cup flour
½ teaspoon baking soda
¼ teaspoon salt
1 package (8 squares) BAKER'S® Semi-Sweet Baking Chocolate, chopped, divided
1 package (6 squares) BAKER'S® Premium White Baking Chocolate, chopped, divided
1 cup chopped walnuts, divided

HEAT oven to 350°F. Line 9-inch square baking pan with foil. Grease foil.

BEAT butter, sugar, egg and vanilla in large bowl with electric mixer on medium speed until light and fluffy. Mix in flour, baking soda and salt. Stir in ½ each of the semi-sweet and white chocolates and ½ cup of the walnuts. Spread in prepared pan.

BAKE 25 minutes or until toothpick inserted in center comes out almost clean. DO NOT OVERBAKE. Remove from oven. Sprinkle with remaining semi-sweet and white chocolates. Cover with foil. Let stand 5 minutes or until chocolates are melted. Swirl with knife to marbleize. Sprinkle with remaining ½ cup walnuts. Cool in pan on wire rack until chocolate is firm. Cut into 2×1-inch bars. Store in tightly covered container.

Makes 3 dozen bars

Prep Time: 20 minutes
Bake Time: 25 minutes

No-Bake Pineapple Marmalade Squares

1 cup graham cracker crumbs
½ cup plus 2 tablespoons sugar, divided
¼ cup light margarine, melted
1 cup fat free or light sour cream
4 ounces light cream cheese, softened
¼ cup orange marmalade or apricot fruit spread, divided
1 can (20 ounces) DOLE® Crushed Pineapple
1 envelope unflavored gelatin

• Combine graham cracker crumbs, 2 tablespoons sugar and margarine in 8-inch square glass baking dish; pat mixture firmly and evenly onto bottom of dish. Freeze 10 minutes.

• Beat sour cream, cream cheese, remaining ½ cup sugar and 1 tablespoon marmalade in medium bowl until smooth and blended; set aside.

• Drain pineapple; reserve ¼ cup juice.

• Sprinkle gelatin over reserved juice in small saucepan; let stand 1 minute. Cook and stir over low heat until gelatin dissolves.

• Beat gelatin mixture into sour cream mixture until well blended. Spoon mixture evenly over crust.

• Stir together pineapple and remaining 3 tablespoons marmalade in small bowl until blended. Evenly spoon over sour cream filling. Cover and refrigerate 2 hours or until firm.

Makes 16 servings

Oat-Y Nut Bars

½ cup butter
½ cup honey
¼ cup corn syrup
¼ cup packed brown sugar
2¾ cups uncooked quick oats
⅔ cup raisins
½ cup salted peanuts

Preheat oven to 300°F. Grease 9-inch square baking pan. Melt butter with honey, corn syrup and brown sugar in medium saucepan over medium heat, stirring constantly. Bring to a boil; boil 8 minutes until mixture thickens slightly. Stir in oats, raisins and peanuts until well blended. Press evenly into prepared pan.

Bake 45 to 50 minutes or until golden brown. Place pan on wire rack; score top into 2-inch squares. Cool completely. Cut into bars.

Makes 16 bars

No-Bake Pineapple Marmalade Squares

Fruit and Nut Bars

- 1 cup unsifted all-purpose flour
- 1 cup quick oats
- ⅔ cup brown sugar
- 2 teaspoons baking soda
- ½ teaspoon salt
- ½ teaspoon cinnamon
- ⅔ cup buttermilk
- 3 tablespoons vegetable oil
- 2 egg whites, lightly beaten
- 1 Washington Golden Delicious apple, cored and chopped
- ½ cup dried cranberries or raisins, chopped
- ¼ cup chopped nuts
- 2 tablespoons flaked coconut (optional)

1. Heat oven to 375°F. Lightly grease 9-inch square baking pan. In large mixing bowl, combine flour, oats, brown sugar, baking soda, salt and cinnamon; stir to blend.

2. Add buttermilk, oil and egg whites; beat with electric mixer just until mixed. Stir in apple, dried fruit and nuts; spread evenly in pan and top with coconut, if desired. Bake 20 to 25 minutes or until cake tester inserted in center comes out clean. Cool and cut into 10 bars. *Makes 10 bars*

Favorite recipe from Washington Apple Commission

Tip

Always use the pan size called for in the recipe. Substituting a different pan will affect the cookies' texture—a smaller pan will give the bars a more cakelike texture and a larger pan will produce a flatter bar with a drier texture.

Fruit and Nut Bars

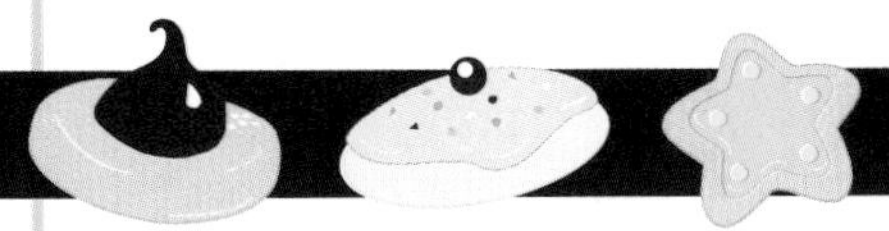

Chippy Chewy Bars

- ½ cup (1 stick) butter or margarine
- 1½ cups graham cracker crumbs
- 1⅔ cups (10-ounce package) REESE'S® Peanut Butter Chips, divided
- 1½ cups MOUNDS® Sweetened Coconut Flakes
- 1 can (14 ounces) sweetened condensed milk (not evaporated milk)
- 1 cup HERSHEY'S Semi-Sweet Chocolate Chips or HERSHEY'S MINI CHIPS™ Semi-Sweet Chocolate
- 1½ teaspoons shortening (do not use butter, margarine, spread or oil)

1. Heat oven to 350°F.

2. Place butter in 13×9×2-inch baking pan. Heat in oven until melted. Remove pan from oven. Sprinkle graham cracker crumbs evenly over butter; press down with fork. Layer 1 cup peanut butter chips over crumbs; sprinkle coconut over peanut butter chips. Layer remaining ⅔ cup peanut butter chips over coconut; drizzle sweetened condensed milk evenly over top. Press down firmly.

3. Bake 20 minutes or until lightly browned.

4. Place chocolate chips and shortening in small microwave-safe bowl. Microwave at HIGH (100%) 1 minute; stir. If necessary, microwave at HIGH an additional 15 seconds at a time, stirring after each heating, just until chips are melted when stirred. Drizzle evenly over top of baked mixture. Cool completely in pan on wire rack. Cut into bars.

Makes about 48 bars

Note: For lighter drizzle, use ½ cup chocolate chips and ¾ teaspoon shortening. Microwave at HIGH 30 seconds to 1 minute; stir. If necessary, microwave at HIGH an additional 15 seconds at a time, stirring after each heating, just until chips are melted when stirred.

Chippy Chewy Bars

Oatmeal Praline Cheese Bars

COOKIE BASE

1¼ cups firmly packed light brown sugar
¾ Butter Flavor* CRISCO® Stick or ¾ cup Butter Flavor* CRISCO® all-vegetable shortening plus additional for greasing
1 egg
⅓ cup milk
1½ teaspoons vanilla
1½ cups quick oats, uncooked
1 cup all-purpose flour
1 cup finely chopped pecans
¼ cup toasted wheat germ
½ teaspoon baking soda
½ teaspoon salt
½ teaspoon cinnamon

TOPPING

1 package (8 ounces) cream cheese, softened
⅓ cup firmly packed light brown sugar
2 eggs
½ teaspoon vanilla
½ teaspoon salt
½ cup almond brickle chips
½ cup finely chopped pecans

**Butter Flavor Crisco® is artificially flavored.*

1. Heat oven to 350°F. Grease 13×9-inch baking pan. Place cooling rack on countertop.

2. For cookie base, place brown sugar, ¾ cup shortening, egg, milk and vanilla in large bowl. Beat at medium speed of electric mixer until well blended.

3. Combine oats, flour, pecans, wheat germ, baking soda, salt and cinnamon. Add to shortening mixture; beat at low speed just until blended.

4. Spread dough onto bottom of prepared pan.

5. Bake at 350°F for 15 to 17 minutes or until surface is light golden brown and edges pull away from sides of pan. *Do not overbake.*

6. For topping, place cream cheese, brown sugar, eggs, vanilla and salt in medium bowl. Beat at medium speed of electric mixer until smooth. Pour mixture over cookie base. Sprinkle with almond brickle chips and pecans.

7. Bake 15 to 17 minutes longer or until topping is set. *Do not overbake.* Cool completely on cooling rack. Cut into 2×1½-inch bars. Refrigerate.

Makes about 3 dozen bars

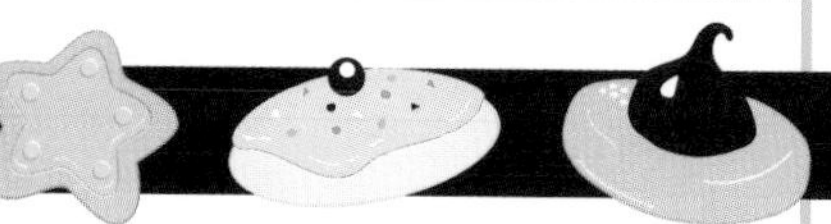

Baker's® Chocolate Pecan Pie Bars

- 2 cups flour
- 2 cups sugar, divided
- 1 cup (2 sticks) butter or margarine, softened
- ¼ teaspoon salt
- 1½ cups corn syrup
- 6 squares BAKER'S® Semi-Sweet Baking Chocolate
- 4 eggs, slightly beaten
- 1½ teaspoons vanilla
- 2½ cups chopped pecans

HEAT oven to 350°F. Lightly grease sides of 15×10×1-inch baking pan.

BEAT flour, ½ cup of the sugar, butter and salt in large bowl with electric mixer on medium speed until mixture resembles coarse crumbs. Press firmly and evenly into prepared baking pan. Bake 20 minutes or until lightly browned.

MICROWAVE corn syrup and chocolate in large microwavable bowl on HIGH 2½ minutes or until chocolate is almost melted, stirring halfway through heating time. Stir until chocolate is completely melted. Mix in remaining 1½ cups sugar, eggs and vanilla until blended. Stir in pecans. Pour filling over hot crust; spread evenly.

BAKE 35 minutes or until filling is firm around edges and slightly soft in center. Cool completely in pan on wire rack.

Makes 48 bars

Melting Chocolate on Top of Stove: Heat corn syrup and chocolate in heavy 3-quart saucepan on very low heat, stirring constantly until chocolate is just melted. Remove from heat. Continue as directed above.

Prep Time: 20 minutes
Bake Time: 55 minutes

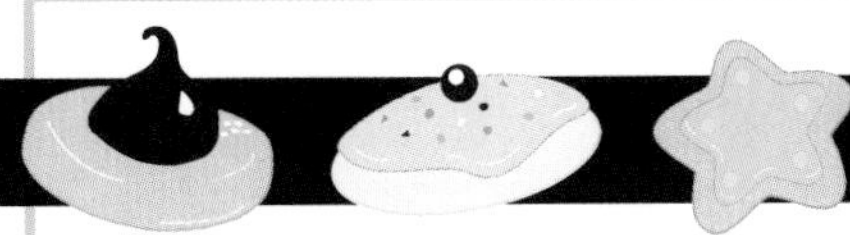

No-Bake Chocolate Oat Bars

- **1 cup butter**
- **½ cup firmly packed brown sugar**
- **1 teaspoon vanilla**
- **3 cups uncooked quick-cooking oats**
- **1 cup semisweet chocolate chips**
- **½ cup crunchy or creamy peanut butter**

Tip

Cookies, brownies and bars always make great gifts. Place them in a paper-lined tin or on a decorative plate covered with plastic wrap and tied with colorful ribbon. For a special touch, include the recipe.

Grease 9-inch square baking pan. Melt butter in large saucepan over medium heat. Add brown sugar and vanilla; mix well.

Stir in oats. Cook over low heat 2 to 3 minutes or until ingredients are well blended. Press half of mixture into prepared pan. Use back of large spoon to spread mixture evenly.

Meanwhile, melt chocolate chips in small heavy saucepan over low heat, stirring occasionally. Stir in peanut butter. Pour chocolate mixture over oat mixture in pan; spread evenly with knife or back of spoon. Crumble remaining oat mixture over chocolate layer, pressing in gently. Cover and refrigerate 2 to 3 hours or overnight.

Bring to room temperature before cutting into bars. (Bars can be frozen; let thaw about 10 minutes or more before serving.)

Makes 32 bars

No-Bake Chocolate Oat Bars

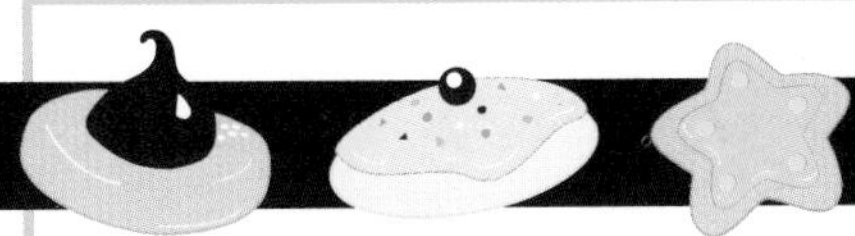

Chocolate Chip Cookie Bars

1¼ cups firmly packed light brown sugar
¾ Butter Flavor* CRISCO® Stick or ¾ cup Butter Flavor* CRISCO® all-vegetable shortening plus additional for greasing
2 tablespoons milk
1 tablespoon vanilla
1 egg
1¾ cups all-purpose flour
1 teaspoon salt
¾ teaspoon baking soda
1 cup (6 ounces) semisweet chocolate chips
1 cup coarsely chopped pecans (optional)**

**Butter Flavor Crisco® is artificially flavored.*

***If pecans are omitted, add an additional ½ cup semisweet chocolate chips.*

1. Heat oven to 350°F. Grease 13×9-inch baking pan. Place cooling rack on countertop.

2. Place brown sugar, shortening, milk and vanilla in large bowl. Beat at medium speed of electric mixer until well blended. Add egg; beat well.

3. Combine flour, salt and baking soda. Add to shortening mixture; beat at low speed just until blended. Stir in chocolate chips and pecans, if desired.

4. Press dough evenly onto bottom of prepared pan.

5. Bake at 350°F for 20 to 25 minutes or until lightly browned and firm in the center. *Do not overbake.* Cool completely on cooling rack. Cut into 2×1½-inch bars.

Makes about 3 dozen bars

Chocolate Chip Cookie Bars

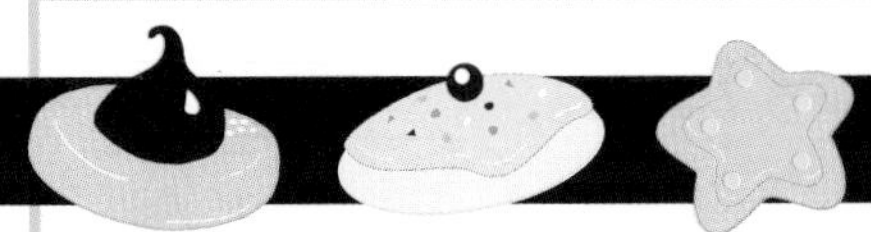

Strawberry Oat Bars

- 1 cup butter, softened
- 1 cup firmly packed light brown sugar
- 2 cups uncooked quick oats
- 1 cup all-purpose flour
- 2 teaspoons baking soda
- ½ teaspoon ground cinnamon
- ¼ teaspoon salt
- 1 can (21 ounces) strawberry pie filling
- ¾ teaspoon almond extract

Preheat oven to 375°F. Beat butter in large bowl with electric mixer at medium speed until smooth. Add brown sugar; beat until well blended.

Combine oats, flour, baking soda, cinnamon and salt in large bowl; mix well. Add flour mixture to butter mixture, beating on low speed until well blended and crumbly.

Spread ⅔ of crumb mixture in bottom of ungreased 13×9-inch baking pan, pressing down to form firm layer. Bake 15 minutes; let cool 5 minutes on wire rack

Meanwhile, place strawberry filling in food processor or blender; process until smooth. Stir in almond extract.

Pour strawberry mixture over partially baked crust. Sprinkle remaining crumb mixture evenly over strawberry layer.

Return pan to oven; bake 20 to 25 minutes or until topping is golden brown and filling is slightly bubbly. Let cool completely on wire rack before cutting into bars.

Makes about 4 dozen bars

Strawberry Oat Bars

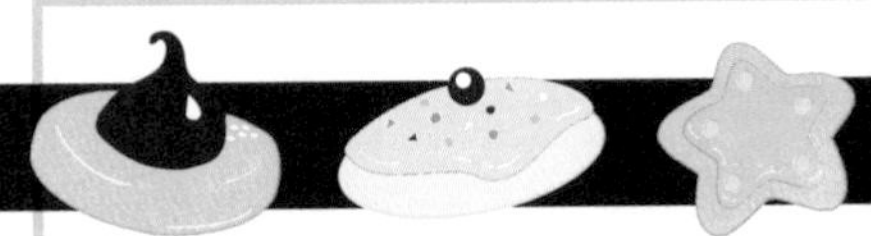

Chocolate Caramel Bars

CRUST

MAZOLA NO STICK® Cooking Spray
2 cups flour
¾ cup (1½ sticks) MAZOLA® Margarine or butter, slightly softened
½ cup packed brown sugar
¼ teaspoon salt
1 cup (6 ounces) semisweet or milk chocolate chips

CARAMEL

¾ cup (1½ sticks) MAZOLA® Margarine or butter
1 cup packed brown sugar
⅓ cup KARO® Light or Dark Corn Syrup
1 teaspoon vanilla
½ cup chopped walnuts

FOR CRUST:
1. Preheat oven to 350°F. Spray 13×9×2-inch baking pan with cooking spray.

2. In large bowl with mixer at medium speed, beat flour, margarine, brown sugar and salt until mixture resembles coarse crumbs; press firmly into prepared pan.

3. Bake 15 minutes or until golden brown. Sprinkle chocolate chips over hot crust; let stand 5 minutes or until shiny and soft. Spread chocolate evenly; set aside.

FOR CARAMEL:
4. In heavy 2-quart saucepan combine margarine, brown sugar, corn syrup and vanilla. Stirring frequently, bring to a boil over medium heat. Without stirring, boil 4 minutes.

5. Pour over chocolate; spread evenly. Sprinkle with walnuts.

6. Cool completely. Refrigerate 1 hour to set chocolate; let stand at room temperature until softened.

7. Cut into 48 (1-inch) bars. Store in tightly covered container at room temperature. *Makes about 4 dozen bars*

Prep Time: 30 minutes
Bake Time: 15 minutes, plus cooling and chilling

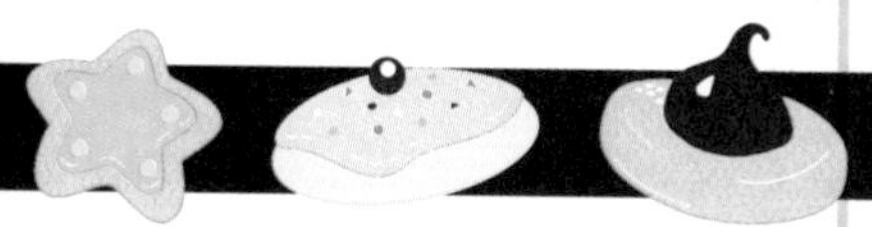

Double Chocolate Crispy Bars

- **6 cups crispy rice cereal**
- **½ cup peanut butter**
- **⅓ cup butter or margarine**
- **2 squares (1 ounce each) unsweetened chocolate**
- **1 package (8 ounces) marshmallows**
- **1 cup (6 ounces) semisweet chocolate chips or 6 ounces bittersweet chocolate, chopped**
- **6 ounces white chocolate, chopped**
- **2 teaspoons shortening, divided**

Preheat oven to 350°F. Line 13×9-inch pan with waxed paper. Spread cereal on cookie sheet; toast in oven 10 minutes or until crispy; place in large bowl. Meanwhile, combine peanut butter, butter and unsweetened chocolate in large heavy saucepan. Stir over low heat until chocolate is melted. Add marshmallows; stir until melted and smooth. Pour chocolate mixture over cereal; mix until evenly coated. Press firmly into prepared pan. Place semisweet and white chocolates into separate bowls. Add 1 teaspoon shortening to each bowl. Place bowls over very warm water; stir until chocolates are melted. Spread top of bars with melted semisweet chocolate; cool until chocolate is set. Turn bars out of pan onto a sheet of waxed paper, chocolate side down. Remove waxed paper from bottom of bars; spread white chocolate over surface. Cool until chocolate is set. Cut into 2×1½-inch bars using sharp, thin knife.

Makes about 3 dozen bars

Cinnamony Apple Streusel Bars

- **1¼ cups graham cracker crumbs**
- **1¼ cups all-purpose flour**
- **¾ cup packed brown sugar, divided**
- **¼ cup granulated sugar**
- **1 teaspoon ground cinnamon**
- **¾ cup butter or margarine, melted**
- **2 cups chopped apples (2 medium apples, cored and peeled)**
- **Glaze (recipe follows)**

Preheat oven to 350°F. Grease 13×9-inch baking pan. Combine graham cracker crumbs, flour, ½ cup brown sugar, granulated sugar, cinnamon and melted butter in large bowl until well blended; reserve 1 cup. Press remaining crumb mixture into bottom of prepared pan.

Bake 8 minutes. Remove from oven; set aside. Toss apples with remaining ¼ cup brown sugar in medium bowl until brown sugar is dissolved; arrange apples over baked crust. Sprinkle reserved 1 cup crumb mixture over filling. Bake 30 to 35 minutes more or until apples are tender. Remove pan to wire rack; cool completely. Drizzle with Glaze. Cut into bars.

Makes 3 dozen bars

Glaze: *Combine ½ cup powdered sugar and 1 tablespoon milk in small bowl until well blended.*

Peachy Oatmeal Bars

CRUMB MIXTURE

- **1½ cups all-purpose flour**
- **1 cup uncooked rolled oats**
- **½ cup sugar**
- **¾ cup butter, melted**
- **½ teaspoon baking soda**
- **¼ teaspoon salt**
- **2 teaspoons almond extract**

FILLING

- **¾ cup peach preserves**
- **⅓ cup flaked coconut**

Preheat oven to 350°F. Grease 9-inch square baking pan.

Combine flour, oats, sugar, butter, baking soda, salt and almond extract in large bowl. Beat with electric mixer at low speed 1 to 2 minutes until mixture is crumbly. Reserve ¾ cup crumb mixture; press remaining crumb mixture onto bottom of prepared baking pan.

Spread peach preserves to within ½ inch of edge of crumb mixture; sprinkle reserved crumb mixture and coconut over top. Bake 22 to 27 minutes or until edges are lightly browned. Cool completely. Cut into bars. *Makes 24 to 30 bars*

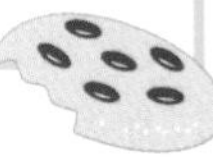

Cinnamony Apple Streusel Bars

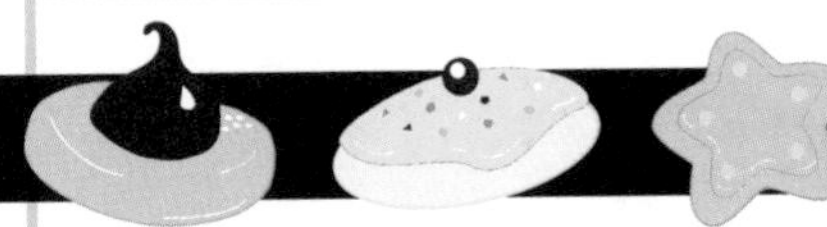

Oatmeal Chocolate Cherry Bars

- **½ cup (1 stick) butter or margarine, softened**
- **¼ cup solid vegetable shortening**
- **1 cup firmly packed light brown sugar**
- **1 large egg**
- **1 teaspoon vanilla extract**
- **2½ cups quick-cooking or old-fashioned oats, uncooked**
- **1 cup all-purpose flour**
- **1 teaspoon baking soda**
- **1¾ cups "M&M's"® Chocolate Mini Baking Bits, divided**
- **1 cup dried cherries, plumped***

**To plump cherries, pour 1½ cups boiling water over cherries and let stand 10 minutes. Drain well and use as directed.*

Preheat oven to 350°F. Lightly grease 13×9×2-inch baking pan; set aside. In large bowl cream butter and shortening until light and fluffy; beat in sugar, egg and vanilla. In medium bowl combine oats, flour and baking soda; blend into creamed mixture. Stir in 1¼ cups "M&M's"® Chocolate Mini Baking Bits and cherries. Spread batter evenly in prepared pan; top with remaining ½ cup "M&M's"® Chocolate Mini Baking Bits. Bake 25 to 30 minutes or until toothpick inserted in center comes out clean. Cool completely. Cut into squares. Store in tightly covered container. *Makes 24 bars*

Variation: *To make cookies, drop dough by rounded tablespoonfuls about 2 inches apart onto lightly greased cookie sheets; place 4 to 5 pieces of remaining ½ cup "M&M's"® Chocolate Mini Baking Bits on top of each cookie. Bake 13 to 15 minutes. Cool 2 to 3 minutes on cookie sheets; remove to wire racks to cool completely. Store in tightly covered container. Makes about 4 dozen cookies.*

Oatmeal Chocolate Cherry Bars

Peanut Butter Chocolate No-Bake Bars

BARS

1 cup peanut butter
½ cup light corn syrup
½ cup powdered sugar
2 tablespoons margarine or butter
2 cups QUAKER® Oats (quick or old fashioned, uncooked)

TOPPING

1 cup (6 ounces) semisweet chocolate pieces
2 tablespoons peanut butter
¼ cup chopped peanuts (optional)

1. For bars, in medium saucepan, heat peanut butter, corn syrup, powdered sugar and margarine over medium-low heat until margarine is melted, stirring frequently. Remove from heat. Stir in oats, mixing well.

2. Spread onto bottom of *ungreased* 8- or 9-inch square pan; set aside.

3. For topping, place chocolate pieces in medium-size microwavable bowl. Microwave on HIGH 1 to 2 minutes, stirring every 30 seconds until smooth.

4. Stir in peanut butter until well blended.

5. Spread evenly over oats layer. Sprinkle with chopped nuts, if desired. Refrigerate 30 minutes or until chocolate is set.

6. Cut into bars with sharp knife. If bars are difficult to cut, let stand about 10 minutes. Store tightly covered at room temperature.

Makes 24 bars

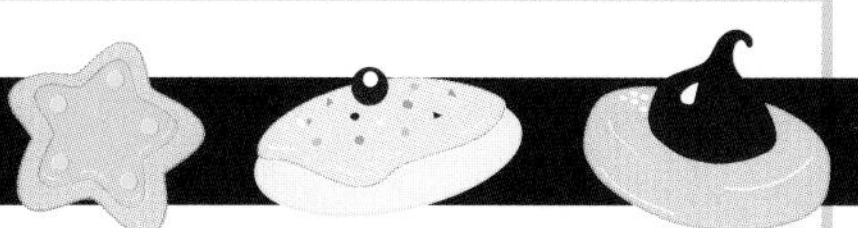

Festive Fruited White Chip Blondies

- ½ cup (1 stick) butter or margarine
- 1⅔ cups (10-ounce package) HERSHEY'S® Premier White Chips, divided
- 2 eggs
- ¼ cup granulated sugar
- 1¼ cups all-purpose flour
- ⅓ cup orange juice
- ¾ cup cranberries, chopped
- ¼ cup chopped dried apricots
- ½ cup coarsely chopped nuts
- ¼ cup packed light brown sugar

1. Heat oven to 325°F. Grease and flour 9-inch square baking pan.

2. Melt butter in medium saucepan; stir in 1 cup white chips. In large bowl, beat eggs until foamy. Add granulated sugar; beat until thick and pale yellow in color. Add flour, orange juice and white chip mixture; beat just until combined. Spread one-half of batter, about 1¼ cups, into prepared pan.

3. Bake 15 minutes until edges are lightly browned; remove from oven.

4. Stir cranberries, apricots and remaining ⅔ cup white chips into remaining one-half of batter; spread over top of hot baked mixture. Stir together nuts and brown sugar; sprinkle over top.

5. Bake 25 to 30 minutes or until edges are lightly browned. Cool completely in pan on wire rack. Cut into bars.

Makes about 16 bars

Praline Bars

- **¾ cup butter or margarine, softened**
- **1 cup sugar, divided**
- **1 teaspoon vanilla, divided**
- **1½ cups flour**
- **2 packages (8 ounces each) PHILADELPHIA® Cream Cheese, softened**
- **2 eggs**
- **½ cup almond brickle chips**
- **3 tablespoons caramel ice cream topping**

MIX butter, ½ cup of the sugar and ½ teaspoon of the vanilla with electric mixer on medium speed until light and fluffy. Gradually add flour, mixing on low speed until blended. Press onto bottom of 13×9-inch pan. Bake at 350°F for 20 to 23 minutes or until lightly browned.

MIX cream cheese, remaining ½ cup sugar and ½ teaspoon vanilla with electric mixer on medium speed until well blended. Add eggs; mix well. Blend in chips. Pour over crust. Dot top of cream cheese mixture with topping. Cut through batter with knife several times for marble effect.

BAKE at 350°F for 30 minutes. Cool in pan on wire rack. Cut into bars.

Makes 2 dozen

Prep Time: 30 minutes
Bake Time: 30 minutes

Microwave Double Peanut Bars

- **½ cup light brown sugar**
- **½ cup light corn syrup or honey**
- **½ cup creamy peanut butter**
- **6 shredded wheat biscuits, coarsely crushed**
- **¾ cup raisins**
- **½ cup chopped peanuts**

In 2-quart microwavable bowl, blend sugar, corn syrup and peanut butter. Microwave on HIGH (100% power) 1 to 1½ minutes until bubbly. Stir until smooth. Quickly stir in cereal, raisins and peanuts. Press evenly into greased 8- or 9-inch square baking pan. Cool. Cut into bars.

Makes 2 dozen bars

Favorite recipe from Peanut Advisory Board

Praline Bars

Oatmeal Carmelita Bars

¾ Butter Flavor* CRISCO® stick or ¾ cup Butter Flavor* CRISCO® all-vegetable shortening, melted, plus additional for greasing
1½ cups quick oats (not instant or old fashioned), uncooked
¾ cup firmly packed brown sugar
½ cup plus 3 tablespoons all-purpose flour, divided
½ cup whole wheat flour
½ teaspoon baking soda
¼ teaspoon cinnamon
1⅓ cups milk chocolate chips
½ cup chopped walnuts
1 jar (12.5 ounces) or ¾ cup caramel ice cream topping

**Butter Flavor Crisco is artificially flavored.*

1. Heat oven to 350°F. Grease bottom and sides of 9-inch square baking pan with shortening. Place wire rack on countertop to cool bars.

2. Combine ¾ cup shortening, oats, sugar, ½ cup all-purpose flour, whole wheat flour, baking soda and cinnamon in large bowl. Mix at low speed of electric mixer until crumbs form. Reserve ½ cup for topping. Press remaining crumbs into prepared pan.

3. Bake at 350°F for 10 minutes. Sprinkle chocolate chips and nuts over crust.

4. Combine caramel topping and remaining 3 tablespoons all-purpose flour. Stir until well blended. Drizzle over chocolate chips and nuts. Sprinkle reserved ½ cup crumbs over caramel topping.

5. Return to oven. Bake for 20 to 25 minutes or until golden brown. *Do not overbake.* Run spatula around edge of pan before cooling. Cool completely in pan on wire rack. Cut into 1½×1½-inch squares. *Makes 3 dozen squares*

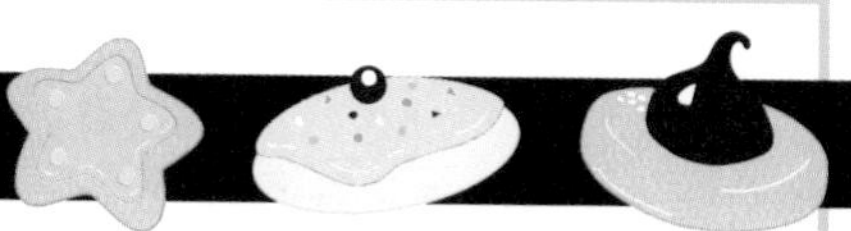

Double-Decker Cereal Treats

- **1⅔ cups (10-ounce package) REESE'S® Peanut Butter Chips**
- **2 tablespoons vegetable oil**
- **2 teaspoons vanilla extract, divided**
- **2 cups (12-ounce package) HERSHEY'S® Semi-Sweet Chocolate Chips**
- **2 cups light corn syrup**
- **1⅓ cups packed light brown sugar**
- **12 cups crisp rice cereal, divided**

1. Line 15½×10½×1-inch jelly-roll pan with foil, extending foil over edges of pan.

2. Place peanut butter chips, oil and 1 teaspoon vanilla in large bowl. Place chocolate chips and remaining 1 teaspoon vanilla in second large bowl. Stir together corn syrup and brown sugar in large saucepan; cook over medium heat, stirring constantly, until mixture comes to full rolling boil. Remove from heat. Immediately pour half of hot mixture into each reserved bowl; stir each mixture until chips are melted and mixture is smooth. Immediately stir 6 cups rice cereal into each of the two mixtures. Spread peanut butter mixture into prepared pan; spread chocolate mixture over top of peanut butter layer.

3. Cool completely. Use foil to lift treats out of pan; peel off foil. Cut treats into bars. Store in tightly covered container in cool, dry place. *Makes about 6 dozen pieces*

Marvelous Cookie Bars

- ½ cup (1 stick) butter or margarine, softened
- 1 cup firmly packed light brown sugar
- 2 large eggs
- 1⅓ cups all-purpose flour
- 1 cup quick-cooking or old-fashioned oats, uncooked
- ⅓ cup unsweetened cocoa powder
- 1 teaspoon baking powder
- ½ teaspoon salt
- ¼ teaspoon baking soda
- ½ cup chopped walnuts, divided
- 1 cup "M&M's"® Semi-Sweet Chocolate Mini Baking Bits, divided
- ½ cup cherry preserves
- ¼ cup shredded coconut

Preheat oven to 350°F. Lightly grease 9×9×2-inch baking pan; set aside. In large bowl cream butter and sugar until light and fluffy; beat in eggs. In medium bowl combine flour, oats, cocoa powder, baking powder, salt and baking soda; blend into creamed mixture. Stir in ¼ cup nuts and ¾ cup "M&M's"® Semi-Sweet Chocolate Mini Baking Bits. Reserve 1 cup dough; spread remaining dough into prepared pan. Combine preserves, coconut and remaining ¼ cup nuts; spread evenly over dough to within ½ inch of edge. Drop reserved dough by rounded teaspoonfuls over preserves mixture; sprinkle with remaining ¼ cup "M&M's"® Semi-Sweet Chocolate Mini Baking Bits. Bake 25 to 30 minutes or until slightly firm near edges. Cool completely. Cut into bars. Store in tightly covered container.

Makes 16 bars

Marvelous Cookie Bars

Chocolate Chips and Raspberry Bars

1½ cups all-purpose flour
½ cup sugar
½ teaspoon baking powder
½ teaspoon salt
½ cup (1 stick) butter or margarine, softened
1 egg, beaten
¼ cup milk
¼ teaspoon vanilla extract
¾ cup raspberry preserves
1 cup HERSHEY'S® Semi-Sweet Chocolate Chips

1. Heat oven to 400°F. Grease 13×9×2-inch baking pan.

2. Stir together flour, sugar, baking powder and salt in large bowl. Cut in butter with pastry blender until mixture resembles coarse crumbs. Add egg, milk and vanilla; beat on medium speed of electric mixer until well blended.

3. Reserve ½ cup mixture for topping. Spread remaining mixture onto bottom of prepared pan (this will be a very thin layer). Spread preserves evenly over dough; sprinkle chocolate chips over top. Drop reserved dough by ½ teaspoons over chips.

4. Bake 25 minutes or until golden. Cool completely in pan on wire rack. Cut into bars. *Makes about 32 bars*

Tip: Rich, buttery bar cookies and brownies freeze extremely well. Freeze in airtight containers or freezer bags for up to three months. Thaw at room temperature.

Chocolate Chips and Raspberry Bars

Holiday Treats

Christmas Tree Platter

1 recipe Christmas Ornament Cookie dough (page 306)
2 cups sifted powdered sugar
2 tablespoons milk or lemon juice
Assorted food colors, colored sugars and assorted small decors

1. Preheat oven to 350°F. Prepare dough; divide dough in half. Reserve 1 half; refrigerate remaining dough. Roll reserved half of dough to ⅛-inch thickness.

2. Cut out tree shapes with cookie cutters. Place on ungreased cookie sheets.

3. Bake 10 to 12 minutes or until edges are lightly browned. Remove to wire racks; cool completely.

4. Repeat with remaining half of dough. Reroll scraps; cut into small circles for ornaments, squares and rectangles for gift boxes and tree trunks.

5. Bake 8 to 12 minutes, depending on size of cookies.

6. Mix sugar and milk for icing. Tint most of icing green and a smaller amount red or other colors for ornaments and boxes. Spread green icing on trees. Sprinkle ornaments and boxes with colored sugars or decorate as desired. Arrange cookies on flat platter to resemble tree as shown in photo.

Makes about 1 dozen cookies

Christmas Tree Platter

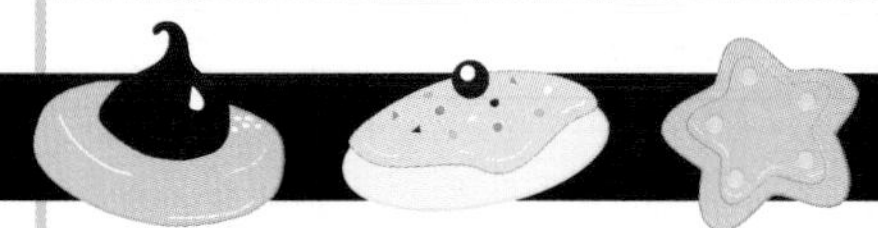

Pinwheels

1 package DUNCAN HINES® Golden Sugar Cookie Mix
1 egg
¼ cup vegetable oil
1½ tablespoons water
1 egg white, lightly beaten
Coarse decorating sugar
18 candied maraschino cherries, halved

1. Preheat oven to 375°F.

2. Combine cookie mix, egg, oil and water in large bowl. Stir until thoroughly blended. Roll dough to ⅛-inch thickness on lightly floured surface. Cut into 2½-inch squares. Place each square 1 inch apart on ungreased baking sheet. Cut 1-inch slits diagonally from each corner towards center. Fold every other corner tip towards center. Brush tops with egg white. Sprinkle with sugar. Place cherry half on center of each pinwheel. Bake at 375°F for 8 to 9 minutes or until edges are lightly golden brown. Remove to cooling racks. Cool completely. Store between layers of waxed paper in airtight containers. *Makes 3 dozen cookies*

Tip: *You may substitute granulated sugar for coarse decorating sugar, if desired.*

Pinwheels

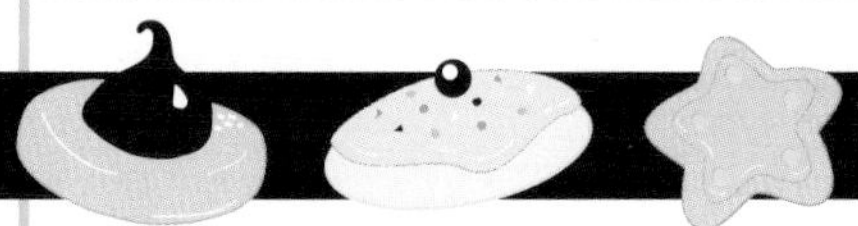

Yuletide Linzer Bars

- **1⅓ cups butter or margarine, softened**
- **¾ cup sugar**
- **1 egg**
- **1 teaspoon grated lemon peel**
- **2½ cups all-purpose flour**
- **1½ cups whole almonds, ground**
- **1 teaspoon ground cinnamon**
- **¾ cup raspberry preserves**
- **Powdered sugar**

Preheat oven to 350°F. Grease 13×9-inch baking pan.

Beat butter and sugar in large bowl with electric mixer until creamy. Beat in egg and lemon peel until blended. Mix in flour, almonds and cinnamon until well blended.

Press 2 cups dough into bottom of prepared pan. Spread preserves over crust. Press remaining dough, a small amount at a time, evenly over preserves.

Bake 35 to 40 minutes until golden brown. Cool in pan on wire rack. Sprinkle with powdered sugar; cut into bars.

Makes 36 bars

Santa's Chocolate Cookies

- **1 cup margarine or butter**
- **⅔ cup semisweet chocolate chips**
- **¾ cup sugar**
- **1 egg**
- **½ teaspoon vanilla**
- **2 cups all-purpose flour**
- **Apricot jam, melted semisweet chocolate, chopped almonds, frosting, coconut or colored sprinkles (optional)**

Preheat oven to 350°F. Melt margarine and chocolate together in small saucepan over low heat or microwave for 2 minutes at HIGH until completely melted. Combine chocolate mixture and sugar in large bowl. Add egg and vanilla; stir well. Add flour; stir well. Refrigerate 30 minutes or until firm.

Shape dough into 1-inch balls. Place 1 inch apart on ungreased cookie sheets. If desired, flatten balls with bottom of drinking glass, shape into logs or make a depression in center and fill with apricot jam.

Bake 8 to 10 minutes or until set. Remove to wire racks to cool completely. Decorate as desired with melted chocolate, almonds, frosting, coconut or colored sprinkles.

Makes about 3 dozen cookies

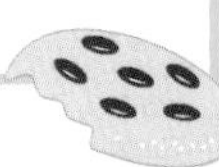

Yuletide Linzer Bars

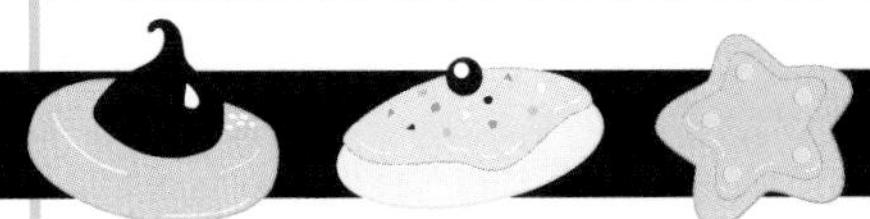

Gingerbread Kids

2 ripe, small DOLE® Bananas
4 cups all-purpose flour
1½ teaspoons ground ginger
1 teaspoon baking soda
1 teaspoon ground cinnamon
½ cup butter, softened
½ cup packed brown sugar
½ cup dark molasses
Prepared icing and candies

• Purée bananas in blender. Combine flour, ginger, baking soda and cinnamon. Cream butter and sugar until light and fluffy. Beat in molasses and bananas until blended. Stir in flour mixture with wooden spoon until completely blended. (Dough will be stiff.) Cover; refrigerate 1 hour.

• Preheat oven to 375°F. Divide dough into 4 parts. Roll out each part to ⅛-inch thickness on lightly floured surface. Cut out cookies using small gingerbread people cutters. Use favorite cookie cutters for any smaller amounts of remaining dough.

• Bake on greased cookie sheets 10 to 15 minutes or until just brown around edges. Cool completely on wire racks. Decorate as desired with favorite icing and candies.

Makes 30 to 35 cookies

Tip

Before measuring molasses, lightly coat a measuring cup with nonstick cooking spray so the molasses will slide out easily instead of clinging to the cup.

Gingerbread Kids

Pumpkin White Chocolate Drops

- **2 cups butter or margarine, softened**
- **2 cups granulated sugar**
- **1 can (16 ounces) solid pack pumpkin**
- **2 eggs**
- **4 cups all-purpose flour**
- **2 teaspoons pumpkin pie spice**
- **1 teaspoon baking powder**
- **½ teaspoon baking soda**
- **1 bag (12 ounces) vanilla baking chips**
- **1 container (16 ounces) ready-to-spread cream cheese frosting**
- **¼ cup packed brown sugar**

1. Preheat oven to 375°F. Grease cookie sheets.

2. Beat butter and sugar in large bowl until light and fluffy. Add pumpkin and eggs; beat until smooth. Add flour, pumpkin pie spice, baking powder and baking soda; beat just until well blended. Stir in chips.

3. Drop dough by teaspoonfuls about 2 inches apart onto cookie sheets. Bake about 16 minutes or until set and bottoms are brown. Cool 1 minute on cookie sheets. Remove from cookie sheets to wire rack to cool.

4. Combine frosting and brown sugar in small bowl. Spread on warm cookies. *Makes about 6 dozen cookies*

Pumpkin White Chocolate Drops

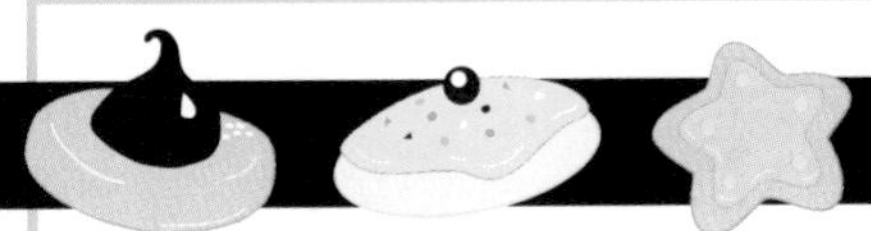

Kringle's Cutouts

1¼ cups granulated sugar
1 Butter Flavor* CRISCO® Stick or 1 cup Butter Flavor* CRISCO® all-vegetable shortening
2 eggs
¼ cup light corn syrup or regular pancake syrup
1 teaspoon vanilla
3 cups plus 4 tablespoons all-purpose flour, divided
¾ teaspoon baking powder
½ teaspoon baking soda
½ teaspoon salt
Colored sugar, decors and prepared frosting (optional)

**Butter Flavor Crisco® is artificially flavored.*

1. Combine sugar and 1 cup shortening in large bowl. Beat at medium speed of electric mixer until well blended. Add eggs, syrup and vanilla. Beat until well blended and fluffy.

2. Combine 3 cups flour, baking powder, baking soda and salt. Add gradually to creamed mixture at low speed. Mix until well blended.

3. Divide dough into 4 quarters. Cover and refrigerate at least two hours or overnight.

4. Heat oven to 375°F. Place sheets of foil on countertop for cooling cookies.

5. Spread 1 tablespoon flour on large sheet of waxed paper. Place one quarter of dough on floured paper. Flatten slightly with hands. Turn dough over. Cover with another large sheet of waxed paper. Roll dough to ¼-inch thickness. Remove top layer of waxed paper. Cut out with seasonal cookie cutters. Place cutouts 2 inches apart on ungreased baking sheets. Roll and cut out remaining dough. Sprinkle with colored sugar and decors or leave plain to frost when cool.

6. Bake at 375°F for 5 to 9 minutes, depending on size of cookies. (Bake small, thin cookies about 5 minutes; larger cookies about 9 minutes.) *Do not overbake.* Cool 2 minutes on baking sheet. Remove cookies to foil to cool completely.

Makes 3 to 4 dozen cookies (depending on size and shape)

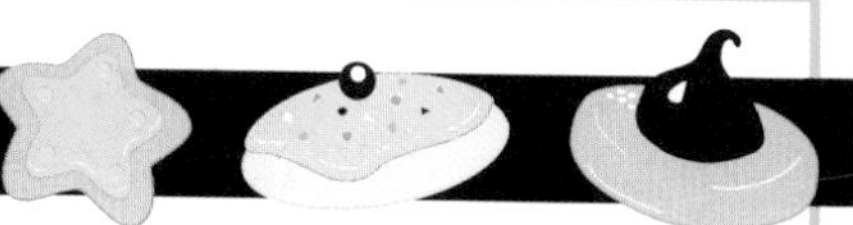

Honey Nut Rugelach

- 1 cup butter or margarine, softened
- 3 ounces cream cheese, softened
- ½ cup honey, divided
- 2 cups flour
- 1 teaspoon lemon juice
- 1 teaspoon ground cinnamon, divided
- 1 cup finely chopped walnuts
- ½ cup dried cherries or cranberries

Cream butter and cream cheese until fluffy. Add 3 tablespoons honey and mix well. Mix in flour until dough holds together. Form into a ball, wrap and refrigerate 2 hours or longer. Divide dough into 4 equal portions. On floured surface, roll one portion of dough into 9-inch circle. Combine 2 tablespoons honey and lemon juice; mix well. Brush dough with ¼ of honey mixture; sprinkle with ¼ teaspoon cinnamon. Combine walnuts and cherries in small bowl; drizzle with remaining 3 tablespoons honey and mix well. Spread ¼ of walnut mixture onto circle of dough, stopping ½ inch from outer edge. Cut circle into 8 triangular pieces. Roll up dough staring at wide outer edge and rolling toward tip. Gently bend both ends to form a crescent. Place on oiled parchment paper-lined baking sheet and refrigerate 20 minutes or longer. Repeat with remaining dough and filling. Bake at 350°F 20 to 25 minutes or until golden brown. Cool on wire racks.

Makes 32 cookies

Freezing Tip: *Unbaked cookies can be placed in freezer-safe containers or bags and frozen until ready to bake.*

Favorite recipe from National Honey Board

Cranberry Cheese Bars

- **2 cups all-purpose flour**
- **1½ cups quick-cooking or old-fashioned oats, uncooked**
- **¾ cup plus 1 tablespoon firmly packed light brown sugar, divided**
- **1 cup (2 sticks) butter or margarine, softened**
- **1¾ cups "M&M's"® Chocolate Mini Baking Bits, divided**
- **1 (8-ounce) package cream cheese**
- **1 (14-ounce) can sweetened condensed milk**
- **¼ cup lemon juice**
- **1 teaspoon vanilla extract**
- **2 tablespoons cornstarch**
- **1 (16-ounce) can whole berry cranberry sauce**

Preheat oven to 350°F. Lightly grease 13×9×2-inch baking pan; set aside. In large bowl combine flour, oats, ¾ cup sugar and butter; mix until crumbly. Reserve 1½ cups crumb mixture for topping. Stir ½ cup "M&M's"® Chocolate Mini Baking Bits into remaining crumb mixture; press into prepared pan. Bake 15 minutes. Cool completely. In large bowl beat cream cheese until light and fluffy; gradually mix in condensed milk, lemon juice and vanilla until smooth. Pour evenly over crust. In small bowl combine remaining 1 tablespoon sugar, cornstarch and cranberry sauce. Spoon over cream cheese mixture. Stir remaining 1¼ cups "M&M's"® Chocolate Mini Baking Bits into reserved crumb mixture. Sprinkle over cranberry mixture. Bake 40 minutes. Cool at room temperature; refrigerate before cutting. Store in refrigerator in tightly covered container.

Makes 32 bars

Cranberry Cheese Bars

Maple Walnut Meringues

- ⅓ cup powdered sugar
- ½ cup plus ⅓ cup ground walnuts, divided
- ¾ cup packed light brown sugar
- 3 egg whites, at room temperature
- Pinch salt
- ⅛ teaspoon cream of tartar
- 1 teaspoon maple extract

Place 1 oven rack in the top third of oven and 1 oven rack in the bottom third of oven; preheat oven to 300°F. Line 2 large cookie sheets with aluminum foil, shiny side up.

Stir powdered sugar and ½ cup walnuts with fork in medium bowl; set aside. Crumble brown sugar into small bowl; set aside.

Beat egg whites and salt in large bowl with electric mixer at high speed until foamy. Add cream of tartar; beat 30 seconds or until mixture forms soft peaks. Sprinkle brown sugar, 1 tablespoon at a time, over egg white mixture; beat at high speed until each addition is completely absorbed. Beat 2 to 3 minutes or until mixture forms stiff peaks. Beat in maple extract at low speed. Fold in walnut mixture with large rubber spatula.

Drop level tablespoonfuls of dough to form mounds about 1 inch apart on prepared cookie sheets. Sprinkle cookies with remaining ⅓ cup ground walnuts. Bake 25 minutes or until cookies feel dry on surface but remain soft inside. (Rotate cookie sheets from top to bottom halfway through baking time.)

Slide foil with cookies onto wire racks; cool completely. Carefully remove cookies from foil. Store in airtight container with waxed paper between layers of cookies. Cookies are best the day they are baked. *Makes about 36 cookies*

Maple Walnut Meringues

Molded Scotch Shortbread

1½ cups all-purpose flour
¼ teaspoon salt
¾ cup butter, softened
⅓ cup sugar
1 egg

1. Preheat oven to temperature recommended by shortbread mold manufacturer. Combine flour and salt in medium bowl.

2. Beat butter and sugar in large bowl with electric mixer at medium speed until light and fluffy. Beat in egg. Gradually add flour mixture. Beat at low speed until well blended.

3. Spray 10-inch ceramic shortbread mold with nonstick cooking spray.* Press dough firmly into mold. Bake, cool and remove from mold according to manufacturer's directions.

Makes 1 shortbread mold or 24 cookies

**If mold is not available, preheat oven to 350°F. Shape tablespoonfuls of dough into 1-inch balls. Place 2 inches apart on ungreased cookie sheets; press with fork to flatten. Bake 18 to 20 minutes or until edges are lightly browned. Let cookies stand on cookie sheets 2 minutes; transfer to wire racks to cool completely. Store tightly covered at room temperature or freeze up to 3 months.*

Tip

To measure flour accurately, spoon it into a dry measure until the measure is overflowing. Then, with a straight-edged metal spatula, sweep across the top of the measure. Don't scoop the flour with the measure or tap the measure on the counter, because this will compact the flour and result in an inaccurate measure.

Molded Scotch Shortbread

Spritz Christmas Trees

- **⅓ cup (3½ ounces) almond paste**
- **1 egg**
- **1 package DUNCAN HINES® Golden Sugar Cookie Mix**
- **8 drops green food coloring**
- **1 container DUNCAN HINES® Vanilla Frosting**
- **Cinnamon candies, for garnish**

1. Preheat oven to 375°F.

2. Combine almond paste and egg in large bowl. Beat at low speed with electric mixer until blended. Add contents of buttery flavor packet from Mix and green food coloring. Beat until smooth and evenly tinted. Add cookie mix. Beat at low speed until thoroughly blended.

3. Fit cookie press with Christmas tree plate; fill with dough. Force dough through press, 2 inches apart, onto ungreased cookie sheets. Bake at 375°F for 6 to 7 minutes or until set but not browned. Cool 1 minute on cookie sheets. Remove to cooling racks. Cool completely.

4. To decorate, fill resealable plastic bag half full with vanilla frosting. Do not seal bag. Cut pinpoint hole in bottom corner of bag. Pipe small dot of frosting onto tip of one cookie tree and top with cinnamon candy. Repeat with remaining cookies. Pipe remaining frosting to form garland on cookie trees. Allow frosting to set before storing between layers of waxed paper in airtight container. *Makes about 5 dozen cookies*

Spritz Christmas Trees

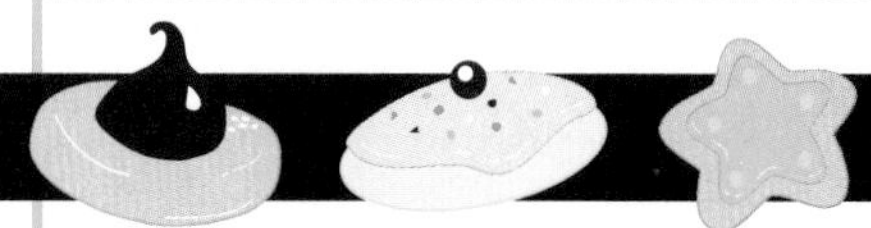

Christmas Stained Glass Cookies

Colored hard candy
¾ cup butter or margarine, softened
¾ cup granulated sugar
2 eggs
1 teaspoon vanilla extract
3 cups all-purpose flour
1 teaspoon baking powder
Frosting (optional)
Small decorative candies (optional)

Separate colors of hard candy into resealable plastic freezer bags. Crush with mallet or hammer to equal about ⅓ cup crushed candy; set aside. In mixing bowl, cream butter and sugar. Beat in eggs and vanilla. In another bowl sift together flour and baking powder. Gradually stir flour mixture into butter mixture until dough is very stiff. Wrap in plastic wrap and chill about 3 hours.

Preheat oven to 375°F. Roll out dough to ⅛-inch thickness on lightly floured surface. Additional flour may be added to dough if necessary. Cut out cookies using large Christmas cookie cutters. Transfer cookies to foil-lined baking sheet. Using small Christmas cookie cutter of the same shape as large one, cut out and remove dough from center of each cookie.* Fill cut out sections with crushed candy. If using cookies as hanging ornaments, make holes at tops of cookies for string with drinking straw or chopstick. Bake 7 to 9 minutes or until cookies are lightly browned and candy is melted. Slide foil off baking sheets. When cool, carefully loosen cookies from foil. Use frosting and candy for additional decorations, if desired.

Makes about 2½ dozen medium-sized cookies

**For different designs, other cookie cutter shapes can be used to cut out center of cookies (i.e., small circle and star-shaped cutters can be used to cut out ornament designs on large Christmas tree cookies).*

Favorite recipe from The Sugar Association, Inc.

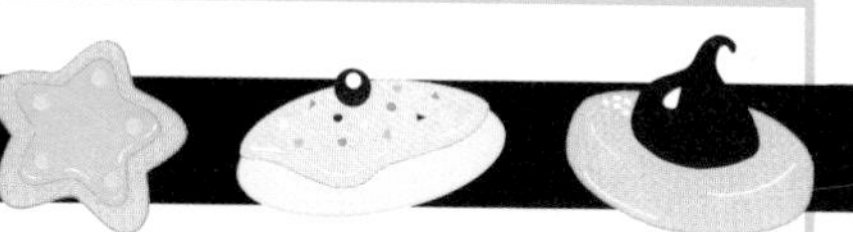

Chocolate Chip Cranberry Cheese Bars

- **1 cup (2 sticks) butter or margarine, softened**
- **1 cup packed brown sugar**
- **2 cups all-purpose flour**
- **1½ cups quick or old-fashioned oats**
- **2 teaspoons grated orange peel**
- **2 cups (12-ounce package) NESTLÉ® TOLL HOUSE® Semi-Sweet Chocolate Morsels**
- **1 cup (4 ounces) dried cranberries**
- **1 package (8 ounces) cream cheese, softened**
- **1¼ cups (14-ounce can) CARNATION® Sweetened Condensed Milk**

BEAT butter and brown sugar in large mixer bowl until creamy. Gradually beat in flour, oats and orange peel until crumbly. Stir in morsels and cranberries; reserve 2 cups mixture. Press remaining mixture onto bottom of greased 13×9-inch baking pan.

BAKE in preheated 350°F. oven for 15 minutes. Beat cream cheese in small mixer bowl until smooth. Gradually beat in sweetened condensed milk. Pour over hot crust; sprinkle with reserved flour mixture. Bake for additional 25 to 30 minutes or until center is set. Cool in pan on wire rack.

Makes about 3 dozen bars

Tip

Cookies, brownies and bars make great gifts. Place them in a paper-lined tin or on a decorative plate covered with plastic wrap and tied with colorful ribbon. For a special touch, include the recipe.

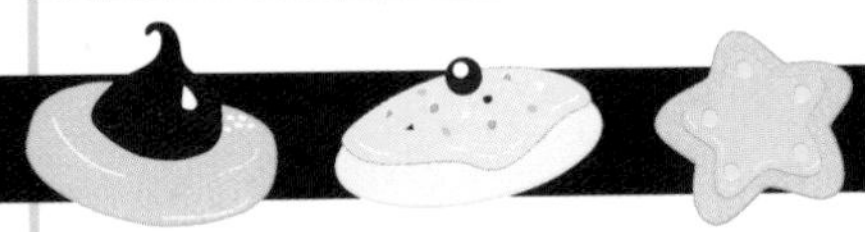

Danish Raspberry Ribbons

1 cup butter, softened
½ cup granulated sugar
1 large egg
2 tablespoons milk
2 tablespoons vanilla
¼ teaspoon almond extract
2⅔ cups all-purpose flour, divided
6 tablespoons seedless raspberry jam
Glaze (recipe follows)

1. Beat butter and sugar in large bowl with electric mixer at medium speed until light and fluffy. Beat in egg, milk, vanilla and almond extract until well blended.

2. Gradually add 1½ cups flour. Beat at low speed until well blended. Stir in enough remaining flour with spoon to form stiff dough. Form dough into disc; wrap in plastic wrap and refrigerate until firm, at least 30 minutes or overnight.

3. Preheat oven to 375°F. Cut dough into 6 equal pieces. Rewrap 3 dough pieces and return to refrigerator. With floured hands, shape each piece of dough into 12-inch-long, ¾-inch-thick rope.

4. Place ropes 2 inches apart on ungreased cookie sheets. Make lengthwise ¼-inch-deep groove down center of each rope with handle of wooden spoon or finger. (Ropes will flatten to ½-inch-thick strips.)

5. Bake 12 minutes. Remove from oven; spoon 1 tablespoon jam into each groove. Return to oven; bake 5 to 7 minutes longer or until strips are light golden brown. Cool strips 15 minutes on cookie sheet.

6. Prepare Glaze. Drizzle strips with Glaze; let stand 5 minutes to dry. Cut cookie strips at 45° angle into 1-inch slices. Place cookies on wire racks; cool completely. Repeat with remaining dough. Store tightly covered between sheets of waxed paper at room temperature.

Makes about 5½ dozen cookies

Glaze: *Blend ½ cup powdered sugar, 1 tablespoon milk and 1 teaspoon vanilla until smooth.*

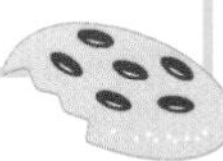

Danish Raspberry Ribbons

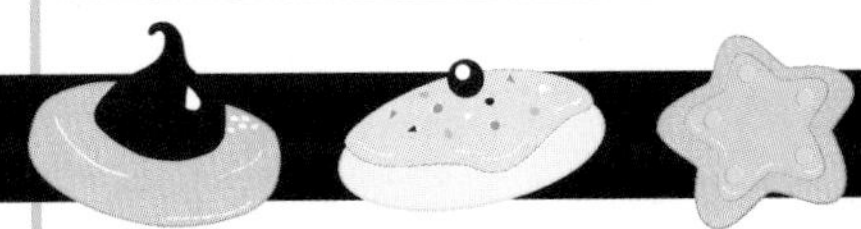

Snowmen

1 package (20 ounces) refrigerated chocolate chip cookie dough
1½ cups sifted powdered sugar
2 tablespoons milk
Candy corn, gum drops, chocolate chips, licorice and other assorted small candies

1. Preheat oven to 375°F.

2. Cut dough into 12 equal sections. Divide each section into 3 balls: large, medium and small for each snowman.

3. For each snowman, place 3 balls in row, ¼ inch apart, on ungreased cookie sheet. Repeat with remaining dough.

4. Bake 10 to 12 minutes or until edges are very lightly browned. Cool 4 minutes on cookie sheets. Remove to wire racks; cool completely.

5. Mix powdered sugar and milk in medium bowl until smooth. Pour over cookies. Let cookies stand 20 minutes or until set.

6. Decorate to create faces, hats and arms with assorted candies.

Makes 1 dozen cookies

Snowmen

Sugar Cookie Wreaths

1 package DUNCAN HINES® Golden Sugar Cookie Mix
1 egg
¼ cup vegetable oil
1 tablespoon water
Green food coloring
Candied or maraschino cherry pieces

1. Preheat oven to 375°F.

2. Combine cookie mix, egg, oil and water in large bowl. Stir until thoroughly blended.

3. Tint dough with green food coloring. Stir until desired color. Form into balls the size of miniature marshmallows. For each wreath, arrange 9 or 10 balls, with sides touching, into a ring. Place wreaths 2 inches apart on ungreased baking sheets. Flatten slightly with fingers. Place small piece of candied cherry on each ball.

4. Bake at 375°F for 5 to 7 minutes or until set but not browned. Cool 1 minute on baking sheets. Remove to cooling racks. Cool completely. Store in airtight container.

Makes 4 dozen cookies

Tip: Instead of tinting dough green, coat balls with green sugar crystals.

Tip

When reusing cookie sheets for several batches of cookies, cool the sheets completely before placing dough on them. The dough will soften and begin to spread on a hot baking sheet.

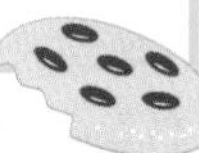

Sugar Cookie Wreaths

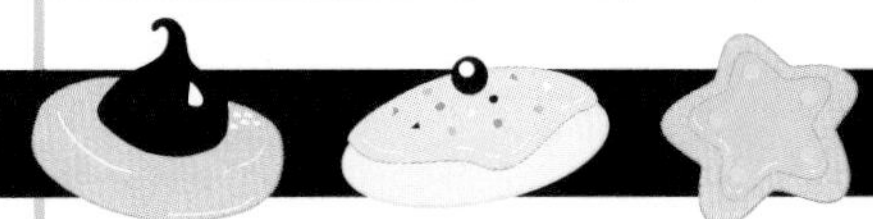

Apple-Cranberry Crescent Cookies

1¼ cups chopped apples
½ cup dried cranberries
½ cup reduced-fat sour cream
¼ cup cholesterol-free egg substitute
¼ cup margarine or butter, melted
3 tablespoons sugar, divided
1 package quick-rise yeast
1 teaspoon vanilla
2 cups all-purpose flour
1 teaspoon ground cinnamon
1 tablespoon reduced-fat (2%) milk

1. Preheat oven to 350°F. Lightly coat cookie sheet with nonstick cooking spray.

2. Place apples and cranberries in food processor or blender; pulse to finely chop. Set aside.

3. Combine sour cream, egg substitute, margarine and 2 tablespoons sugar in medium bowl. Add yeast and vanilla. Add flour; stir to form ball. Turn dough out onto lightly floured work surface. Knead 1 minute. Cover with plastic wrap; allow to stand 10 minutes.

4. Divide dough into thirds. Roll one portion into 12-inch circle. Spread with ⅓ apple mixture (about ¼ cup). Cut dough to make 8 wedges. Roll up each wedge beginning at outside edge. Place on prepared cookie sheet; turn ends of cookies to form crescents. Repeat with remaining dough and apple mixture.

5. Combine remaining 1 tablespoon sugar and cinnamon in small bowl. Lightly brush cookies with milk; sprinkle with sugar-cinnamon mixture. Bake cookies 18 to 20 minutes or until lightly browned. *Makes 24 cookies*

Apple-Cranberry Crescent Cookies

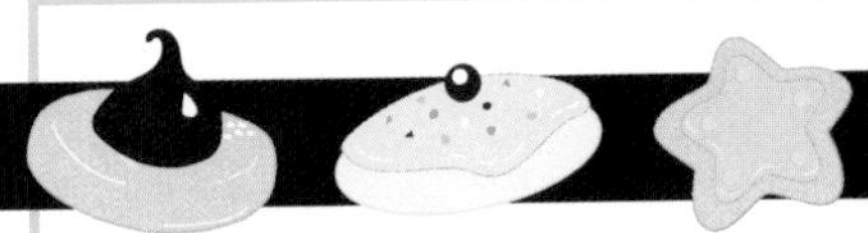

Apricot-Filled Pastries

Apricot Filling (recipe follows)
2¼ cups flour
⅔ cup sugar
1 cup (2 sticks) cold MAZOLA® Margarine or butter
2 egg yolks, lightly beaten
½ cup sour cream
Confectioners sugar

1. Prepare Apricot Filling; set aside.

2. In large bowl combine flour and sugar. With pastry blender or 2 knives, cut in margarine until mixture resembles coarse crumbs. Stir in egg yolks and sour cream until mixed.

3. Turn onto floured surface; knead just until smooth. Divide dough into quarters. Cover; refrigerate 20 minutes.

4. Preheat oven to 375°F. On floured pastry cloth with stockinette-covered rolling pin, roll one piece of dough at a time into 10-inch square. (Keep remaining dough refrigerated.)

5. Cut dough into 2-inch squares. Place ½ teaspoon Apricot Filling diagonally across each square. Moisten 2 opposite corners with water; fold over filling, overlapping slightly. Place on ungreased cookie sheets.

6. Bake 10 to 12 minutes or until edges are lightly browned. Cool on wire racks.

7. Just before serving, sprinkle with confectioners sugar. Store in tightly covered container up to 3 weeks.

Makes about 8 dozen pastries

Apricot Filling: *In 1-quart saucepan bring 1 cup dried apricots and 1 cup water to boil over medium-high heat. Reduce heat; cover and simmer 5 minutes. Drain. Place apricots and ½ cup KARO® Light Corn Syrup in blender container or food processor. Cover and blend on high speed 2 minutes or until smooth. Cool completely.*

Prep Time: 90 minutes, plus chilling
Bake Time: 10 minutes, plus cooling

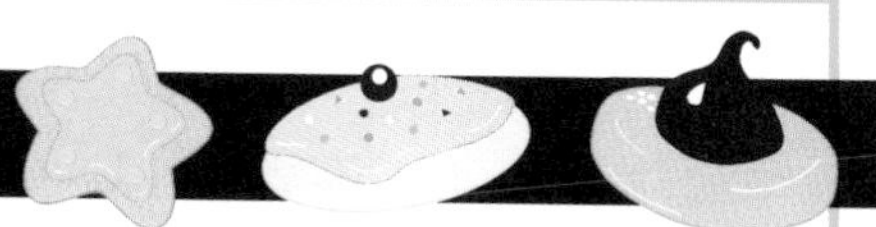

Chocolate Raspberry Thumbprints

½ cup (1 stick) butter or margarine, softened
½ cup granulated sugar
½ cup firmly packed light brown sugar
1 large egg
1 teaspoon vanilla extract
2 cups all-purpose flour
½ teaspoon baking powder
1¾ cups "M&M's"® Chocolate Mini Baking Bits, divided
Powdered sugar
½ cup raspberry jam

In large microwave-safe bowl melt butter in microwave; add sugars and mix well. Stir in egg and vanilla. In medium bowl combine flour and baking powder; blend into butter mixture. Stir in 1¼ cups "M&M's"® Chocolate Mini Baking Bits; refrigerate dough 1 hour. Preheat oven to 350°F. Lightly grease cookie sheets. Roll dough into 1-inch balls and place about 2 inches apart onto prepared cookie sheets. Make an indentation in center of each ball with thumb. Bake 8 to 10 minutes. Remove from oven and reindent, if necessary; transfer to wire racks. Lightly dust warm cookies with powdered sugar; fill each indentation with ½ teaspoon raspberry jam. Sprinkle with remaining ½ cup "M&M's"® Chocolate Mini Baking Bits. Cool completely. Dust with additional powdered sugar, if desired. Store in tightly covered container.

Makes about 4 dozen cookies

Jolly Peanut Butter Gingerbread Cookies

1⅔ cups (10-ounce package) REESE'S® Peanut Butter Chips
¾ cup (1½ sticks) butter or margarine, softened
1 cup packed light brown sugar
1 cup dark corn syrup
2 eggs
5 cups all-purpose flour
1 teaspoon baking soda
½ teaspoon ground cinnamon
¼ teaspoon ground ginger
¼ teaspoon salt

1. Place peanut butter chips in small microwave-safe bowl. Microwave at HIGH (100%) 1 to 2 minutes or until chips are melted when stirred. In large bowl, beat melted peanut butter chips and butter until well blended. Add brown sugar, corn syrup and eggs; beat until light and fluffy. Stir together flour, baking soda, cinnamon, ginger and salt. Add half of flour mixture to butter mixture; beat on low speed of electric mixer until smooth. With wooden spoon, stir in remaining flour mixture until well blended. Divide into thirds; wrap each in plastic wrap. Refrigerate at least 1 hour or until dough is firm enough to roll.

2. Heat oven to 325°F.

3. Roll 1 dough portion at a time to ⅛-inch thickness on lightly floured surface; with floured cookie cutters, cut into holiday shapes. Place on ungreased cookie sheet.

4. Bake 10 to 12 minutes or until set and lightly browned. Cool slightly; remove from cookie sheet to wire rack. Cool completely. Frost and decorate as desired.

Makes about 6 dozen cookies

Jolly Peanut Butter Gingerbread Cookies

Pfeffernusse

- 3½ cups all-purpose flour
- 2 teaspoons baking powder
- 1½ teaspoons ground cinnamon
- 1 teaspoon ground ginger
- ½ teaspoon baking soda
- ½ teaspoon salt
- ½ teaspoon ground cloves
- ½ teaspoon ground cardamom
- ¼ teaspoon black pepper
- 1 cup butter, softened
- 1 cup granulated sugar
- ¼ cup dark molasses
- 1 egg
- Powdered sugar

Combine flour, baking powder, cinnamon, ginger, baking soda, salt, cloves, cardamom and pepper in large bowl.

Beat butter and sugar in large bowl with electric mixer at medium speed until light and fluffy. Beat in molasses and egg. Gradually add flour mixture. Beat at low speed until dough forms. Shape dough into disk; wrap in plastic wrap and refrigerate until firm, 30 minutes or up to 3 days.

Preheat oven to 350°F. Grease cookie sheets. Roll dough into 1-inch balls. Place 2 inches apart on prepared cookie sheets.

Bake 12 to 14 minutes or until golden brown. Transfer cookies to wire racks; dust with sifted powdered sugar. Cool completely. Store tightly covered at room temperature or freeze up to 3 months. *Makes about 60 cookies*

Pfeffernusse

Pumpkin Jingle Bars

¾ cup MIRACLE WHIP® Salad Dressing
1 package (2-layer size) spice cake mix
1 can (16 ounces) can pumpkin
3 eggs
Sifted powdered sugar
Vanilla frosting
Red and green gum drops, sliced

• Mix first 4 ingredients in large bowl at medium speed of electric mixer until well blended. Pour into greased 15½×10½×1-inch baking pan.

• Bake at 350°F 18 to 20 minutes or until edges pull away from sides of pan. Cool.

• Sprinkle with sugar. Cut into bars. Decorate with frosting and gum drops. *Makes about 3 dozen bars*

Prep Time: 5 minutes
Cook Time: 20 minutes

Gingersnaps

2½ cups all-purpose flour
1½ teaspoons ground ginger
1 teaspoon baking soda
1 teaspoon ground allspice
½ teaspoon salt
1½ cups sugar
2 tablespoons margarine, softened
½ cup MOTT'S® Apple Sauce
¼ cup GRANDMA'S® Molasses

1. Preheat oven to 375°F. Spray cookie sheet with nonstick cooking spray.

2. In medium bowl, sift together flour, ginger, baking soda, allspice and salt.

3. In large bowl, beat sugar and margarine with electric mixer at medium speed until blended. Whisk in apple sauce and molasses.

4. Add flour mixture to apple sauce mixture; stir until well blended.

5. Drop rounded tablespoonfuls of dough 1 inch apart onto prepared cookie sheet. Flatten each slightly with moistened fingertips.

6. Bake 12 to 15 minutes or until firm. Cool completely on wire rack. *Makes 3 dozen cookies*

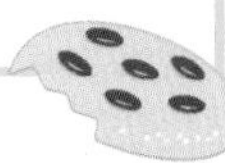

Pumpkin Jingle Bars

Date-Nut Cookies

- **1 cup chopped dates**
- **½ cup water**
- **1¾ cups all-purpose flour**
- **½ teaspoon baking powder**
- **⅛ teaspoon salt**
- **½ cup butter, softened**
- **½ cup packed dark brown sugar**
- **1 egg**
- **2 teaspoons rum extract**
- **½ cup walnut pieces, chopped**

Soak dates in water in small bowl at least 30 minutes or up to 2 hours.

Preheat oven to 350°F. Grease cookie sheets. Combine flour, baking powder and salt in medium bowl.

Beat butter in large bowl at medium speed until smooth. Gradually beat in brown sugar; increase speed to high and beat until light and fluffy. Beat in egg and rum extract until fluffy. Gradually stir in flour mixture alternately with date mixture, mixing just until combined after each addition. Stir in walnuts until blended.

Drop level tablespoonfuls of dough about 1½ inches apart onto prepared cookie sheets. Bake 14 minutes or until just set. Transfer to wire racks to cool completely. Store in airtight container. *Makes 24 cookies*

Date-Nut Cookies

Pumpkin Cheesecake Bars

BASE AND TOPPING

- **2 cups all-purpose flour**
- **⅔ cup packed light brown sugar**
- **½ cup (1 stick) butter or margarine**
- **1 cup finely chopped pecans**

PUMPKIN CREAM CHEESE FILLING

- **11 ounces (one 8-ounce package and one 3-ounce package) cream cheese, softened**
- **1¼ cups granulated sugar**
- **1½ teaspoons vanilla extract**
- **1½ teaspoons ground cinnamon**
- **½ teaspoon ground allspice**
- **¾ cup LIBBY'S® Solid Pack Pumpkin**
- **3 eggs**
- **Glazed Pecans (recipe follows)**

FOR BASE AND TOPPING

COMBINE flour and brown sugar in medium bowl. Cut in butter with pastry blender or two knives until mixture resembles coarse crumbs; stir in nuts. Reserve 1½ cups mixture for topping; press remaining mixture onto bottom of ungreased 13×9-inch baking pan. Bake in preheated 350°F. oven for 15 minutes.

FOR PUMPKIN CREAM CHEESE FILLING

BEAT cream cheese, granulated sugar, vanilla, cinnamon and allspice in large mixer bowl. Beat in pumpkin and eggs. Spread over crust; sprinkle with reserved topping. Bake in 350°F. oven for 25 to 30 minutes or until center is set. Cool in pan on wire rack; chill for several hours or until firm. Cut into bars; place Glazed Pecan half on each bar.

Makes 32 bars or 64 triangles

Glazed Pecans: PLACE waxed paper under greased wire rack. Bring ¼ cup dark corn syrup to a boil in medium saucepan; boil, stirring constantly, for 1 minute. Remove from heat; stir in 30 pecan halves. Remove pecan halves to wire rack. Turn right side up; separate. Cool.

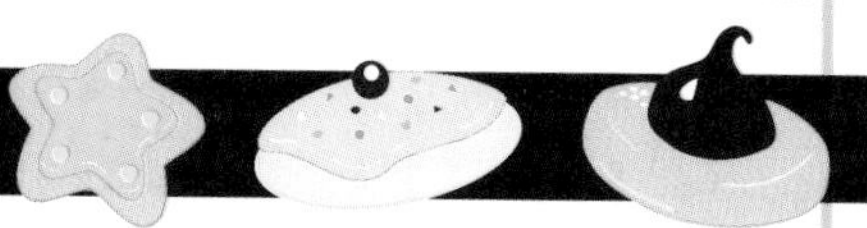

Peanut Butter Cut-Outs

- **½ cup SKIPPY® Creamy Peanut Butter**
- **6 tablespoons MAZOLA® Margarine or butter, softened**
- **½ cup packed brown sugar**
- **⅓ cup KARO® Light or Dark Corn Syrup**
- **1 egg**
- **2 cups flour, divided**
- **1½ teaspoons baking powder**
- **1 teaspoon cinnamon (optional)**
- **⅛ teaspoon salt**

1. In large bowl with mixer at medium speed, beat peanut butter, margarine, brown sugar, corn syrup and egg until smooth. Reduce speed; beat in 1 cup flour, baking powder, cinnamon and salt. With spoon stir in remaining 1 cup flour.

2. Divide dough in half. Between two sheets of waxed paper on large cookie sheets, roll each half of dough ¼ inch thick. Refrigerate until firm, about 1 hour.

3. Preheat oven to 350°F. Remove top piece of waxed paper. With floured cookie cutters, cut dough into shapes. Place on ungreased cookie sheets.

4. Bake 10 minutes or until lightly browned. Do not overbake. Let stand on cookie sheets 2 minutes. Remove from cookie sheets; cool completely on wire racks. Reroll dough trimmings and cut additional cookies. Decorate as desired.

Makes about 5 dozen cookies

Note: Use scraps of dough to create details on cookies.

Prep Time: 20 minutes, plus chilling and decorating
Bake Time: 10 minutes, plus cooling

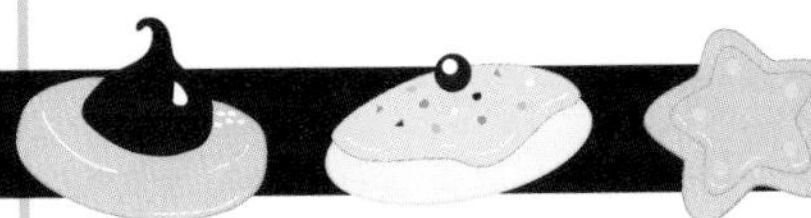

Linzer Sandwich Cookies

1⅓ cups all-purpose flour
¼ teaspoon baking powder
¼ teaspoon salt
¾ cup granulated sugar
½ cup butter, softened
1 large egg
1 teaspoon vanilla
Powdered sugar (optional)
Seedless raspberry jam

Place flour, baking powder and salt in small bowl; stir to combine. Beat granulated sugar and butter in medium bowl with electric mixer at medium speed until light and fluffy. Beat in egg and vanilla. Gradually add flour mixture. Beat at low speed until dough forms. Divide dough in half; cover and refrigerate 2 hours or until firm.

Preheat oven to 375°F. Working with 1 portion at a time, roll out dough on lightly floured surface to 3/16-inch thickness. Cut dough into desired shapes with floured cookie cutters. Cut out equal numbers of each shape. (If dough becomes too soft, refrigerate several minutes before continuing.) Cut 1-inch centers out of half the cookies of each shape. Reroll trimmings and cut out more cookies. Place cookies 1½ to 2 inches apart on ungreased cookie sheets. Bake 7 to 9 minutes or until edges are lightly brown. Let cookies stand on cookie sheets 1 to 2 minutes. Remove cookies to wire racks; cool completely.

Sprinkle cookies with holes with powdered sugar, if desired. Spread 1 teaspoon jam on flat side of whole cookies, spreading almost to edges. Place cookies with holes, flat side down, over jam. Store tightly covered at room temperature or freeze up to 3 months. *Makes about 2 dozen cookies*

Linzer Sandwich Cookies

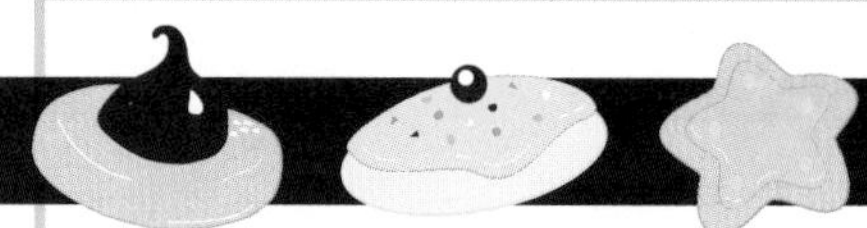

Chocolate Sugar Spritz

- **2 squares (1 ounce each) unsweetened chocolate, coarsely chopped**
- **2¼ cups all-purpose flour**
- **¼ teaspoon salt**
- **1 cup butter or margarine, softened**
- **¾ cup granulated sugar**
- **1 large egg**
- **1 teaspoon almond extract**
- **½ cup powdered sugar**
- **1 teaspoon ground cinnamon**

1. Preheat oven to 400°F.

2. Melt chocolate in small, heavy saucepan over low heat, stirring constantly.

3. Combine flour and salt in small bowl; stir to combine.

4. Beat butter and granulated sugar in large bowl with electric mixer at medium speed until light and fluffy. Beat in egg and almond extract. Beat in chocolate. Gradually add flour mixture with mixing spoon. (Dough will be stiff.)

5. Fit cookie press with desired plate (or change plates for different shapes after first batch). Fill press with dough; press dough 1 inch apart onto ungreased cookie sheets.

6. Bake 7 minutes or until just set.

7. Combine powdered sugar and cinnamon in small bowl. Transfer to fine-mesh strainer and sprinkle over hot cookies while they are still on cookie sheets. Remove cookies to wire racks; cool completely.

8. Store tightly covered at room temperature. These cookies do not freeze well.

Makes 4 to 5 dozen cookies

Chocolate Sugar Spritz

Rum Fruitcake Cookies

- **1 cup sugar**
- **¾ cup vegetable shortening**
- **3 large eggs**
- **⅓ cup orange juice**
- **1 tablespoon rum extract**
- **3 cups all-purpose flour**
- **2 teaspoons baking powder**
- **1 teaspoon baking soda**
- **1 teaspoon salt**
- **2 cups (8 ounces) candied fruit**
- **1 cup raisins**
- **1 cup nuts, coarsely chopped**

1. Preheat oven to 375°F. Lightly grease cookie sheets; set aside. Beat sugar and shortening in large bowl until fluffy. Add eggs, orange juice and rum extract; beat 2 minutes longer.

2. Combine flour, baking powder, baking soda and salt in small bowl. Add fruit, raisins and nuts. Stir into creamed mixture. Drop dough by rounded teaspoonfuls 2 inches apart onto prepared cookie sheets. Bake 10 to 12 minutes or until golden. Let cookies stand on cookie sheets 2 minutes. Remove to wire rack; cool completely.

Makes about 6 dozen cookies

Linzer Tarts

- **1 cup margarine or butter, softened**
- **1 cup granulated sugar**
- **2 cups all-purpose flour**
- **1 cup PLANTERS® Slivered Almonds, chopped**
- **1 teaspoon grated lemon peel**
- **¼ teaspoon ground cinnamon**
- **⅓ cup raspberry preserves**
- **Powdered sugar**

In large bowl with electric mixer at high speed, beat margarine and sugar until light and fluffy. Stir in flour, almonds, lemon peel and cinnamon until blended. Cover; refrigerate 2 hours.

Divide dough in half. On floured surface, roll out half of dough to ⅛-inch thickness. Using 2½-inch round cookie cutter, cut circles from dough. Reroll scraps to make additional rounds. Cut out ½-inch circles from centers of half the rounds. Repeat with remaining dough. Place on ungreased cookie sheets.

Bake at 325°F for 12 to 15 minutes or until lightly browned. Remove from cookie sheets; cool on wire racks. Spread preserves on flat side of whole cookies. Top with cut-out cookies to make sandwiches. Dust with powdered sugar.

Makes about 2 dozen cookies

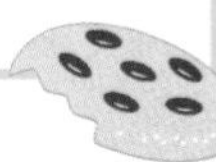

Rum Fruitcake Cookies

Christmas Ornament Cookies

2¼ cups all-purpose flour
¼ teaspoon salt
1 cup sugar
¾ cup butter, softened
1 large egg
1 teaspoon vanilla
1 teaspoon almond extract
Icing (recipe follows)
Assorted candies or decors

Place flour and salt in medium bowl; stir to combine. Beat sugar and butter in large bowl with electric mixer at medium speed until light and fluffy. Beat in egg, vanilla and almond extract. Gradually add flour mixture. Beat at low speed until well blended. Divide dough in half; cover and refrigerate 30 minutes or until firm.

Preheat oven to 350°F. Working with 1 portion at a time, roll out dough on lightly floured surface to ¼-inch thickness. Cut dough into desired shapes with assorted floured cookie cutters. Reroll trimmings and cut out more cookies. Place cutouts on ungreased baking sheets. Using drinking straw or tip of sharp knife, cut hole near top of each cookie to allow for piece of ribbon or string to be inserted for hanger. Bake 10 to 12 minutes or until edges are golden brown. Let cookies stand on baking sheets 1 minute. Remove cookies to wire racks; cool completely.

Prepare Icing. Spoon Icing into small resealable plastic food storage bag. Cut off very tiny corner of bag; pipe Icing decoratively over cookies. Decorate with candies as desired. Let stand at room temperature 40 minutes or until set. Thread ribbon through each cookie hole to hang as Christmas tree ornaments. *Makes about 2 dozen cookies*

Icing: *Blend 2 cups powdered sugar and 2 tablespoons milk or lemon juice; stir until smooth. Tint with food color, if desired.*

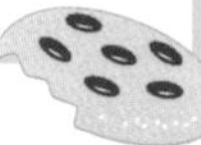

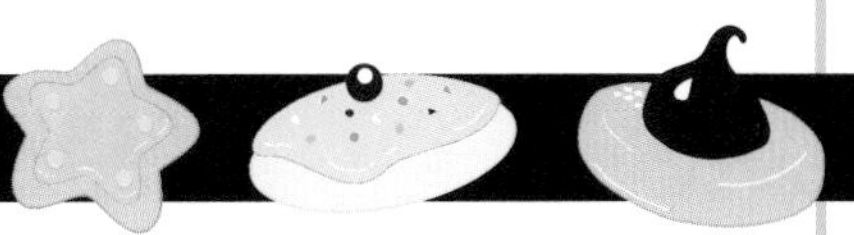

Holiday Truffles

- 3 tablespoons heavy cream
- 1 tablespoon instant coffee granules
- 2 cups semisweet or milk chocolate chips
- ½ cup FLEISCHMANN'S® Original Margarine
- 1 teaspoon vanilla extract
- Crushed cookie crumbs, chopped nuts, toasted coconut, melted white chocolate, colored sprinkles

1. Blend heavy cream and coffee in small bowl; let stand 5 minutes to dissolve.

2. Melt chocolate chips in medium saucepan over low heat until smooth. Remove from heat. With wire whisk, beat in margarine, heavy cream mixture and vanilla until smooth. Place in bowl; refrigerate until firm, about 3 hours.

3. Shape teaspoonfuls of mixture into balls and coat with cookie crumbs, chopped nuts, coconut, melted white chocolate or colored sprinkles until well coated. Store in airtight container in refrigerator.

Makes 2½ dozen cookies

Prep Time: 30 minutes
Cook Time: 5 minutes
Chill Time: 3 hours
Total Time: 3 hours and 35 minutes

Peanut Butter Bears

1 cup SKIPPY® Creamy Peanut Butter
1 cup (2 sticks) MAZOLA® Margarine or butter, softened
1 cup packed brown sugar
⅔ cup KARO® Light or Dark Corn Syrup
2 eggs
4 cups flour, divided
1 tablespoon baking powder
1 teaspoon cinnamon (optional)
¼ teaspoon salt

1. In large bowl with mixer at medium speed, beat peanut butter, margarine, brown sugar, corn syrup and eggs until smooth. Reduce speed; beat in 2 cups flour, baking powder, cinnamon and salt. With spoon, stir in remaining 2 cups flour. Wrap dough in plastic wrap; refrigerate 2 hours.

2. Preheat oven to 325°F. Divide dough in half; set aside half.

3. On floured surface roll out half the dough to ⅛-inch thickness. Cut with floured bear cookie cutter. Repeat with remaining dough.

4. Use scraps of dough to make bear faces. Make one small ball of dough for muzzle. Form 3 smaller balls of dough and press gently to create eyes and nose.

5. Bake bears on ungreased cookie sheets 10 minutes or until lightly browned. Remove from cookie sheets; cool completely on wire rack. Decorate as desired using frosting to create paws, ears and bow ties. *Makes about 3 dozen bears*

Prep Time: 35 minutes plus chilling
Bake Time: 10 minutes plus cooling

Peanut Butter Bears

Almost Homemade

Quick Chocolate Softies

- **1 package (18.25 ounces) devil's food cake mix**
- **⅓ cup water**
- **¼ cup butter, softened**
- **1 egg**
- **1 cup white chocolate baking chips**
- **½ cup coarsely chopped walnuts**

Preheat oven to 350°F. Grease cookie sheets. Combine cake mix, water, butter and egg in large bowl. Beat with electric mixer at low speed until moistened. Increase speed to medium; beat 1 minute. (Dough will be thick.) Stir in chips and nuts; mix until well blended. Drop dough by heaping teaspoonfuls 2 inches apart onto prepared cookie sheets.

Bake 10 to 12 minutes or until set. Let cookies stand on cookie sheets 1 minute. Remove cookies to wire racks; cool completely. *Makes about 4 dozen cookies*

Quick Chocolate Softies

Lemon Bars

- 1 package DUNCAN HINES® Moist Deluxe Lemon Supreme Cake Mix
- 3 eggs, divided
- ⅓ cup butter-flavor shortening
- ½ cup granulated sugar
- ¼ cup lemon juice
- 2 teaspoons grated lemon peel
- ½ teaspoon baking powder
- ¼ teaspoon salt
- Confectioners' sugar

Preheat oven to 350°F.

Combine cake mix, 1 egg and shortening in large mixing bowl. Beat at low speed with electric mixer until crumbs form. Reserve 1 cup. Pat remaining mixture lightly into *ungreased* 13×9-inch pan. Bake 15 minutes or until lightly browned.

Combine remaining 2 eggs, granulated sugar, lemon juice, lemon peel, baking powder and salt in medium mixing bowl. Beat at medium speed with electric mixer until light and foamy. Pour over hot crust. Sprinkle with reserved crumb mixture.

Bake 15 minutes or until lightly browned. Sprinkle with confectioners' sugar. Cool in pan. Cut into bars.

Makes 30 to 32 bars

Tip: These bars are also delicious using DUNCAN HINES® Moist Deluxe Yellow Cake Mix.

Lemon Bars

Chocolate Mint Ravioli Cookies

1 package (15 ounces) refrigerated pie crusts
1 bar (7 ounces) cookies 'n' mint chocolate candy
1 egg
1 tablespoon water
Powdered sugar

Tip

Don't like mint? Just use your favorite candy bar for the filling instead of the cookies 'n' mint bar.

1. Preheat oven to 400°F. Unfold 1 pie crust on lightly floured surface. Roll into 13-inch circle. Using 2½-inch cutters, cut pastry into 24 (2½-inch) circles with cookie cutters, rerolling scraps if necessary. Repeat with remaining pie crust.

2. Separate candy bar into pieces marked in chocolate. Cut each chocolate piece in half. Beat egg and water together in small bowl with fork. Brush half of pastry circles lightly with egg mixture. Place 1 piece of chocolate in center of each circle (there will be some candy bar left over). Top with remaining pastry circles. Seal edges with tines of fork.

3. Place on ungreased baking sheets. Brush with egg mixture.

4. Bake 8 to 10 minutes or until golden brown. Remove from cookie sheets; cool completely on wire rack. Dust with powdered sugar.

Makes 2 dozen cookies

Prep and Cook Time: 30 minutes

Chocolate Mint Ravioli Cookies

Sugar Doodles

1 package (22.3 ounces) golden sugar cookie mix
2 eggs
⅓ cup oil
1 teaspoon water
½ cup (of each) HERSHEY'S® Butterscotch Chips, HERSHEY'S® Semi-Sweet Chocolate Chips and REESE'S® Peanut Butter Chips
5 tablespoons colored sugar
1 tablespoon granulated sugar

1. Heat oven to 375°F.

2. Empty cookie mix into large bowl. Break up any lumps. Add eggs, oil and water to mix; stir with spoon or fork until well blended. Stir in butterscotch chips, chocolate chips and peanut butter chips. Cover; refrigerate dough about 1 hour.

3. Shape dough into 1½-inch balls. Place colored sugar and granulated sugar in large reclosable plastic bag; shake well to blend. Place 2 balls into bag; reclose bag and shake well. Place balls 2 inches apart on ungreased cookie sheet. Repeat until all balls are coated with sugar mixture.

4. Bake 8 to 10 minutes or until set. Cool slightly; remove from cookie sheet to wire rack. Cool completely.

Makes about 2½ dozen cookies

Cocoa Sugar Doodles: Substitute 5 tablespoons granulated sugar and ¾ teaspoon HERSHEY'S® Cocoa or HERSHEY'S® European Style Cocoa for amounts of colored and granulated sugars above.

Rainbow Sugar Doodles: Substitute about 1¾ teaspoons each of blue, pink and yellow colored sugar for the 5 tablespoons colored sugar called for above.

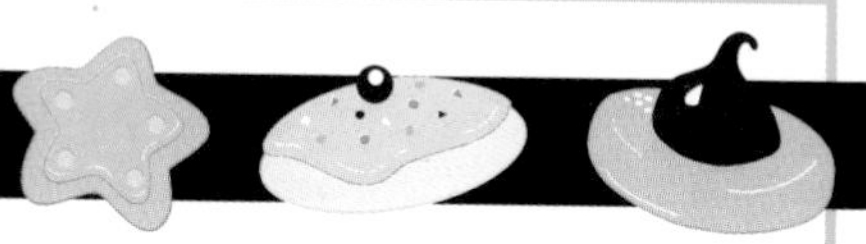

Elephant Ears

- 1 package (17¼ ounces) frozen puff pastry, thawed according to package directions
- 1 egg, beaten
- ¼ cup sugar, divided
- 2 squares (1 ounce each) semisweet chocolate

Preheat oven to 375°F. Grease cookie sheets; sprinkle lightly with water. Roll one sheet of pastry to 12×10-inch rectangle. Brush with egg; sprinkle with 1 tablespoon sugar. Tightly roll up 10-inch sides, meeting in center. Brush center with egg and seal rolls tightly together; turn over. Cut into ⅜-inch-thick slices. Place slices on prepared cookie sheets. Sprinkle with 1 tablespoon sugar. Repeat with remaining pastry, egg and sugar. Bake 16 to 18 minutes until golden brown. Remove to wire racks; cool completely.

Melt chocolate in small saucepan over low heat, stirring constantly. Remove from heat. Spread bottoms of cookies with chocolate. Place on wire rack, chocolate side up. Let stand until chocolate is set. Store between layers of waxed paper in airtight containers. *Makes about 4 dozen cookies*

Peanutty Picnic Brownies

- 1 package DUNCAN HINES® Double Fudge Brownie Mix
- 1 cup quick-cooking oats (not instant or old-fashioned)
- 1 egg
- ⅓ cup water
- ⅓ cup vegetable oil plus additional for greasing
- ¾ cup peanut butter chips
- ⅓ cup chopped peanuts

1. Preheat oven to 350°F. Grease bottom of 13×9-inch pan.

2. Combine brownie mix, oats, egg, water and oil in large bowl. Stir with spoon until well blended, about 50 strokes. Stir in peanut butter chips. Spread in prepared pan. Sprinkle with peanuts. Bake at 350°F for 25 to 28 minutes or until set. *Do not overbake.* Cool completely. Cut into bars.

Makes about 24 brownies

Crispy Thumbprint Cookies

1 package (18.25 ounces) yellow cake mix
½ cup vegetable oil
1 egg
3 cups crisp rice cereal, crushed
½ cup chopped walnuts
Raspberry or strawberry preserves or thin chocolate mint candies, cut in half

1. Preheat oven to 375°F.

2. Combine cake mix, oil, egg and ¼ cup water. Beat at medium speed of electric mixer until well blended. Add cereal and walnuts; mix until well blended.

3. Drop by heaping teaspoonfuls about 2 inches apart onto ungreased baking sheets. Use thumb to make indentation in each cookie. Spoon about ½ teaspoon preserves into center of each cookie. (Or, place ½ of mint candy in center of each cookie).

4. Bake 9 to 11 minutes or until golden brown. Cool cookies 1 minute on baking sheet; remove from baking sheet to wire rack to cool completely. *Makes 3 dozen cookies*

Prep and Cook Time: 30 minutes

Chewy Chocolate Cookies

1 package (2-layer size) chocolate cake mix
2 eggs
1 cup MIRACLE WHIP® or MIRACLE WHIP® LIGHT Dressing
1 cup BAKER'S® Semi-Sweet Real Chocolate Chips
½ cup chopped walnuts

• Mix cake mix, eggs and dressing in large bowl with electric mixer on medium speed until blended. Stir in remaining ingredients. Drop by rounded teaspoonfuls onto greased cookie sheets.

• Bake at 350°F for 10 to 12 minutes or until edges are lightly browned. *Makes 4 dozen cookies*

Prep Time: 10 minutes
Bake Time: 12 minutes

Crispy Thumbprint Cookies

Orange Pecan Gems

- **1 package DUNCAN HINES® Moist Deluxe Orange Supreme Cake Mix**
- **1 container (8 ounces) vanilla low fat yogurt**
- **1 egg**
- **2 tablespoons butter or margarine, softened**
- **1 cup finely chopped pecans**
- **1 cup pecan halves**

1. Preheat oven to 350°F. Grease cookie sheets.

2. Combine cake mix, yogurt, egg, butter and chopped pecans in large bowl. Beat at low speed with electric mixer until blended. Drop by rounded teaspoonfuls 2 inches apart onto prepared cookie sheets. Press pecan half onto center of each cookie. Bake at 350°F for 11 to 13 minutes or until golden brown. Cool 1 minute on cookie sheets. Remove to cooling racks. Cool completely. Store in airtight container.

Makes about 4½ to 5 dozen cookies

Creamy Cappuccino Brownies

- **1 package (21 to 24 ounces) brownie mix**
- **1 tablespoon coffee crystals *or* 1 teaspoon espresso powder**
- **2 tablespoons warm water**
- **1 cup (8 ounces) Wisconsin Mascarpone cheese**
- **3 tablespoons sugar**
- **1 egg**
- **Powdered sugar**

Grease bottom of 13×9-inch baking pan. Prepare brownie mix according to package directions. Pour half of batter into prepared pan. Dissolve coffee crystals in water; add Mascarpone, sugar and egg. Blend until smooth. Drop by spoonfuls over brownie batter; top with remaining brownie batter. With knife, swirl cheese mixture through brownies creating a marbled effect. Bake at 375°F 30 to 35 minutes or until toothpick inserted in center comes out clean. Sprinkle with powdered sugar.

Makes 2 dozen brownies

Favorite recipe from Wisconsin Milk Marketing Board

Orange Pecan Gems

Pumpkin Snack Bars

CAKE
- **1 package (2-layer size) spice cake mix**
- **1 can (16 ounces) pumpkin**
- **¾ cup MIRACLE WHIP® or MIRACLE WHIP® LIGHT Dressing**
- **3 eggs**

FROSTING
- **3½ cups powdered sugar**
- **½ cup (1 stick) butter or margarine, softened**
- **2 tablespoons milk**
- **1 teaspoon vanilla**

CAKE
- Heat oven to 350°F.
- Blend cake mix, pumpkin, dressing and eggs with electric mixer on medium speed until well blended. Pour into greased 15×10×1-inch baking pan.
- Bake 18 to 20 minutes or until toothpick inserted in center comes out clean. Cool completely on wire rack.

FROSTING
- Blend all ingredients with electric mixer on low speed until moistened. Beat on high speed until light and fluffy. Spread over cake. Cut into bars. *Makes about 3 dozen bars*

Prep Time: 20 minutes
Cook Time: 20 minutes

Tip

A 1-pound bag of powdered sugar contains 4 cups unsifted powdered sugar (4½ cups sifted).

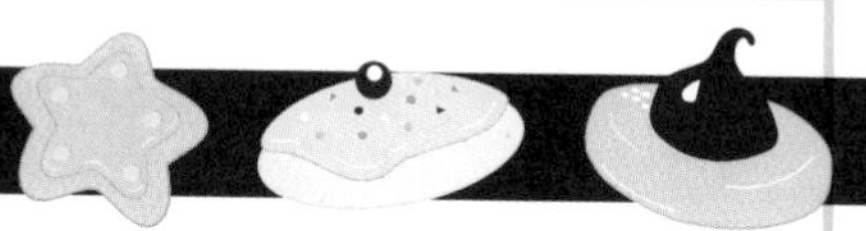

Fudgy Walnut Cookie Wedges

1 package (20 ounces) refrigerated cookie dough, any flavor
2 cups (12-ounce package) HERSHEY'®S Semi-Sweet Chocolate Chips
2 tablespoons butter or margarine
1 can (14 ounces) sweetened condensed milk (not evaporated milk)
1 teaspoon vanilla extract
½ cup chopped walnuts

1. Heat oven to 350°F.

2. Divide cookie dough into thirds. With floured hands, press on bottom of 3 aluminum foil-lined 9-inch round cake pans or press into 9-inch circles on ungreased cookie sheets.

3. Bake 10 to 20 minutes or until golden. Cool. Melt chips and butter with sweetened condensed milk in heavy saucepan over medium heat. Cook and stir until thickened, about 5 minutes. Remove from heat; add vanilla.

4. Spread over cookie circles. Top with walnuts. Chill. Cut into wedges. Store loosely covered at room temperature.

Makes about 36 wedges

Strawberry Streusel Squares

1 package (about 18 ounces) yellow cake mix, divided
3 tablespoons uncooked old-fashioned oats
1 tablespoon margarine
1½ cups sliced strawberries
¾ cup plus 2 tablespoons water, divided
¾ cup diced strawberries
3 egg whites
⅓ cup unsweetened applesauce
½ teaspoon cinnamon
⅛ teaspoon nutmeg

1. Preheat oven to 350°F. Spray 13×9-inch baking pan with nonstick cooking spray; lightly coat with flour.

2. Combine ½ cup cake mix and oats in small bowl. Cut in margarine until mixture resembles coarse crumbs; set aside.

3. Place 1½ cups sliced strawberries and 2 tablespoons water in blender or food processor. Process until smooth. Transfer to small bowl and stir in ¾ cup diced strawberries. Set aside.

4. Place remaining cake mix in large bowl. Add ¾ cup water, egg whites, applesauce, cinnamon and nutmeg. Blend 30 seconds at low speed or just until moistened. Beat at medium speed 2 minutes. Pour batter into prepared pan.

5. Spoon strawberry mixture evenly over batter, spreading lightly. Sprinkle evenly with oat mixture. Bake 31 to 34 minutes or until wooden toothpick inserted into center comes out clean. Cool completely in pan on wire rack.

Makes 12 servings

Strawberry Streusel Squares

Cookie Pizza

- **1 package (20 ounces) refrigerated sugar or peanut butter cookie dough**
- **All-purpose flour (optional)**
- **6 ounces (1 cup) semisweet chocolate chips**
- **1 tablespoon plus 2 teaspoons shortening, divided**
- **¼ cup white chocolate chips**
- **Gummy fruit, chocolate-covered peanuts, assorted roasted nuts, raisins, jelly beans and other assorted candies**

1. Preheat oven to 350°F. Generously grease 12-inch pizza pan. Remove dough from wrapper according to package directions.

2. Sprinkle dough with flour to minimize sticking, if necessary. Press dough into bottom of prepared pan, leaving about ¼-inch space between edge of dough and pan.

3. Bake 14 to 23 minutes or until golden brown and set in center. Cool completely in pan on wire rack, running spatula between cookie crust and pan after 10 to 15 minutes to loosen.

4. Melt semisweet chocolate chips and 1 tablespoon shortening in microwavable bowl on HIGH (100%) 1 minute; stir. Repeat process at 10- to 20-second intervals until smooth.

5. Melt white chocolate chips and remaining 2 teaspoons shortening in another microwavable bowl on MEDIUM-HIGH (70%) 1 minute; stir. Repeat process at 10- to 20-second intervals until smooth.

6. Spread melted semisweet chocolate mixture over crust to within 1 inch of edge. Decorate with desired toppings.

7. Drizzle melted white chocolate over toppings to resemble melted mozzarella cheese. Cut and serve.

Makes 10 to 12 pizza slices

Cookie Pizza

Vanilla Butter Crescents

1 package DUNCAN HINES® Moist Deluxe French Vanilla Flavor Cake Mix
¾ cup butter, softened
1 vanilla bean, very finely chopped (see Tip)
1 cup finely chopped pecans or walnuts
Confectioners' sugar

1. Preheat oven to 350°F.

2. Place cake mix and butter in large bowl. Cut in butter with pastry blender or 2 knives. Stir in vanilla bean and pecans. Since mixture is crumbly, it may be helpful to work dough with hands to blend until mixture holds together. Shape dough into balls. Roll 1 ball between palms until 4 inches long. Shape into crescent. Repeat with remaining balls. Place 2 inches apart on ungreased baking sheets. Bake at 350°F for 10 to 12 minutes or until light golden brown around edges. Cool 2 minutes on baking sheets. Remove to cooling racks. Dust with confectioners' sugar. Cool completely. Dust with additional confectioners' sugar, if desired. Store in airtight container. *Makes 4 dozen cookies*

Tip: To quickly chop vanilla bean, place in work bowl of food processor fitted with knife blade. Process until finely chopped.

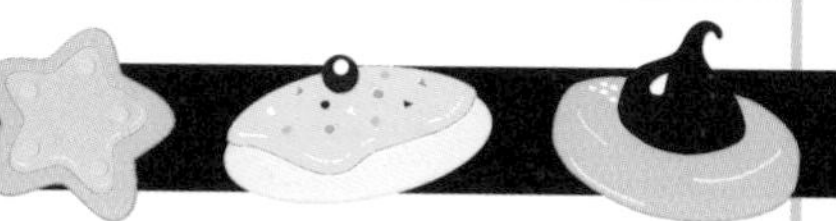

Rocky Road Squares

1 package (21.5 ounces) fudge brownie mix calling for ½ cup water
Vegetable oil, per package directions
Egg(s), per package directions
½ cup CARNATION® Evaporated Milk
2 cups miniature marshmallows
1½ cups coarsely chopped DIAMOND® Walnuts
1 cup (6 ounces) NESTLÉ® TOLL HOUSE® Semi-Sweet Chocolate Morsels

PREPARE brownie mix according to package directions, using oil and egg(s); substitute evaporated milk for water. Spread into greased 13×9-inch baking pan. Bake according to package directions; do not overbake. Remove from oven. Top with marshmallows, walnuts and morsels.

BAKE for 3 to 5 minutes or just until topping is warm and begins to melt together. Cool for 20 to 30 minutes before cutting into squares. *Makes 24 brownies*

Tip

You can prevent marshmallows from drying out by storing them in a tightly sealed plastic bag in the freezer.

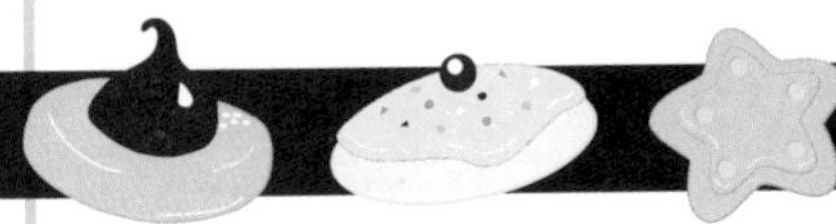

Chocolate Caramel Nut Bars

1 package (18¼ ounces) devil's food cake mix
¾ cup butter or margarine, melted
½ cup milk, divided
60 vanilla caramels
1 cup cashews
1 cup semisweet chocolate chips

Preheat oven to 350°F. Grease 13×9-inch baking pan. Combine cake mix, butter and ¼ cup milk in medium bowl; mix well. Press half of batter into bottom of prepared pan.

Bake 7 to 8 minutes or until batter just begins to form crust. Remove from oven.

Meanwhile, combine caramels and remaining ¼ cup milk in heavy medium saucepan. Cook over low heat, stirring often, about 5 minutes or until caramels are melted and mixture is smooth.

Pour melted caramel mixture over partially baked crust. Combine cashews and chocolate chips in small bowl; sprinkle over caramel mixture.

Drop spoonfuls of remaining batter evenly over nut mixture. Return pan to oven; bake 18 to 20 minutes more or until top cake layer springs back when lightly touched. (Caramel center will be soft.) Let cool on wire rack before cutting into squares or bars. (Bars can be frozen; let thaw 20 to 25 minutes before serving.) *Makes about 48 bars*

Chocolate Caramel Nut Bars

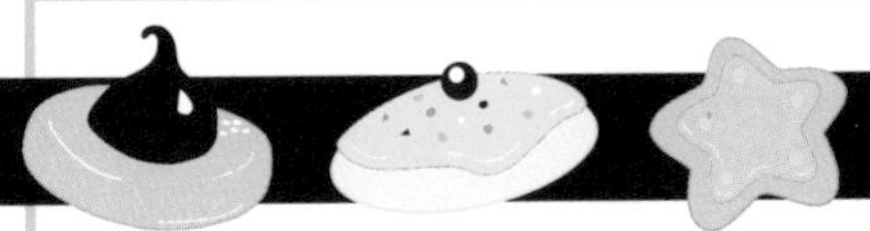

Surprise Cookies

1 package (about 18 ounces) refrigerated sugar cookie dough
All-purpose flour (optional)
Any combination of walnut halves, whole almonds, chocolate-covered raisins or caramel candy squares
Assorted colored sugars

1. Grease cookie sheets. Remove dough from wrapper according to package directions.

2. Divide dough into 4 equal sections. Reserve 1 section; cover and refrigerate remaining 3 sections.

3. Roll reserved dough to ¼-inch thickness. Sprinkle with flour to minimize sticking, if necessary.

4. Cut out 3-inch square cookie with sharp knife. Transfer cookie to prepared cookie sheet.

5. Place desired "surprise" filling in center of cookie. (If using caramel candy square, place so that caramel forms diamond shape within square.)

6. Bring up 4 corners of dough towards center; pinch gently to seal. Repeat steps with remaining dough and fillings, placing cookies about 2 inches apart on prepared cookie sheets. Sprinkle with colored sugar, if desired.

7. Freeze cookies 20 minutes. Preheat oven to 350°F.

8. Bake 9 to 11 minutes or until edges are lightly browned. Remove to wire racks; cool completely.

Makes about 14 cookies

Tip: *Make extra batches of these simple cookies and store in freezer in heavy-duty freezer bags. Take out a few at a time for kids' after-school treats.*

Surprise Cookies

Banana Berry Brownie Pizza

- ⅓ cup cold water
- 1 package (15 ounces) brownie mix
- ¼ cup oil
- 1 egg
- 1 package (8 ounces) PHILADELPHIA® Cream Cheese, softened
- ¼ cup sugar
- 1 egg
- 1 teaspoon vanilla
- Strawberry slices
- Banana slices
- 2 squares (1 ounce each) BAKER'S® Semi-Sweet Chocolate, melted

PREHEAT oven to 350°F. Bring water to boil.

MIX together brownie mix, boiled water, oil and egg in large bowl until well blended.

POUR into greased and floured 12-inch pizza pan.

BAKE 25 minutes.

BEAT cream cheese, sugar, egg and vanilla in small mixing bowl at medium speed with electric mixer until well blended. Pour over crust.

BAKE 15 minutes. Cool. Top with fruit; drizzle with chocolate. Garnish with mint leaves, if desired.

Makes 10 to 12 servings

Microwave Tip: To melt chocolate, place unwrapped chocolate squares in small bowl. Microwave on HIGH 1 to 2 minutes or until almost melted. Stir until smooth.

Prep Time: 35 minutes
Cook Time: 40 minutes

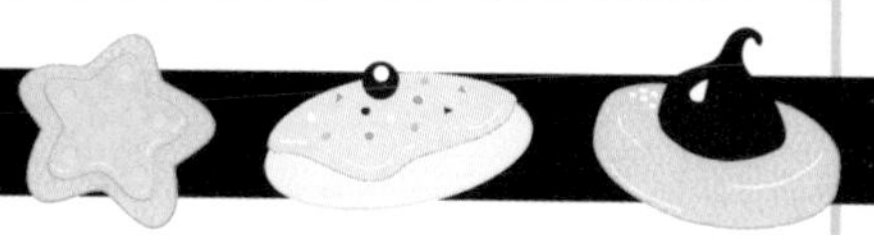

Sweet Walnut Maple Bars

CRUST

1 package DUNCAN HINES® Moist Deluxe Yellow Cake Mix, divided
⅓ cup butter or margarine, melted
1 egg

TOPPING

1⅓ cups MRS. BUTTERWORTH'S® Maple Syrup
3 eggs
⅓ cup firmly packed light brown sugar
½ teaspoon maple flavoring or vanilla extract
1 cup chopped walnuts

1. Preheat oven to 350°F. Grease 13×9×2-inch pan.

2. **For crust,** reserve ⅔ cup cake mix; set aside. Combine remaining cake mix, melted butter and egg in large bowl. Stir until thoroughly blended. (Mixture will be crumbly.) Press into pan. Bake at 350°F for 15 to 20 minutes or until light golden brown.

3. **For topping,** combine reserved cake mix, maple syrup, eggs, brown sugar and maple flavoring in large bowl. Beat at low speed with electric mixer for 3 minutes. Pour over crust. Sprinkle with walnuts. Bake at 350°F for 30 to 35 minutes or until filling is set. Cool completely. Cut into bars. Store leftover cookie bars in refrigerator. *Makes 24 bars*

Ultimate Brownies

½ cup MIRACLE WHIP® Salad Dressing
2 eggs, beaten
¼ cup cold water
1 package (21.5 ounces) fudge brownie mix
3 milk chocolate bars (7 ounces each), divided
Walnut halves (optional)

- Preheat oven to 350°F.
- Mix together salad dressing, eggs and water until well blended. Stir in brownie mix, mixing just until moistened.
- Coarsely chop 2 chocolate bars; stir into brownie mixture. Pour into greased 13×9-inch baking pan.
- Bake 30 to 35 minutes or until edges begin to pull away from sides of pan. Immediately top with remaining chocolate bar, chopped. Let stand about 5 minutes or until melted; spread evenly over brownies. Garnish with walnut halves, if desired. Cool. Cut into squares.

Makes about 24 brownies

Easy Peanutty Snickerdoodles

3 tablespoons sugar
3 teaspoons ground cinnamon
1 package (22.3 ounces) golden sugar cookie mix
2 eggs
⅓ cup vegetable oil
1 teaspoon water
1 cup REESE'S® Peanut Butter Chips

1. Heat oven to 375°F. Stir together sugar and cinnamon in small bowl; set aside.
2. Empty cookie mix into large bowl. Break up any lumps. Add eggs, oil and water; stir with spoon or fork until well blended. Stir in peanut butter chips. Shape dough into 1-inch balls. (If dough is too soft, cover and refrigerate about 1 hour.) Roll balls in cinnamon-sugar; place on ungreased cookie sheet.
3. Bake 9 to 11 minutes or until set. Cool slightly; remove from cookie sheet to wire rack. Cool completely.

Makes about 3½ dozen cookies

Ultimate Brownies

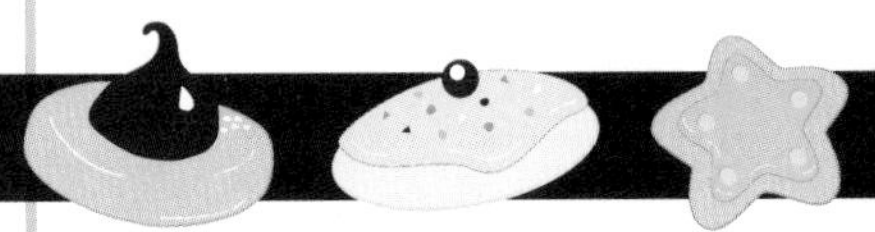

Oatmeal Brownie Gems

2¾ cups quick-cooking or old-fashioned oats, uncooked
1 cup all-purpose flour
1 cup firmly packed light brown sugar
1 cup coarsely chopped walnuts
1 teaspoon baking soda
1 cup butter or margarine, melted
1¾ cups "M&M's"® Semi-Sweet Chocolate Mini Baking Bits
1 (19- to 21-ounce) package fudge brownie mix, prepared according to package directions for fudge-like brownies

Preheat oven to 350°F. In large bowl combine oats, flour, sugar, nuts and baking soda; add butter until mixture forms coarse crumbs. Toss in "M&M's"® Semi-Sweet Chocolate Mini Baking Bits until evenly distributed. Reserve 3 cups mixture. Pat remaining mixture onto bottom of 15×10×1-inch pan to form crust. Pour prepared brownie mix over crust, carefully spreading into thin layer. Sprinkle reserved crumb mixture over top of brownie mixture; pat down lightly. Bake 25 to 30 minutes or until toothpick inserted in center comes out with moist crumbs. Cool completely. Cut into bars. Store in tightly covered container.

Makes 48 bars

Tip

To melt butter in the microwave, place 1 cup (2 sticks) of butter in a microwavable dish. Cover with plastic wrap and heat at HIGH 1½ to 2 minutes.

Oatmeal Brownie Gems

Chocolate Caramel Brownies

1 package (18¼ to 18½ ounces) devil's food or chocolate cake mix
1 cup chopped nuts
½ cup (1 stick) butter or margarine, melted
1 cup *undiluted* CARNATION® Evaporated Milk, divided
35 light caramels (10 ounces)
1 cup (6-ounce package) NESTLÉ® TOLL HOUSE® Semi-Sweet Chocolate Morsels

COMBINE cake mix and nuts in large bowl; stir in butter. Stir in ½ cup evaporated milk (batter will be thick). Spread half of batter in greased 13×9-inch baking pan.

BAKE in preheated 350°F. oven for 15 minutes.

COMBINE caramels and remaining evaporated milk in small saucepan; cook over low heat, stirring occasionally, until caramels are melted. Sprinkle morsels over baked layer. Drizzle melted caramels over chocolate morsels, carefully spreading to cover chocolate layer. Drop remaining half of batter in heaping teaspoons over caramel mixture.

RETURN to oven; bake 20 to 25 minutes longer (top layer will be soft). Cool completely before cutting.

Makes 48 brownies

Banana Chocolate Chip Cookies

2 extra-ripe, medium DOLE® Bananas, peeled
1 package (17.5 ounces) chocolate chip cookie mix
½ teaspoon ground cinnamon
1 egg, lightly beaten
1 teaspoon vanilla extract
1 cup toasted wheat germ

- Mash bananas with fork. Measure 1 cup.
- Combine cookie mix and cinnamon. Stir in contents of enclosed flavoring packet, mashed bananas, egg and vanilla until well blended. Stir in wheat germ.
- Drop batter by heaping tablespoonfuls 2 inches apart onto cookie sheets coated with cooking spray. Shape cookies with back of spoon. Bake in 375°F oven 10 to 12 minutes until lightly browned. Cool on wire racks. *Makes 18 cookies*

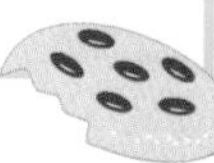

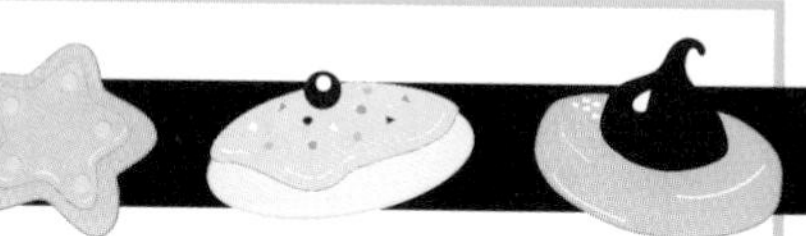

Peanut Maple Triangles

1¼ cups powdered sugar, divided
½ cup creamy peanut butter
¼ cup plus 3 tablespoons maple-flavored syrup, divided
1 package (17½ ounces) frozen puff pastry dough, thawed

1. Preheat oven to 400°F. Combine ¼ cup powdered sugar, peanut butter and ¼ cup maple syrup in small bowl until well blended; set aside.

2. Cut pastry dough into 3-inch-wide strips. Place rounded teaspoon peanut butter mixture about 1 inch from 1 end of each strip.

3. Starting at end of each strip with filling, fold corner of pastry dough over filling so it lines up with other side of strip, forming a triangle. Continue folding like a flag in triangular shape, using entire strip. Repeat process with remaining pastry dough and filling.

4. Place triangles about 2 inches apart onto ungreased baking sheets, seam-side down; spray with cooking spray. Bake 6 to 8 minutes or until golden brown. Remove from baking sheets to wire rack to cool.

5. Combine remaining 1 cup powdered sugar, 3 tablespoons syrup and 1 to 2 tablespoons water in small bowl. Glaze cookies just before serving. *Makes 28 cookies*

Note: *For longer storage, do not glaze cookies and store loosely covered so pastry dough remains crisp. Glaze before serving.*

Prep and Bake Time: 30 minutes

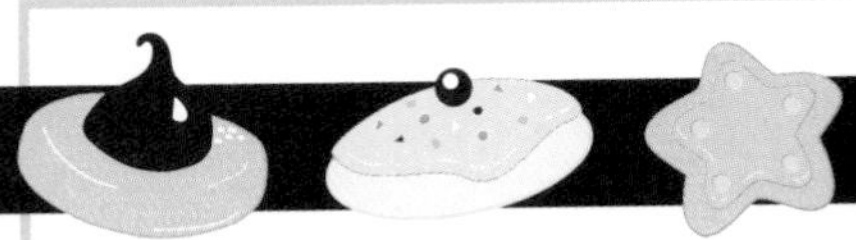

Festive Fudge Blossoms

¼ cup butter or margarine, softened
1 box (18.25 ounces) chocolate fudge cake mix
1 egg, slightly beaten
2 tablespoons water
¾ to 1 cup finely chopped walnuts
48 chocolate star candies

1. Preheat oven to 350°F. Cut butter into cake mix in large bowl until mixture resembles coarse crumbs. Stir in egg and water until well blended.

2. Shape dough into ½-inch balls; roll in walnuts, pressing nuts gently into dough. Place about 2 inches apart on ungreased baking sheets.

3. Bake cookies 12 minutes or until puffed and nearly set. Place chocolate star in center of each cookie; bake 1 minute more. Cool 2 minutes on baking sheet. Remove cookies from baking sheets to wire rack to cool completely.

Makes 4 dozen cookies

Spicy Sour Cream Cookies

1 package DUNCAN HINES® Moist Deluxe Spice Cake Mix
1 cup sour cream
1 cup chopped pecans or walnuts
¼ cup butter or margarine, softened
1 egg

1. Preheat oven to 350°F. Grease cookie sheets.

2. Combine cake mix, sour cream, pecans, butter and egg in large bowl. Mix at low speed with electric mixer until blended.

3. Drop dough by rounded teaspoonfuls onto prepared cookie sheets. Bake 9 to 11 minutes or until lightly browned. Cool 2 minutes on cookie sheets. Remove to cooling racks; cool completely.

Makes about 4½ dozen cookies

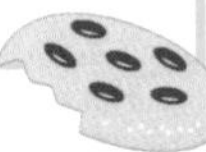

Festive Fudge Blossoms

Especially for Kids

Crayon Cookies

1 cup butter, softened
2 teaspoons vanilla
½ cup powdered sugar
2¼ cups all-purpose flour
¼ teaspoon salt
Assorted paste food colorings
1½ cups chocolate chips
1½ teaspoons shortening

1. Preheat oven to 350°F. Grease cookie sheets. Beat butter and vanilla in large bowl at high speed of electric mixer until fluffy. Add sugar; beat at medium speed until blended. Combine flour and salt in small bowl. Gradually add to butter mixture.

2. Divide dough into 10 equal sections. Reserve 1 section; cover and refrigerate remaining 9 sections. Combine reserved section and desired food coloring in small bowl; blend well.

3. Cut dough into 2 equal sections. Roll each section into 5-inch log. Pinch one end to resemble crayon tip. Place cookies 2 inches apart on prepared cookie sheets. Repeat with remaining 9 sections of dough and desired food colorings.

4. Bake 15 to 18 minutes or until edges are lightly browned. Cool completely on cookie sheets.

5. Combine chocolate chips and shortening in small microwavable bowl. Microwave at HIGH 1 to 1½ minutes or until smooth. Decorate with chocolate mixture as shown in photo.

Makes 20 cookies

Crayon Cookies

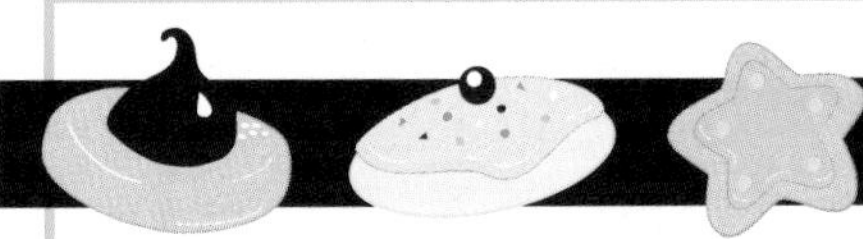

Happy Cookie Pops

- **1½ cups granulated sugar**
- **1 cup butter-flavored solid vegetable shortening**
- **2 large eggs**
- **1 teaspoon vanilla extract**
- **2¾ cups all-purpose flour**
- **1 teaspoon baking powder**
- **½ teaspoon baking soda**
- **1¾ cups "M&M's"® Chocolate Mini Baking Bits, divided**
- **Additional granulated sugar**
- **2½ dozen flat wooden ice cream sticks**
- **Prepared frostings**
- **Tubes of decorator's icing**

In large bowl cream 1½ cups sugar and shortening until light and fluffy; beat in eggs and vanilla. In medium bowl combine flour, baking powder and baking soda; blend into creamed mixture. Stir in 1¼ cups "M&M's"® Chocolate Mini Baking Bits. Wrap and refrigerate dough 1 hour.

Preheat oven to 375°F. Roll 1½ tablespoons dough into ball and roll in granulated sugar. Insert ice cream stick into each ball. Place about 2 inches apart onto ungreased cookie sheets; gently flatten, using bottom of small plate. On half the cookies, make a smiling face by placing some of the remaining "M&M's"® Chocolate Mini Baking Bits on the surface; leave other cookies for decorating after baking. Bake all cookies 10 to 12 minutes or until golden. Cool 2 minutes on cookie sheets; cool completely on wire racks. Decorate cookies as desired using frostings, decorator's icing and remaining "M&M's"® Chocolate Mini Baking Bits. Store in single layer in tightly covered container.

Makes 2½ dozen cookies

Variation: *For chocolate cookies, combine ⅓ cup unsweetened cocoa powder with flour, baking powder and baking soda; continue as directed.*

Happy Cookie Pops

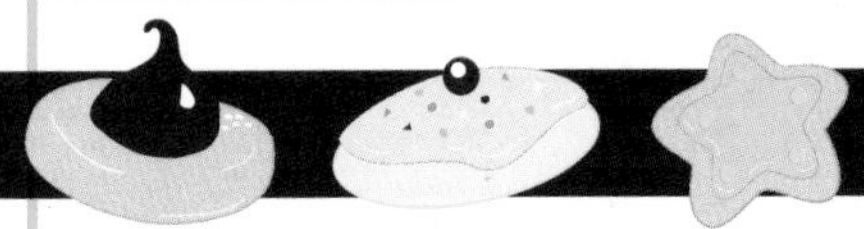

Moons and Stars

- **1 cup butter, softened**
- **1 cup sugar**
- **1 egg**
- **2 teaspoons lemon peel**
- **½ teaspoon almond extract**
- **3 cups all-purpose flour**
- **½ cup ground almonds**
- **All-purpose flour (optional)**
- **Assorted colored icings, hard candies and colored sprinkles**

1. Preheat oven to 350°F. Grease cookie sheets.

2. Beat butter, sugar, egg, lemon peel and almond extract in large bowl at medium speed of electric mixer until light and fluffy.

3. Combine flour and almonds in medium bowl. Add flour mixture to butter mixture; stir just until combined.

4. Roll dough on lightly floured surface to ⅛- to ¼-inch thickness. Cut out cookies using moon and star cookie cutters. Place cookies 2 inches apart on prepared cookie sheets.

5. Bake 7 to 9 minutes or until set but not browned. Cool on cookie sheets 2 minutes. Remove to wire rack; cool completely.

6. Decorate cookies with icings, sugars and sprinkles as shown in photo. *Makes about 4 dozen cookies*

Moons and Stars

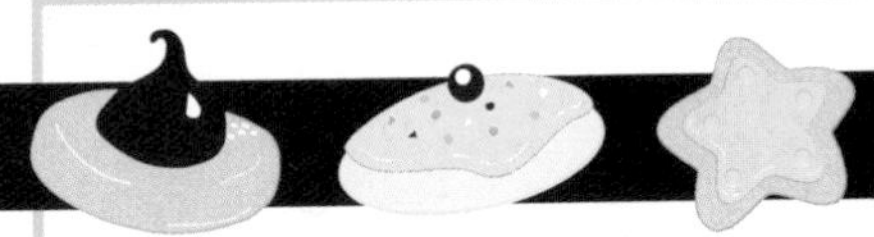

Chocolate Surprise Cookies

2¾ cups all-purpose flour
¾ cup unsweetened cocoa powder
½ teaspoon baking powder
½ teaspoon baking soda
1 cup (2 sticks) butter or margarine, softened
1½ cups packed light brown sugar
½ cup plus 1 tablespoon granulated sugar, divided
2 eggs
1 teaspoon vanilla
1 cup chopped pecans, divided
1 package (9 ounces) caramels coated in milk chocolate
3 squares (1 ounce each) white chocolate, coarsely chopped

Preheat oven to 375°F. Combine flour, cocoa, baking powder and baking soda in medium bowl; set aside.

Beat butter, brown sugar and ½ cup granulated sugar with electric mixer at medium speed until light and fluffy; beat in eggs and vanilla. Gradually add flour mixture and ½ cup pecans; beat well. Cover dough; refrigerate 15 minutes or until firm enough to roll into balls.

Place remaining ½ cup pecans and 1 tablespoon sugar in shallow dish. Roll tablespoonful of dough around 1 caramel candy, covering completely; press one side into nut mixture. Place, nut side up, on ungreased cookie sheet. Repeat with additional dough and candies, placing 3 inches apart.

Bake 10 to 12 minutes or until set and slightly cracked. Let stand on cookie sheet 2 minutes. Transfer cookies to wire rack; cool completely.

Place white chocolate pieces in small resealable plastic freezer bag; seal bag. Microwave at MEDIUM (50% power) 2 minutes. Turn bag over; microwave 2 to 3 minutes or until melted. Knead bag until chocolate is smooth. Cut off tiny corner of bag; drizzle chocolate onto cookies. Let stand about 30 minutes or until chocolate is set.

Makes about 3½ dozen cookies

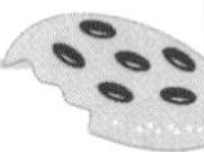

Chocolate Surprise Cookies

Sugar Cookie Pizza

1 package DUNCAN HINES® Golden Sugar Cookie Mix
½ cup semisweet mini chocolate coated candy pieces
1 container DUNCAN HINES® Vanilla or Chocolate Frosting (optional)

Preheat oven to 350°F.

Prepare cookie mix as directed on package. Spread onto lightly greased 12-inch pizza pan. Sprinkle candy pieces evenly over cookie dough; press down gently. Bake 15 to 20 minutes or until golden brown. Cool 3 to 4 minutes in pan. Remove from pan; cool completely. Decorate with frosting, if desired. *Makes 12 servings*

Flourless Peanut Butter Cookies

1 cup peanut butter
1 cup packed light brown sugar
1 egg
24 milk chocolate candy stars or other solid milk chocolate candy

Preheat oven to 350°F. Combine peanut butter, sugar and egg in medium bowl until blended and smooth.

Shape dough into 24 balls about 1½ inches in diameter. Place 2 inches apart on ungreased cookie sheets. Press one chocolate star on top of each cookie. Bake 10 to 12 minutes or until set. Transfer to wire racks to cool completely.
Makes about 2 dozen cookies

Sugar Cookie Pizza

Peanut Butter and Jelly Sandwich Cookies

1 package (about 18 ounces) refrigerated sugar cookie dough
1 tablespoon unsweetened cocoa powder
All-purpose flour (optional)
1¾ cups creamy peanut butter
½ cup grape jam or jelly

1. Remove dough from wrapper according to package directions. Reserve ¼ section of dough; cover and refrigerate remaining ¾ section of dough. Combine reserved dough and cocoa in small bowl; refrigerate.

2. Shape remaining ¾ section dough into 5½-inch log. Sprinkle with flour to minimize sticking, if necessary. Remove chocolate dough from refrigerator; roll on sheet of waxed paper to 9½×6½-inch rectangle. Place dough log in center of rectangle.

3. Bring waxed paper edges and chocolate dough up and together over log. Press gently on top and sides of dough so entire log is wrapped in chocolate dough. Flatten log slightly to form square. Wrap in waxed paper. Freeze 10 minutes.

4. Preheat oven to 350°F. Remove waxed paper from dough. Cut dough into ¼-inch slices. Place slices 2 inches apart on ungreased cookie sheets. Reshape dough edges into square, if necessary. Press dough slightly to form indentation so dough resembles slice of bread.

5. Bake 8 to 11 minutes or until lightly browned. Remove from oven and straighten cookie edges with spatula. Cool 2 minutes on cookie sheets. Remove to wire racks; cool.

6. To make sandwich, spread about 1 tablespoon peanut butter on underside of 1 cookie. Spread about ½ tablespoon jam over peanut butter; top with second cookie, pressing gently. Repeat with remaining cookies.

Makes 11 sandwich cookies

Tip: Cut each sandwich diagonally in half for a smaller cookie and fun look.

Peanut Butter and Jelly Sandwich Cookies

Cookie Pops

1 package (20 ounces) refrigerated sugar cookie dough
All-purpose flour (optional)
20 (4-inch) lollipop sticks
Assorted colored sugars, frostings, glazes and gels

1. Preheat oven to 350°F. Grease cookie sheets.

2. Remove dough from wrapper according to package directions. Sprinkle with flour to minimize sticking, if necessary.

3. Cut dough in half. Reserve 1 half; refrigerate remaining dough. Roll reserved dough to ⅛-inch thickness. Cut out cookies using 3½-inch cookie cutters.

4. Place lollipop sticks on cookies so that tips of sticks are imbedded in cookies. Carefully turn cookies so sticks are in back; place on prepared cookie sheets. Repeat with remaining dough.

5. Bake 7 to 11 minutes or until edges are lightly browned. Cool cookies on cookie sheets 2 minutes. Remove cookies to wire racks; cool completely.

6. Decorate with colored sugars, frostings, glazes and gels as desired. *Makes 20 cookies*

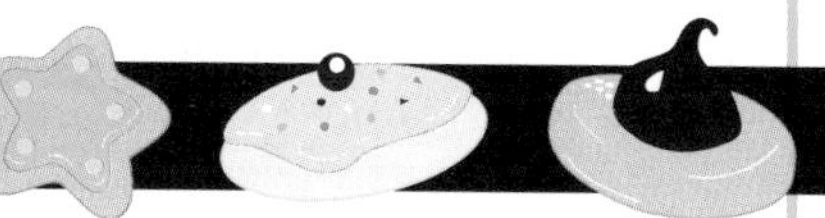

Caramel Marshmallow Bars

CRUMB MIXTURE

1¼ cups all-purpose flour
½ cup sugar
½ cup butter or margarine, softened
¼ cup graham cracker crumbs
¼ teaspoon salt
½ cup chopped salted peanuts

FILLING

¾ cup caramel ice cream topping
½ cup salted peanuts
½ cups miniature marshmallows
½ cup milk chocolate chips

Preheat oven to 350°F. Grease and flour 9-inch square baking pan. For crumb mixture, combine flour, sugar, butter, graham cracker crumbs and salt in small mixer bowl. Beat with electric mixer at low speed 1 to 2 minutes until mixture is crumbly. Stir in nuts. Reserve ¾ cup crumb mixture. Press remaining crumb mixture onto bottom of prepared pan. Bake 10 to 12 minutes or until lightly browned.

For filling, spread caramel topping evenly over hot crust. Sprinkle with nuts, marshmallows and chocolate chips. Crumble ¾ cup reserved crumb mixture over chocolate chips. Continue baking 10 to 12 minutes or until marshmallows just start to brown. Cool on wire rack about 30 minutes. Cover; refrigerate 1 to 2 hours or until firm. Cut into bars.

Makes about 30 bars

Tip: For an extra special treat, serve these kid-pleasing bars with a scoop of ice cream.

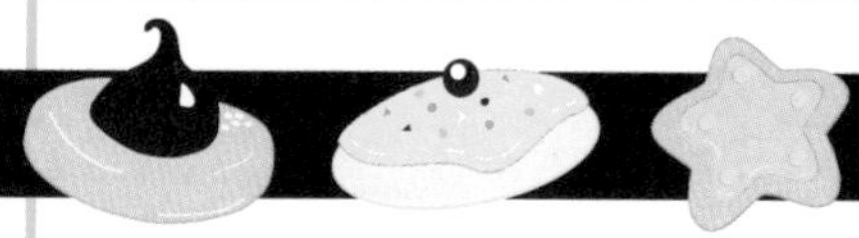

Peanuts

½ cup butter or margarine, softened
¼ cup shortening
¼ cup creamy peanut butter
1 cup powdered sugar, sifted
1 egg yolk
1 teaspoon vanilla
1¾ cups all-purpose flour
1 cup finely ground honey-roasted peanuts, divided
Peanut Buttery Frosting (recipe follows)

1. Beat butter, shortening and peanut butter in large bowl at medium speed of electric mixer. Gradually add sugar, beating until smooth. Add egg yolk and vanilla; beat well. Add flour; mix well. Stir in ⅓ cup ground peanuts. Cover dough; refrigerate 1 hour.

2. Prepare Peanut Buttery Frosting. Preheat oven to 350°F. Grease cookie sheets. Shape dough into 1-inch balls. Place 2 balls, side by side and slightly touching, on prepared cookie sheet. Gently flatten balls with fingertips and form into "peanut" shape. Repeat steps with remaining dough.

3. Bake 16 to 18 minutes or until edges are lightly browned. Cool on cookie sheets 5 minutes. Remove cookies to wire racks; cool completely.

4. Place remaining ⅔ cup ground peanuts in shallow dish. Spread about 2 teaspoons Peanut Buttery Frosting evenly over top of each cookie. Coat with ground peanuts.

Makes about 2 dozen cookies

Peanut Buttery Frosting

½ cup butter or margarine, softened
½ cup creamy peanut butter
2 cups powdered sugar, sifted
½ teaspoon vanilla
3 to 6 tablespoons milk

Beat butter and peanut butter in medium bowl at medium speed of electric mixer until smooth. Gradually add sugar and vanilla until blended but crumbly. Add milk, 1 tablespoon at a time, until smooth. Refrigerate until ready to use.

Makes 1⅓ cups frosting

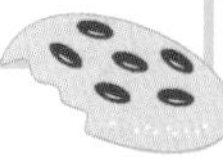

Peanuts

Handprints

- **1 package (20 ounces) refrigerated cookie dough, any flavor**
- **All-purpose flour (optional)**
- **Cookie glazes, frostings, nondairy whipped topping, peanut butter and assorted candies**

1. Grease cookie sheets. Remove dough from wrapper according to package directions.

2. Cut dough into 4 equal sections. Reserve 1 section; refrigerate remaining 3 sections. Sprinkle reserved dough with flour to minimize sticking, if necessary.

3. Roll dough on prepared cookie sheet to 5×7-inch rectangle.

4. Place hand, palm-side down, on dough. Carefully cut around outline of hand with knife. Remove scraps. Separate fingers as much as possible using small spatula. Pat fingers outward to lengthen slightly. Repeat steps with remaining dough.

5. Freeze dough 15 minutes. Preheat oven to 350°F.

6. Bake 7 to 13 minutes or until cookies are set and edges are golden brown. Cool completely on cookie sheets.

7. Decorate as desired. *Makes 4 adult handprint cookies*

Tip: To get the kids involved, let them use their hands to make the handprints. Be sure that an adult is available to cut around the outline with a knife. The kids will enjoy seeing how their handprints bake into big cookies.

Handprints

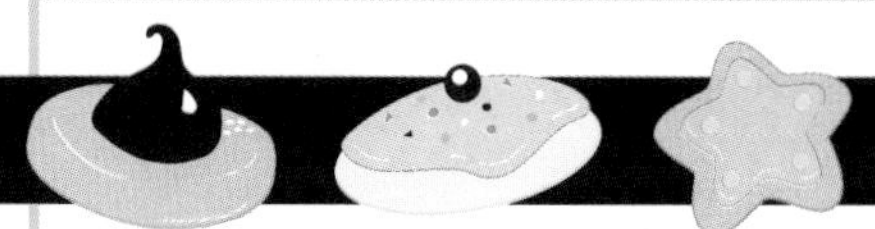

Sandwich Cookies

1 package (20 ounces) refrigerated cookie dough, any flavor
All-purpose flour (optional)
Any combination of colored frostings, peanut butter or assorted ice creams
Colored sprinkles, chocolate-covered raisins, miniature candy-coated chocolate pieces and other assorted small candies

1. Preheat oven to 350°F. Grease cookie sheets.

2. Remove dough from wrapper according to package directions.

3. Cut dough into 4 equal sections. Reserve 1 section; refrigerate remaining 3 sections.

4. Roll reserved dough to ¼-inch thickness. Sprinkle with flour to minimize sticking, if necessary.

5. Cut out cookies using ¾-inch round cookie cutter. Transfer cookies to prepared cookie sheets, placing about 2 inches apart. Repeat steps with remaining dough.

6. Bake 8 to 11 minutes or until edges are lightly browned. Remove to wire racks; cool completely.

7. To make sandwich, spread about 1 tablespoon desired filling on bottom of 1 cookie. Top with second cookie, pressing gently.

8. Roll side of sandwich in desired decorations. Repeat with remaining cookies.

Makes about 20 to 24 sandwich cookies

Tip: Be creative—make sandwich cookies using 2 or more flavors of refrigerated cookie dough. Mix and match to see how many flavor combinations you can come up with.

Sandwich Cookies

Mini Pizza Cookies

1 20-ounce tube of refrigerated sugar cookie dough
2 cups (16 ounces) prepared pink frosting
"M&M's"® Chocolate Mini Baking Bits
Variety of additional toppings such as shredded coconut, granola, raisins, nuts, small pretzels, snack mixes, sunflower seeds, popped corn and mini marshmallows

Preheat oven to 350°F. Lightly grease cookie sheets; set aside. Divide dough into 8 equal portions. On lightly floured surface, roll each portion of dough into ¼-inch-thick circle; place about 2 inches apart onto prepared cookie sheets. Bake 10 to 13 minutes or until golden brown on edges. Cool completely on wire racks. Spread top of each pizza with frosting; sprinkle with "M&M's"® Chocolate Mini Baking Bits and 2 or 3 suggested toppings. *Makes 8 cookies*

Tip

These cookies are a great activity for a kids' party, or even for a special after-school treat—kids will love creating and eating their own masterpieces!

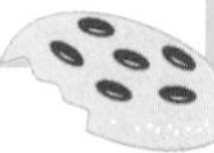

Mini Pizza Cookies

Peanut Butter Pizza Cookies

- 1¼ cups firmly packed light brown sugar
- ¾ cup creamy peanut butter
- ½ CRISCO® Stick or ½ cup CRISCO® all-vegetable shortening
- 3 tablespoons milk
- 1 tablespoon vanilla
- 1 egg
- 1¾ cups all-purpose flour
- ¾ teaspoon salt
- ¾ teaspoon baking soda
- 8 ounces white baking chocolate, chopped
- Decorative candies

1. Heat oven to 375°F. Place sheets of foil on countertop for cooling cookies.

2. Combine brown sugar, peanut butter, shortening, milk and vanilla in large bowl. Beat at medium speed of electric mixer until well blended. Add egg. Beat just until blended.

3. Combine flour, salt and baking soda. Add to creamed mixture at low speed. Mix just until blended.

4. Divide dough in half. Form each half into a ball. Place 1 ball of dough onto center of ungreased pizza pan or baking sheet. Spread dough with fingers to form a 12-inch circle. Repeat with other ball of dough.

5. Bake one baking sheet at a time at 375°F for 10 to 12 minutes, or until lightly browned. *Do not overbake.* Cool 2 minutes on baking sheet. Remove with large spatula to foil to cool completely.

6. Place white chocolate in a shallow microwave-safe bowl. Microwave on 100% (HIGH) for 30 seconds. Stir. Repeat at 30 second intervals until white chocolate is melted.

7. Spread melted white chocolate on center of cooled cookies to within ½ inch of edge. Decorate with candies. Set completely. Cut into wedges.

Makes 2 pizzas

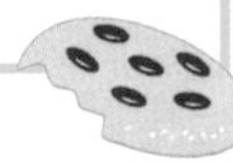

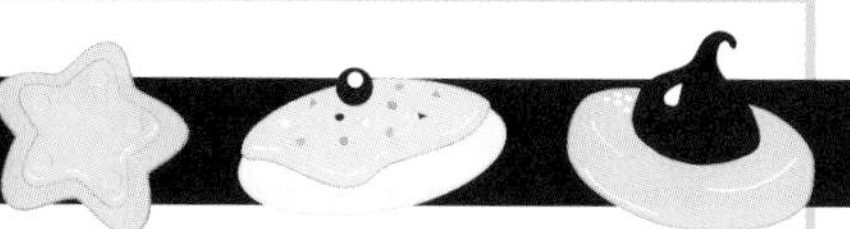

PB & J Cookie Sandwiches

- **½ cup butter or margarine, softened**
- **½ cup creamy peanut butter**
- **¼ cup solid vegetable shortening**
- **1 cup firmly packed light brown sugar**
- **1 large egg**
- **1 teaspoon vanilla extract**
- **1⅔ cups all-purpose flour**
- **1 teaspoon baking soda**
- **½ teaspoon baking powder**
- **1 cup "M&M's"® Milk Chocolate Mini Baking Bits**
- **½ cup finely chopped peanuts**
- **½ cup grape or strawberry jam**

Preheat oven to 350°F. In large bowl cream butter, peanut butter, shortening and sugar until light and fluffy; beat in egg and vanilla. In medium bowl combine flour, baking soda and baking powder; blend into creamed mixture. Stir in "M&M's"® Milk Chocolate Mini Baking Bits and nuts. Drop by rounded teaspoonfuls onto ungreased cookie sheets. Bake 8 to 10 minutes or until light golden. Let cool 2 minutes on cookie sheets; remove to wire racks to cool completely. Just before serving, spread ½ teaspoon jam on bottom of one cookie; top with second cookie. Store in tightly covered container.

Makes about 2 dozen sandwich cookies

Fruity Cookie Rings and Twists

1 package (20 ounces) refrigerated sugar cookie dough
3 cups fruit-flavored cereal, crushed and divided

Tip

Be creative! Try making the cookies in a variety of shapes in addition to rings and twists: form the ropes of dough into pretzels, snails, hearts or alphabet letters.

1. Remove dough from wrapper according to package directions.

2. Combine dough and ½ cup cereal in large bowl. Divide dough into 32 balls. Refrigerate 1 hour.

3. Preheat oven to 375°F. Roll dough balls into 6- to 8-inch-long ropes. Roll ropes in remaining cereal to coat; shape into rings or fold in half and twist.

4. Place cookies 2 inches apart on ungreased cookie sheets.

5. Bake 10 to 11 minutes or until lightly browned. Remove to wire racks; cool completely.

Makes 32 cookies

Tip: These cookie rings can be transformed into Christmas tree ornaments by poking a hole in each unbaked ring using a drinking straw. Bake cookies and decorate with colored gels and small candies to resemble wreaths. Loop thin ribbon through holes and tie together.

Fruity Cookie Rings and Twists

Critters-in-Holes

48 chewy caramel candies coated in milk chocolate
48 pieces candy corn
Miniature candy-coated chocolate pieces
1 container frosting, any flavor
1 package (20 ounces) refrigerated peanut butter cookie dough

1. Cut slit into side of 1 caramel candy using sharp knife.

2. Carefully insert 1 piece candy corn into slit. Repeat with remaining caramel candies and candy corn.

3. Attach miniature chocolate pieces to caramel candies to resemble "eyes," using frosting as glue. Decorate as desired.

4. Preheat oven to 350°F. Grease 12 (1¾-inch) muffin cups.

5. Remove dough from wrapper according to package directions. Cut dough into 12 (1-inch) slices. Cut each slice into 4 equal sections. Place 1 section of dough into each muffin cup.

6. Bake 9 minutes. Remove from oven and immediately press 1 decorated caramel candy into center of each cookie. Repeat with remaining ingredients. Remove to wire racks; cool completely. *Makes 4 dozen cookies*

Critters-in-Holes

Kids' Favorite Jumbo Chippers

- **1 cup butter, softened**
- **¾ cup granulated sugar**
- **¾ cup packed brown sugar**
- **2 eggs**
- **1 teaspoon vanilla**
- **2¼ cups all-purpose flour**
- **1 teaspoon baking soda**
- **¾ teaspoon salt**
- **1 package (9 ounces) candy-coated chocolate pieces**
- **1 cup peanut butter flavored chips**

Preheat oven to 375°F. Beat butter, granulated sugar and brown sugar in large bowl until light and fluffy. Beat in eggs and vanilla. Add flour, baking soda and salt. Beat until well blended. Stir in chocolate pieces and peanut butter chips. Drop by rounded tablespoonfuls 3 inches apart onto ungreased cookie sheets. Bake 10 to 12 minutes or until edges are golden brown. Let cookies stand on cookie sheets 2 minutes. Remove cookies to wire racks; cool completely.

Makes 3 dozen cookies

Note: *For a change of pace, substitute white chocolate chips, chocolate chips, chocolate-covered raisins, toffee bits or any of your kids' favorite candy pieces for the candy-coated chocolate pieces.*

Crispy Cocoa Bars

- **¼ cup (½ stick) margarine**
- **¼ cup HERSHEY'S® Cocoa**
- **5 cups miniature marshmallows**
- **5 cups crisp rice cereal**

Spray 13×9×2-inch pan with vegetable cooking spray.

Melt margarine in large saucepan over low heat; stir in cocoa and marshmallows. Cook over low heat, stirring constantly, until marshmallows are melted and mixture is smooth and well blended. Continue cooking 1 minute, stirring constantly. Remove from heat.

Add cereal; stir until coated. Lightly spray spatula with vegetable cooking spray; press mixture into prepared pan. Cool completely. Cut into bars.

Makes 24 bars

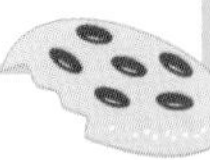

Kids' Favorite Jumbo Chippers

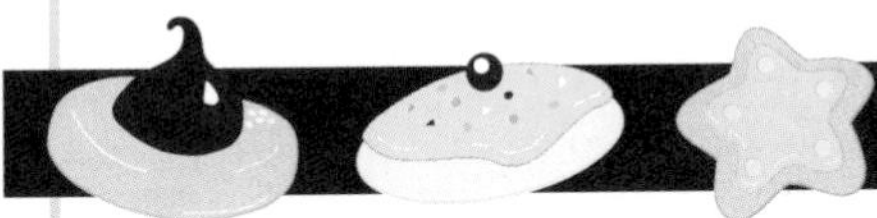

Acknowledgments

The publishers would like to thank the companies and organizations listed below for the use of their recipes and photographs in this publication.

Arm & Hammer Division, Church & Dwight Co., Inc.
Bestfoods
California Prune Board
ConAgra Grocery Products Company
Dole Food Company, Inc.
Duncan Hines® and Moist Deluxe® are registered trademarks of Aurora Foods Inc.
Egg Beaters®
Fleischmann's® Original Spread
Hershey Foods Corporation
Kraft Foods, Inc.
M&M/MARS
McIlhenny Company (TABASCO® brand Pepper Sauce)
MOTT'S® Inc., a division of Cadbury Beverages Inc.
National Honey Board
Nestlé USA, Inc.
Peanut Advisory Board
PLANTERS® Baking Nuts
The Procter & Gamble Company
The Quaker® Oatmeal Kitchens
Reckitt Benckiser
The J.M. Smucker Company
The Sugar Association, Inc.
Washington Apple Commission
Wisconsin Milk Marketing Board

Index

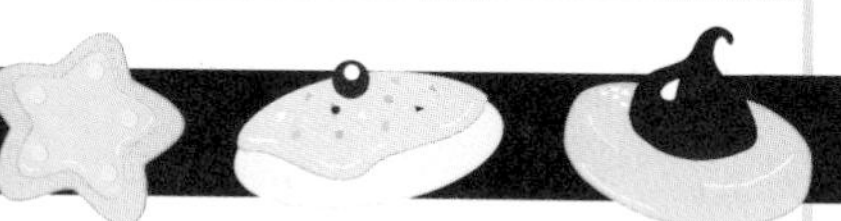

A
Almonds
Almond Crescents, 146
Almond Milk Chocolate Chippers, 78
Banana Crescents, 136
Chocolate Almond Biscotti, 164
Chocolate Chip Almond Biscotti, 70
Chocolate Edged Lace Cookies, 110
Double Chocolate Banana Cookies, 76
Fabulous Blonde Brownies, 170
Linzer Tarts, 304
Marbled Biscotti, 128
Mexican Chocolate Macaroons, 158
Moons and Stars, 348
Oatmeal Chocolate Chip Cookies, 86
Pineapple Raisin Jumbles, 151
Raspberry Almond Sandwich Cookies, 132
Snow-Covered Almond Crescents, 134
Spicy Lemon Crescents, 118
Apple-Cranberry Crescent Cookies, 286
Apple Pie Wedges, 114
Apricot-Filled Pastries, 288
Apricot Filling, 288

B
Baker's® Chocolate Pecan Pie Bars, 235
Baker's® Chocolate Sugar Cookies, 50
Baker's® Coconut Chocolate Jumbles, 12
Baker's® Double Chocolate Chunk Cookies, 93
Baker's® Mississippi Mud Bars, 227
Baker's® One Bowl® Coconut Macaroons, 29
Baker's® One Bowl® Super Chunk Cookies, 43
Baker's® Raspberry Truffle Brownies, 185
Banana Berry Brownie Pizza, 334
Banana Chocolate Chip Cookies, 340
Banana Chocolate Chip Softies, 66
Banana Crescents, 136
Brownie Caramel Pecan Bars, 219
Brownie Turtle Cookies, 172
Butterscotch Blondies, 214
Butterscotch Brownies, 178
Buttery Lemon Bars, 206

C
Cappuccino Cookies, 160
Caramel Apple Bars, 226
Caramel Filling, 154
Caramel Marshmallow Bars, 357
Caramel Topping, 219
Cashew-Lemon Shortbread Cookies, 126
Chewy Chocolate Brownies, 190
Chewy Chocolate Cookies, 318
Chippy Chewy Bars, 232
Choco-Caramel Delights, 154
Choco Cheesecake Squares, 206
Chocolate (*see also* Chocolate Chips; Cocoa; White Chocolate)
Baker's® Chocolate Pecan Pie Bars, 235
Baker's® Chocolate Sugar Cookies, 50
Baker's® Coconut Chocolate Jumbles, 12
Baker's® Double Chocolate Chunk Cookies, 93
Baker's® Mississippi Mud Bars, 227
Baker's® One Bowl® Super Chunk Cookies, 43

Chocolate *(continued)*
Baker's® Raspberry Truffle Brownies, 185
Banana Berry Brownie Pizza, 334
Brownie Turtle Cookies, 172
Chewy Chocolate Brownies, 190
Chewy Chocolate Cookies, 318
Chocolate Biscotti Nuggets, 156
Chocolate-Caramel Sugar Cookies, 51
Chocolate Chocolate Cookies, 40
Chocolate Crackletops, 30
Chocolate-Dipped Cinnamon Thins, 15
Chocolate Dipped Macaroons, 29
Chocolate Edged Lace Cookies, 110
Chocolate Espresso Brownies, 198
Chocolate-Flecked Pirouettes, 144
Chocolate Macaroons, 29
Chocolate Peanut Butter Cup Cookies, 130
Chocolate-Raspberry Kolachy, 148
Chocolate-Raspberry Kolachy Cups, 148
Chocolate Sugar Spritz, 302
Chunky Chocolate Cookies, 46
Creamy Cappuccino Brownies, 320
Creamy Quick Chocolate Frosting, 182
Derby Brownies, 168
Double Chocolate Cookies, 52
Double Chocolate Crispy Bars, 243
Elephant Ears, 317
Festive Fudge Blossoms, 342
Fudge Frosting, 59
Fudge Meringues, 138
German Chocolate Brownies, 186
Irish Brownies, 180
Jam-Filled Chocolate Sugar Cookies, 50

Index

Chocolate *(continued)*
- Mexican Chocolate Macaroons, 158
- Mini Kisses™ Coconut Macaroon Bars, 208
- Mrs. J's Chip Cookies, 68
- Nuggets o' Gold Brownies, 178
- Orange Cappuccino Brownies, 174
- Peanut Butter Chip Brownies, 176
- Peanut Butter Spritz Sandwiches, 163
- Peanutty Picnic Brownies, 317
- Quick & Easy Fudgey Brownies, 182
- Quick Chocolate Softies, 310
- Simpler Than Sin Peanut Chocolate Cookies, 51
- Spiced Chocolate Pecan Squares, 222
- Triple Chocolate Brownies, 202
- Triple Chocolate Cookies, 136
- Ultimate Brownies, 336

Chocolate Almond Biscotti, 164
Chocolate & Peanut Butter Tweed Cookies, 32
Chocolate Biscotti Nuggets, 156
Chocolate Caramel Bars, 242
Chocolate Caramel Brownies, 340
Chocolate Caramel Nut Bars, 330
Chocolate-Caramel Sugar Cookies, 51
Chocolate Cheesecake Bars, 210

Chocolate Chips
- Almond Milk Chocolate Chippers, 78
- Banana Chocolate Chip Cookies, 340
- Banana Chocolate Chip Softies, 66
- Banana Crescents, 136
- Brownie Caramel Pecan Bars, 219
- Brownie Turtle Cookies, 172

Chocolate Chips *(continued)*
- Butterscotch Brownies, 178
- Caramel Marshmallow Bars, 357
- Chewy Chocolate Cookies, 318
- Chippy Chewy Bars, 232
- Choco-Caramel Delights, 154
- Choco Cheesecake Squares, 206
- Chocolate & Peanut Butter Tweed Cookies, 32
- Chocolate Caramel Bars, 242
- Chocolate Caramel Brownies, 340
- Chocolate Caramel Nut Bars, 330
- Chocolate Chip Almond Biscotti, 70
- Chocolate Chip 'n Oatmeal Cookies, 96
- Chocolate Chip Cookie Bars, 238
- Chocolate Chip Cranberry Cheese Bars, 279
- Chocolate Chip Drizzle, 200
- Chocolate Chip Macaroons, 86
- Chocolate Chips and Raspberry Bars, 256
- Chocolate Chip Shortbread, 82
- Chocolate Clouds, 44
- Chocolate Crackletops, 30
- Chocolate-Dipped Oat Cookies, 10
- Chocolate Glaze, 146
- Chocolate Macadamia Chewies, 90
- Chocolate Peanut Butter Cup Cookies, 130
- Chocolate-Pecan Angels, 74
- Chocolate Raspberry Thumbprints, 289
- Coconut Pecan Bars, 212
- Cookie Pizza, 326
- Cowboy Cookies, 102
- Cranberry Cheese Bars, 270
- Crayon Cookies, 344
- Crispy Oat Drops, 38
- Crunchy Chocolate Chip Cookies, 69

Chocolate Chips *(continued)*
- Devil's Fudge Brownies, 177
- Double Chocolate Banana Cookies, 76
- Double Chocolate Cookies, 52
- Double Chocolate Crispy Bars, 243
- Double Chocolate Oat Drops, 92
- Double Chocolate Walnut Drops, 8
- Double-Decker Cereal Treats, 253
- Double-Decker Confetti Brownies, 194
- Double Fudge Brownie Bars, 197
- "Everything but the Kitchen Sink" Bar Cookies, 216
- Forgotten Chips Cookies, 77
- Fudge Cookies, 59
- Fudgy Walnut Cookie Wedges, 323
- Giant Cookies, 64
- Giant Raisin-Chip Frisbees, 77
- Great American Ice Cream Sandwiches, 84
- Happy Cookie Pops, 346
- Heavenly Oatmeal Hearts, 124
- Hershey®s Classic Milk Chocolate Chip Cookies, 34
- Hershey®s Great American Chocolate Chip Cookies, 84
- Hershey®s Great American Chocolate Chip Pan Cookies, 84
- Hershey®s "Perfectly Chocolate" Chocolate Chip Cookies, 72
- Holiday Truffles, 307
- Kids' Favorite Jumbo Chippers, 372
- Loaded Oatmeal Cookies, 48
- Marbled Biscotti, 128
- Marvelous Cookie Bars, 254
- Medium-Size Refrigerator Cookies, 64
- Milk Chocolate Florentine Cookies, 125

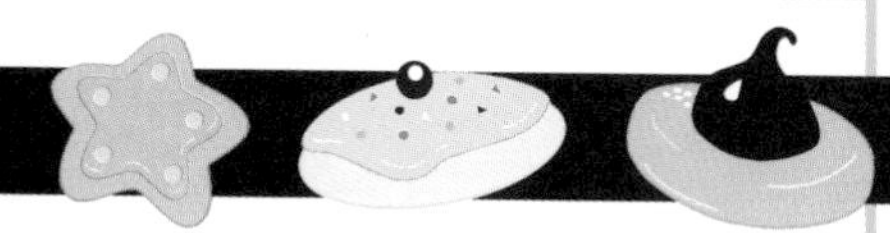

Chocolate Chips *(continued)*
- Miniature Cookies, 64
- Mini Chip Snowball Cookies, 74
- Mini Pizza Cookies, 364
- Minted Chocolate Chip Brownies, 188
- Mrs. J's Chip Cookies, 68
- No-Bake Chocolate Oat Bars, 236
- Oatmeal Brownie Gems, 338
- Oatmeal Candied Chippers, 82
- Oatmeal Carmelita Bars, 252
- Oatmeal Chocolate Cherry Bars, 246
- Oatmeal Chocolate Chip Cookies, 86
- Oatmeal Scotch Chippers, 62
- Oatmeal Treasures, 100
- Orange Cappuccino Brownies, 174
- Orange-Walnut Chippers, 98
- Original Nestlé® Toll House® Chocolate Chip Cookies, 56
- PB & J Cookie Sandwiches, 367
- Peanut Butter Chip Brownies, 176
- Peanut Butter Chocolate Chippers, 88
- Peanut Butter Chocolate No-Bake Bars, 248
- Peanut Butter Knockouts, 112
- Peanutty Double Chip Cookies, 85
- Philadelphia® Marble Brownies, 188
- Raspberry Coconut Layer Bars, 224
- Rich Chocolate Caramel Brownies, 196
- Rich Chocolate Chip Toffee Bars, 204
- Rocky Road Squares, 328
- San Francisco Cookies, 96
- Santa's Chocolate Cookies, 262
- Skor® & Chocolate Chip Cookies, 84

Chocolate Chips *(continued)*
- Snow Caps, 113
- Spicy Lemon Crescents, 118
- Sugar Cookie Pizza, 352
- Sugar Doodles, 316
- Three Great Tastes Blond Brownies, 200
- Three-in-One Chocolate Chip Cookies, 64
- Tracy's Pizza-Pan Cookies, 94
- Triple Chocolate Brownies, 202
- Triple Chocolate Cookies, 136

Chocolate Chocolate Cookies, 40
Chocolate Clouds, 44
Chocolate Crackletops, 30
Chocolate-Dipped Cinnamon Thins, 152
Chocolate Dipped Macaroons, 29
Chocolate-Dipped Oat Cookies, 10
Chocolate Edged Lace Cookies, 110
Chocolate Espresso Brownies, 198
Chocolate-Flecked Pirouettes, 144
Chocolate Glaze, 146
Chocolate Macadamia Chewies, 90
Chocolate Macadamia Cookies, 104
Chocolate Macaroons, 29
Chocolate Malted Cookies, 54
Chocolate Mint Ravioli Cookies, 314
Chocolate Peanut Butter Cup Cookies, 130
Chocolate-Pecan Angels, 74
Chocolate Peppermint Bars, 218
Chocolate-Raspberry Kolachy, 148
Chocolate-Raspberry Kolachy Cups, 148
Chocolate Raspberry Thumbprints, 289
Chocolate Sugar Drops, 126
Chocolate Sugar Spritz, 302
Chocolate Surprise Cookies, 350
Christmas Ornament Cookies, 306
Christmas Stained Glass Cookies, 278
Christmas Tree Platter, 258
Chunky Chocolate Cookies, 46
Cinnamony Apple Streusel Bars, 244
Classic Peanut Butter Cookies, 28
Classic Refrigerator Cookies, 14

Cocoa
- Choco-Caramel Delights, 154
- Chocolate Almond Biscotti, 164
- Chocolate Cheesecake Bars, 210
- Chocolate Clouds, 44
- Chocolate Macadamia Cookies, 104
- Chocolate Malted Cookies, 54
- Chocolate Peppermint Bars, 218
- Chocolate Sugar Drops, 126
- Chocolate Surprise Cookies, 350
- Cocoa Crinkle Sandwiches, 116
- Cocoa Sugar Doodles, 316
- Creamy Cocoa Icing, 184
- Crispy Cocoa Bars, 372
- Deep Dish Brownies, 186
- Devil's Fudge Brownies, 177
- Double Chocolate Banana Cookies, 76
- Double Chocolate Walnut Drops, 8
- Double-Decker Confetti Brownies, 194
- Drizzled Raspberry Crinkles, 142
- Fudge Meringues, 138
- Giant Raisin-Chip Frisbees, 77
- Greeting Card Cookies, 166
- Heavenly Hash Brownies, 184
- Hershey®s "Perfectly Chocolate" Chocolate Chip Cookies, 72
- Hershey®s White Chip Brownies, 192
- Hershey®s White Chip Chocolate Cookies, 80
- Marbled Biscotti, 128
- Peanut Butter and Chocolate Cookie Sandwich Cookies, 150
- Peanut Butter and Chocolate Spirals, 16

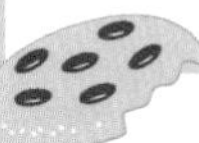

Index

Cocoa *(continued)*
Reese's® Chewy Chocolate Cookie Ice Cream Sandwiches, 18
Reese's® Chewy Chocolate Cookies, 18
Reese's® Chewy Chocolate Pan Cookies, 18
Sensational Peppermint Pattie Brownies, 176
Sugar Doodles, 316

Coconut
Baker's® Coconut Chocolate Jumbles, 12
Baker's® One Bowl® Coconut Macaroons, 29
Chippy Chewy Bars, 232
Chocolate Chip Macaroons, 86
Chocolate Dipped Macaroons, 29
Chocolate Macadamia Chewies, 90
Chocolate Macaroons, 29
Coconut Pecan Bars, 212
Crispy Oat Drops, 38
Date-Nut Macaroons, 52
Double Chocolate Oat Drops, 92
Double Fudge Brownie Bars, 197
German Chocolate Brownies, 186
Granola Apple Cookies, 19
Macaroon Kiss Cookies, 134
Mini Kisses™ Coconut Macaroon Bars, 208
Oatmeal Chocolate Chip Cookies, 86
Oatmeal Treasures, 100
Ranger Cookies, 42
Raspberry Coconut Layer Bars, 224
White Chocolate Coconut Macaroons, 29

Cookie Pizza, 326
Cookie Pops, 356

Cookies, Bar
Apple Pie Wedges, 114
Banana Berry Brownie Pizza, 334

Cookies, Bar *(continued)*
Caramel Marshmallow Bars, 357
Chocolate Caramel Nut Bars, 330
Chocolate Chip Cranberry Cheese Bars, 279
Chocolate Chip Shortbread, 82
Cookie Pizza, 326
Cranberry Cheese Bars, 270
Crispy Cocoa Bars, 372
Fudgy Walnut Cookie Wedges, 323
Giant Cookies, 64
Hershey®s Great American Chocolate Chip Pan Cookies, 84
Lemon Bars, 312
Oatmeal Brownie Gems, 338
Pumpkin Cheesecake Bars, 298
Pumpkin Jingle Bars, 294
Pumpkin Snack Bars, 322
Reese's® Chewy Chocolate Pan Cookies, 18
Rocky Road Squares, 328
Strawberry Streusel Squares, 324
Sugar Cookie Pizza, 352
Sweet Walnut Maple Bars, 335
Tracy's Pizza-Pan Cookies, 94
Yuletide Linzer Bars, 262

Cookies, Cutout
Chocolate Mint Ravioli Cookies, 314
Chocolate-Raspberry Kolachy, 148
Christmas Ornament Cookies, 306
Christmas Stained Glass Cookies, 278
Christmas Tree Platter, 258
Cookie Pops, 356
Gingerbread Kids, 264
Greeting Card Cookies, 166
Handprints, 360
Jam-Up Oatmeal Cookies, 108
Jolly Peanut Butter Gingerbread Cookies, 290
Kringle's Cutouts, 268
Linzer Tarts, 304

Cookies, Cutout *(continued)*
Moons and Stars, 348
Peanut Butter Bears, 308
Peanut Butter Cut-Outs, 299
Smucker's® Grandmother's Jelly Cookies, 28

Cookies, Drop
Almond Milk Chocolate Chippers, 78
Baker's® Coconut Chocolate Jumbles, 12
Baker's® Double Chocolate Chunk Cookies, 93
Baker's One Bowl® Coconut Macaroons, 29
Baker's® One Bowl® Super Chunk Cookies, 43
Banana Chocolate Chip Softies, 66
Brownie Turtle Cookies, 172
Chewy Chocolate Cookies, 318
Chocolate Chip 'n Oatmeal Cookies, 96
Chocolate Chip Macaroons, 86
Chocolate Chocolate Cookies, 40
Chocolate Clouds, 44
Chocolate Dipped Macaroons, 29
Chocolate Edged Lace Cookies, 110
Chocolate Macadamia Chewies, 90
Chocolate Macadamia Cookies, 104
Chocolate Macaroons, 29
Chocolate-Pecan Angels, 74
Chunky Chocolate Cookies, 46
Cowboy Cookies, 102
Crispy Oat Drops, 38
Crunchy Chocolate Chip Cookies, 69
Date-Nut Cookies, 296
Date-Nut Macaroons, 52
Double Chocolate Banana Cookies, 76
Double Chocolate Cookies, 52

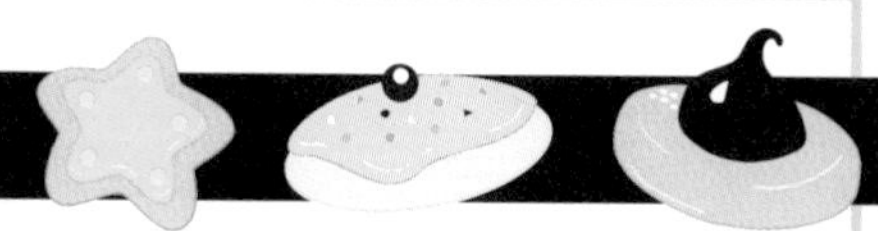

Cookies, Drop *(continued)*
Double Chocolate Oat Drops, 92
Double Chocolate Walnut Drops, 8
Drizzled Raspberry Crinkles, 142
Forgotten Chips Cookies, 77
Fudge Cookies, 59
Fudge Meringues, 138
Giant Raisin-Chip Frisbees, 77
Gingersnaps, 294
Golden Gingersnaps, 48
Granola Apple Cookies, 19
Hermits, 13
Hershey®s Classic Milk Chocolate Chip Cookies, 34
Hershey®s Great American Chocolate Chip Cookies, 84
Hershey®s "Perfectly Chocolate" Chocolate Chip Cookies, 72
Hershey®s Soft & Chewy Cookies, 40
Hershey®s White Chip Chocolate Cookies, 80
Kids' Favorite Jumbo Chippers, 372
Lemon Pecan Cookies, 58
Loaded Oatmeal Cookies, 48
Maple Walnut Meringues, 272
Miniature Cookies, 64
Mocha Cookies, 120
Oatmeal Apple Cookies, 140
Oatmeal Butterscotch Cookies, 24
Oatmeal Candied Chippers, 82
Oatmeal Chocolate Chip Cookies, 86
Oatmeal Pecan Scotchies, 30
Oatmeal Scotch Chippers, 62
Oatmeal Treasures, 100
Orange Pecan Gems, 320
Orange-Walnut Chippers, 98
Original Nestlé® Toll House® Chocolate Chip Cookies, 56
Peanut Butter Chewies, 22
Peanut Butter Chip Oatmeal Cookies, 100

Cookies, Drop *(continued)*
Peanut Butter Chip Orange Cookies, 106
Peanut Gems, 10
Peanutty Double Chip Cookies, 85
Pineapple Raisin Jumbles, 151
Pumpkin White Chocolate Drops, 266
Quick Chocolate Softies, 310
Ranger Cookies, 42
Reese's® Chewy Chocolate Cookies, 18
Rum Fruitcake Cookies, 304
San Francisco Cookies, 96
Skor® & Chocolate Chip Cookies, 84
Snow Caps, 113
Southern Belle White Chocolate Cookies, 162
Spicy Oatmeal Raisin Cookies, 32
Spicy Sour Cream Cookies, 342
Triple Chocolate Cookies, 136
White Chocolate Coconut Macaroons, 29

Cookies, Refrigerator
Cappuccino Cookies, 160
Chocolate & Peanut Butter Tweed Cookies, 32
Chocolate-Dipped Cinnamon Thins, 152
Classic Refrigerator Cookies, 14
Date Pinwheel Cookies, 122
Lip-Smacking Lemon Cookies, 20
Medium-Size Refrigerator Cookies, 64
Peanut Butter and Chocolate Spirals, 16
Peppersass Cookies, 125
Slice 'n' Bake Ginger Wafers, 135

Cookies, Sandwich
Cocoa Crinkle Sandwiches, 116
Great American Ice Cream Sandwiches, 84

Cookies, Sandwich *(continued)*
Linzer Sandwich Cookies, 300
Milk Chocolate Florentine Cookies, 125
PB & J Cookie Sandwiches, 367
Peanut Butter and Chocolate Cookie Sandwich Cookies, 150
Peanut Butter and Jelly Sandwich Cookies, 354
Peanut Butter Spritz Sandwiches, 163
Raspberry Almond Sandwich Cookies, 132
Reese's® Chewy Chocolate Cookie Ice Cream Sandwiches, 18
Sandwich Cookies, 362

Cookies, Shaped
Almond Crescents, 146
Apple-Cranberry Crescent Cookies, 286
Apricot-Filled Pastries, 288
Baker's® Chocolate Sugar Cookies, 50
Banana Crescents, 136
Cashew-Lemon Shortbread Cookies, 126
Choco-Caramel Delights, 154
Chocolate-Caramel Sugar Cookies, 51
Chocolate Crackletops, 30
Chocolate-Dipped Oat Cookies, 10
Chocolate-Flecked Pirouettes, 144
Chocolate Malted Cookies, 54
Chocolate Peanut Butter Cup Cookies, 130
Chocolate-Raspberry Kolachy Cups, 148
Chocolate Raspberry Thumbprints, 289
Chocolate Sugar Drops, 126
Chocolate Sugar Spritz, 302
Chocolate Surprise Cookies, 350
Classic Peanut Butter Cookies, 28

Index

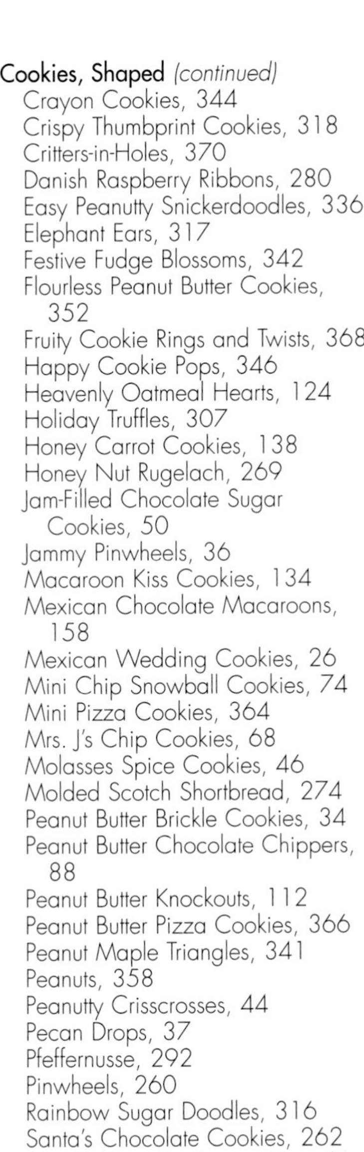

Cookies, Shaped *(continued)*
- Crayon Cookies, 344
- Crispy Thumbprint Cookies, 318
- Critters-in-Holes, 370
- Danish Raspberry Ribbons, 280
- Easy Peanutty Snickerdoodles, 336
- Elephant Ears, 317
- Festive Fudge Blossoms, 342
- Flourless Peanut Butter Cookies, 352
- Fruity Cookie Rings and Twists, 368
- Happy Cookie Pops, 346
- Heavenly Oatmeal Hearts, 124
- Holiday Truffles, 307
- Honey Carrot Cookies, 138
- Honey Nut Rugelach, 269
- Jam-Filled Chocolate Sugar Cookies, 50
- Jammy Pinwheels, 36
- Macaroon Kiss Cookies, 134
- Mexican Chocolate Macaroons, 158
- Mexican Wedding Cookies, 26
- Mini Chip Snowball Cookies, 74
- Mini Pizza Cookies, 364
- Mrs. J's Chip Cookies, 68
- Molasses Spice Cookies, 46
- Molded Scotch Shortbread, 274
- Peanut Butter Brickle Cookies, 34
- Peanut Butter Chocolate Chippers, 88
- Peanut Butter Knockouts, 112
- Peanut Butter Pizza Cookies, 366
- Peanut Maple Triangles, 341
- Peanuts, 358
- Peanutty Crisscrosses, 44
- Pecan Drops, 37
- Pfeffernusse, 292
- Pinwheels, 260
- Rainbow Sugar Doodles, 316
- Santa's Chocolate Cookies, 262
- Simpler Than Sin Peanut Chocolate Cookies, 51

Cookies, Shaped *(continued)*
- Snow-Covered Almond Crescents, 134
- Snowmen, 282
- Soft Spicy Molasses Cookies, 37
- Spicy Lemon Crescents, 118
- Spritz Christmas Trees, 276
- Sugar Cookie Wreaths, 284
- Sugar Doodles, 316
- Surprise Cookies, 332
- Tiny Mini Kisses™ Peanut Blossoms, 60
- Vanilla Butter Crescents, 328
- Walnut Crescents, 151

Cowboy Cookies, 102
Cranberry Cheese Bars, 270
Crayon Cookies, 344
Creamy Cappuccino Brownies, 320
Creamy Cocoa Icing, 184
Creamy Quick Chocolate Frosting, 182
Crispy Cocoa Bars, 372
Crispy Oat Drops, 38
Crispy Thumbprint Cookies, 318
Critters-in-Holes, 370
Crunchy Chocolate Chip Cookies, 69

D

Danish Raspberry Ribbons, 280
Date-Nut Cookies, 296
Date-Nut Macaroons, 52
Date Pinwheel Cookies, 122
Decorative Frosting, 166
Deep Dish Brownies, 186
Derby Brownies, 168
Devil's Fudge Brownies, 177
Double Chocolate Banana Cookies, 76
Double Chocolate Cookies, 52
Double Chocolate Crispy Bars, 243
Double Chocolate Oat Drops, 92
Double Chocolate Walnut Drops, 8
Double-Decker Cereal Treats, 253
Double-Decker Confetti Brownies, 194
Double Fudge Brownie Bars, 197
Drizzled Raspberry Crinkles, 142

E

Easy Peanutty Snickerdoodles, 336
Elephant Ears, 317
"Everything but the Kitchen Sink" Bar Cookies, 216

F

Fabulous Blonde Brownies, 170
Festive Fruited White Chip Blondies, 249
Festive Fudge Blossoms, 342
Flourless Peanut Butter Cookies, 352
Forgotten Chips Cookies, 77

Frostings, Icings & Glazes
- Chocolate Chip Drizzle, 200
- Chocolate Glaze, 146
- Creamy Cocoa Icing, 184
- Creamy Quick Chocolate Frosting, 182
- Decorative Frosting, 166
- Fudge Frosting, 59
- Glaze, 244, 280
- Icing, 306
- Irish Cream Frosting, 180
- Lemon Drizzle, 58
- Peanut Buttery Frosting, 358

Fruit and Nut Bars, 230
Fruit and Oat Squares, 216
Fruity Cookie Rings and Twists, 368
Fudge Cookies, 59
Fudge Frosting, 59
Fudge Meringues, 138
Fudgy Walnut Cookie Wedges, 323

G

German Chocolate Brownies, 186
Giant Cookies, 64
Giant Raisin-Chip Frisbees, 77
Gingerbread Kids, 264

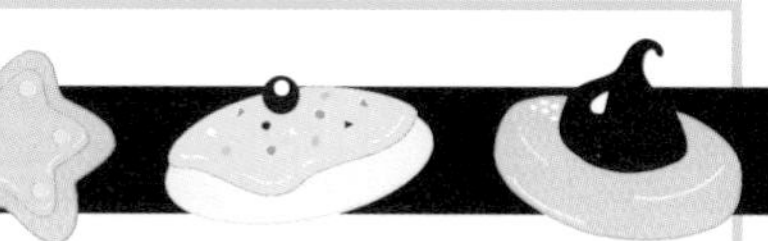

Gingersnaps, 294
Glaze, 244, 280
Glazed Pecans, 298
Golden Gingersnaps, 48
Granola Apple Cookies, 19
Great American Ice Cream Sandwiches, 84
Greeting Card Cookies, 166

H
Handprints, 360
Happy Cookie Pops, 346
Heavenly Hash Brownies, 184
Heavenly Oatmeal Hearts, 124
Hermits, 13
Hershey®s Classic Milk Chocolate Chip Cookies, 34
Hershey®s Great American Chocolate Chip Cookies, 84
Hershey®s Great American Chocolate Chip Pan Cookies, 84
Hershey®s "Perfectly Chocolate" Chocolate Chip Cookies, 72
Hershey®s Soft & Chewy Cookies, 40
Hershey®s White Chip Brownies, 192
Hershey®s White Chip Chocolate Cookies, 80
Holiday Truffles, 307
Honey Carrot Cookies, 138
Honey Nut Rugelach, 269

I
Icing, 306
Irish Brownies, 180
Irish Cream Frosting, 180

J
Jam-Filled Chocolate Sugar Cookies, 50
Jammy Pinwheels, 36
Jam-Up Oatmeal Cookies, 108
Jolly Peanut Butter Gingerbread Cookies, 290

K
Kids' Favorite Jumbo Chippers, 372
Kringle's Cutouts, 268

L
Lemon Bars, 312
Lemon Drizzle, 58
Lemon Pecan Cookies, 58
Linzer Sandwich Cookies, 300
Linzer Tarts, 304
Lip-Smacking Lemon Cookies, 20
Loaded Oatmeal Cookies, 48

M
Macaroon Kiss Cookies, 134
Maple Walnut Meringues, 272
Marbled Biscotti, 128
Marvelous Cookie Bars, 254
Medium-Size Refrigerator Cookies, 64
Mexican Chocolate Macaroons, 158
Mexican Wedding Cookies, 26
Microwave Double Peanut Bars, 250
Milk Chocolate Florentine Cookies, 125
Miniature Cookies, 64
Mini Chip Snowball Cookies, 74
Mini Kisses™ Coconut Macaroon Bars, 208
Mini Pizza Cookies, 364
Minted Chocolate Chip Brownies, 188
Mrs. J's Chip Cookies, 68
Mocha Cookies, 120
Molasses Spice Cookies, 46
Molded Scotch Shortbread, 274
Moons and Stars, 348
Mott's® Chewy Oatmeal Raisin Squares, 211

N
No-Bake Chocolate Oat Bars, 236
No-Bake Pineapple Marmalade Squares, 228
Nuggets o' Gold Brownies, 178

O
Oatmeal Apple Cookies, 140
Oatmeal Brownie Gems, 338
Oatmeal Butterscotch Cookies, 24
Oatmeal Candied Chippers, 82
Oatmeal Carmelita Bars, 252
Oatmeal Chocolate Cherry Bars, 246
Oatmeal Chocolate Chip Cookies, 86
Oatmeal Pecan Sandies, 30
Oatmeal Praline Cheese Bars, 234
Oatmeal Scotch Chippers, 62
Oatmeal Toffee Bars, 220
Oatmeal Treasures, 100
Oat-Y Nut Bars, 228
Orange Cappuccino Brownies, 174
Orange Chess Bars, 214
Orange Pecan Gems, 320
Orange-Walnut Chippers, 98
Original Nestlé® Toll House® Chocolate Chip Cookies, 56

P
PB & J Cookie Sandwiches, 367
Peachy Oatmeal Bars, 244
Peanut Butter
- Classic Peanut Butter Cookies, 28
- Double Chocolate Crispy Bars, 243
- "Everything but the Kitchen Sink" Bar Cookies, 216
- Flourless Peanut Butter Cookies, 352
- Microwave Double Peanut Bars, 250
- No-Bake Chocolate Oat Bars, 236
- Oatmeal Scotch Chippers, 62
- PB & J Cookie Sandwiches, 367
- Peanut Butter and Chocolate Spirals, 16
- Peanut Butter and Jelly Sandwich Cookies, 354
- Peanut Butter Bears, 308

Peanut Butter *(continued)*
Peanut Butter Brickle Cookies, 34
Peanut Butter Chewies, 22
Peanut Butter Chocolate Chippers, 88
Peanut Butter Chocolate No-Bake Bars, 248
Peanut Butter Cut-Outs, 299
Peanut Butter Knockouts, 112
Peanut Butter Marbled Brownies, 190
Peanut Butter Pizza Cookies, 366
Peanut Butter Spritz Sandwiches, 163
Peanut Buttery Frosting, 358
Peanut Maple Triangles, 341
Peanutty Crisscrosses, 44
Peanutty Double Chip Cookies, 85
Simpler Than Sin Peanut Chocolate Cookies, 51
Southern Belle White Chocolate Cookies, 162
Tiny Mini Kisses™ Peanut Blossoms, 60

Peanut Butter Chips
Chippy Chewy Bars, 232
Chocolate & Peanut Butter Tweed Cookies, 32
Double-Decker Cereal Treats, 253
Double Fudge Brownie Bars, 197
Easy Peanutty Snickerdoodles, 336
Jolly Peanut Butter Gingerbread Cookies, 290
Kids' Favorite Jumbo Chippers, 372
Peanut Butter and Chocolate Cookie Sandwich Cookies, 150
Peanut Butter Chip Brownies, 176
Peanut Butter Chip Oatmeal Cookies, 100
Peanut Butter Chip Orange Cookies, 106
Peanutty Double Chip Cookies, 85
Peanutty Picnic Brownies, 317

Peanut Butter Chips *(continued)*
Reese's® Chewy Chocolate Cookie Ice Cream Sandwiches, 18
Reese's® Chewy Chocolate Cookies, 18
Reese's® Chewy Chocolate Pan Cookies, 18
Sugar Doodles, 316
Three Great Tastes Blond Brownies, 200

Peanuts
Caramel Marshmallow Bars, 357
Chocolate Peanut Butter Cup Cookies, 130
Heavenly Oatmeal Hearts, 124
Microwave Double Peanut Bars, 250
Oat-Y Nut Bars, 228
PB & J Cookie Sandwiches, 367
Peanut Butter Marbled Brownies, 190
Peanut Gems, 10
Peanuts, 358

Peanutty Crisscrosses, 44
Peanutty Double Chip Cookies, 85
Peanutty Picnic Brownies, 317

Pecans
Baker's® Chocolate Pecan Pie Bars, 235
Brownie Caramel Pecan Bars, 219
Brownie Turtle Cookies, 172
Choco-Caramel Delights, 154
Chocolate Biscotti Nuggets, 156
Chocolate Chip Cookie Bars, 238
Chocolate-Pecan Angels, 74
Chocolate Surprise Cookies, 350
Coconut Pecan Bars, 212
Crispy Oat Drops, 38
Date-Nut Macaroons, 52
Devil's Fudge Brownies, 177
Double Fudge Brownie Bars, 197
Fudge Cookies, 59
German Chocolate Brownies, 186

Pecans *(continued)*
Glazed Pecans, 298
Jam-Up Oatmeal Cookies, 108
Lemon Pecan Cookies, 58
Mexican Wedding Cookies, 26
Oatmeal Pecan Scotchies, 30
Oatmeal Praline Cheese Bars, 234
Orange Pecan Gems, 320
Peanut Butter Chewies, 22
Pecan Drops, 37
Pumpkin Cheesecake Bars, 298
Spiced Chocolate Pecan Squares, 222
Spicy Sour Cream Cookies, 342
Triple Chocolate Cookies, 136
Vanilla Butter Crescents, 328

Peppersass Cookies, 125
Pfeffernusse, 292
Philadelphia® Marble Brownies, 188
Pineapple Raisin Jumbles, 151
Pinwheels, 260
Praline Bars, 250
Prune Purée, 198

Pumpkin
Pumpkin Cheesecake Bars, 298
Pumpkin Jingle Bars, 294
Pumpkin Snack Bars, 322
Pumpkin White Chocolate Drops, 266

Q

Quick & Easy Fudgey Brownies, 182
Quick Chocolate Softies, 310

R

Rainbow Sugar Doodles, 316
Ranger Cookies, 42
Raspberry Almond Sandwich Cookies, 132
Raspberry Coconut Layer Bars, 224
Reese's® Chewy Chocolate Cookie Ice Cream Sandwiches, 18

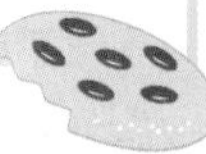

Reese's® Chewy Chocolate Cookies, 18
Reese's® Chewy Chocolate Pan Cookies, 18
Rich Chocolate Caramel Brownies, 196
Rich Chocolate Chip Toffee Bars, 204
Rocky Road Squares, 328
Rum Fruitcake Cookies, 304

S
Sandwich Cookies, 362
San Francisco Cookies, 96
Santa's Chocolate Cookies, 262
Sensational Peppermint Pattie Brownies, 176
Simpler Than Sin Peanut Chocolate Cookies, 51
Skor® & Chocolate Chip Cookies, 84
Slice 'n' Bake Ginger Wafers, 135
Smucker's® Grandmother's Jelly Cookies, 28
Snow Caps, 113
Snow-Covered Almond Crescents, 134
Snowmen, 282
Soft Spicy Molasses Cookies, 37
Southern Belle White Chocolate Cookies, 162
Spiced Chocolate Pecan Squares, 222
Spicy Lemon Crescents, 118
Spicy Oatmeal Raisin Cookies, 32
Spicy Sour Cream Cookies, 342
Spritz Christmas Trees, 276
Strawberry Oat Bars, 240
Strawberry Streusel Squares, 324
Sugar Cookie Pizza, 352
Sugar Cookie Wreaths, 284
Sugar Doodles, 316
Surprise Cookies, 332
Sweet Walnut Maple Bars, 335

T
Three Great Tastes Blond Brownies, 200
Three-in-One Chocolate Chip Cookies, 64
Tiny Mini Kisses™ Peanut Blossoms, 60
Tracy's Pizza-Pan Cookies, 94
Triple Chocolate Brownies, 202
Triple Chocolate Cookies, 136

U
Ultimate Brownies, 336

V
Vanilla Butter Crescents, 328

W
Walnuts
- Baker's® Coconut Chocolate Jumbles, 12
- Baker's® Mississippi Mud Bars, 227
- Chewy Chocolate Cookies, 318
- Chocolate Caramel Bars, 242
- Chocolate-Dipped Oat Cookies, 10
- Chunky Chocolate Cookies, 46
- Crispy Thumbprint Cookies, 318
- Date-Nut Cookies, 296
- Double Chocolate Cookies, 52
- Double Chocolate Oat Drops, 92
- Double Chocolate Walnut Drops, 8
- Festive Fudge Blossoms, 342
- Fudgy Walnut Cookie Wedges, 323
- Giant Raisin-Chip Frisbees, 77
- Heavenly Hash Brownies, 184
- Hermits, 13
- Honey Nut Rugelach, 269
- Loaded Oatmeal Cookies, 48
- Maple Walnut Meringues, 272
- Marvelous Cookie Bars, 254
- Mrs. J's Chip Cookies, 68
- Oatmeal Brownie Gems, 338

Walnuts *(continued)*
- Oatmeal Carmelita Bars, 252
- Oatmeal Scotch Chippers, 62
- Orange-Walnut Chippers, 98
- Peanut Butter Chip Oatmeal Cookies, 100
- Quick Chocolate Softies, 310
- Rocky Road Squares, 328
- Sweet Walnut Maple Bars, 335
- Tracy's Pizza-Pan Cookies, 94
- Walnut Crescents, 151

White Chocolate
- Baker's® Mississippi Mud Bars, 227
- Chocolate Surprise Cookies, 350
- Double Chocolate Crispy Bars, 243
- Fabulous Blonde Brownies, 170
- Festive Fruited White Chip Blondies, 249
- Heavenly Oatmeal Hearts, 124
- Hershey®s White Chip Brownies, 192
- Hershey®s White Chip Chocolate Cookies, 80
- Lemon Pecan Cookies, 58
- Peanut Butter Pizza Cookies, 366
- Pumpkin White Chocolate Drops, 266
- Quick Chocolate Softies, 310
- Raspberry Coconut Layer Bars, 224
- Snow Caps, 113
- Southern Belle White Chocolate Cookies, 162
- Three Great Tastes Blond Brownies, 200
- Triple Chocolate Cookies, 136
- White Chocolate Coconut Macaroons, 29

Y
Yuletide Linzer Bars, 262

METRIC CONVERSION CHART

VOLUME MEASUREMENTS (dry)

1/8 teaspoon = 0.5 mL
1/4 teaspoon = 1 mL
1/2 teaspoon = 2 mL
3/4 teaspoon = 4 mL
1 teaspoon = 5 mL
1 tablespoon = 15 mL
2 tablespoons = 30 mL
1/4 cup = 60 mL
1/3 cup = 75 mL
1/2 cup = 125 mL
2/3 cup = 150 mL
3/4 cup = 175 mL
1 cup = 250 mL
2 cups = 1 pint = 500 mL
3 cups = 750 mL
4 cups = 1 quart = 1 L

VOLUME MEASUREMENTS (fluid)

1 fluid ounce (2 tablespoons) = 30 mL
4 fluid ounces (1/2 cup) = 125 mL
8 fluid ounces (1 cup) = 250 mL
12 fluid ounces (1 1/2 cups) = 375 mL
16 fluid ounces (2 cups) = 500 mL

WEIGHTS (mass)

1/2 ounce = 15 g
1 ounce = 30 g
3 ounces = 90 g
4 ounces = 120 g
8 ounces = 225 g
10 ounces = 285 g
12 ounces = 360 g
16 ounces = 1 pound = 450 g

DIMENSIONS

1/16 inch = 2 mm
1/8 inch = 3 mm
1/4 inch = 6 mm
1/2 inch = 1.5 cm
3/4 inch = 2 cm
1 inch = 2.5 cm

OVEN TEMPERATURES

250°F = 120°C
275°F = 140°C
300°F = 150°C
325°F = 160°C
350°F = 180°C
375°F = 190°C
400°F = 200°C
425°F = 220°C
450°F = 230°C

BAKING PAN SIZES

Utensil	Size in Inches/Quarts	Metric Volume	Size in Centimeters
Baking or Cake Pan (square or rectangular)	8×8×2	2 L	20×20×5
	9×9×2	2.5 L	23×23×5
	12×8×2	3 L	30×20×5
	13×9×2	3.5 L	33×23×5
Loaf Pan	8×4×3	1.5 L	20×10×7
	9×5×3	2 L	23×13×7
Round Layer Cake Pan	8×1½	1.2 L	20×4
	9×1½	1.5 L	23×4
Pie Plate	8×1¼	750 mL	20×3
	9×1¼	1 L	23×3
Baking Dish or Casserole	1 quart	1 L	—
	1½ quart	1.5 L	—
	2 quart	2 L	—